THE GOOD IN IT

A Year of Prompted Gratitude

Book 1 of 4: Days 1 – 91

MELINDA COLLIER

Disclaimer:
I have changed some names to protect individuals' privacy. To maintain the anonymity of individuals involved, I have changed some details. The author does not assume liability for loss or damage caused by errors or omissions. Some of the statements are memories, from my perspective, and I have tried to represent events as faithfully as possible. Some scenarios mentioned in this book are fictitious. Regarding these scenarios, any similarity to actual persons, living or dead, is coincidental.

Copyright © 2023 Melinda Collier

All rights reserved.
No part of this book may be reproduced or used in any manner without the prior written permission of the copyright owner, except for the use of brief quotations in a book review.

ISBN 9798394622182 (paperback)
Imprint: Independently published

Kindle Direct Publishing

Acknowledgements:

I am grateful God has put this on my heart
and given me the ability to write it
and determination to put in the work.

Kasey Hand and Nikki Martin, thank you
for being willing to assist and proofread this work for me.

Thank you, Emily "Peaceful Waters" Woodall, for asking me to
proofread your book and being the final "nudge" for me to write this.

Thank you, Rachel Matthews, for your helpfulness and willingness to
answer any questions I had in creating the cover.

Special thanks to Telisha White for reviewing my work and allowing
me to use your quote on the back cover.
Thank you to others who read my work prior to publishing and shared
their thoughts and opinions with me.

A big thank you to everyone
who has ever commented that I should write a book
and to all the teachers and loved ones who encouraged me.

Thank you, Phillip, for letting me use your laptop
and for being supportive of me. I love you!

Author's Recommendation:

Book 1 contains a few themes that I, as a parent, would find inappropriate for readers under a certain age. My recommendation would be for ages 15 years and up based on the content, depending upon maturity level and mental and/or emotional triggers. As the author and as a parent, I recommend using discretion.

There are some instances and themes in this book including but not limited to: different mental health conditions, self-harm, death, different types of abuse, domestic violence, among other difficult topics including child welfare. **Please proceed with caution if any of these topics pose an issue for you**. I believe most of my writings show early-on any evidence of these topics, but as someone who knows words themselves can cause mental and emotional distress, I wanted to add this before the book begins.

Introduction:

I have prayed for a way to glorify God and not to put the focus solely on myself or my story. I don't want that. I want God's hand to be seen and felt through the whole thing. I have sat down several times and tried to write something like a biography. It didn't happen. I've tried to find all the short devotionals I've posted on social media, and it seems I accidentally deleted the document I'd saved them to.

In late 2022, I was asked to proofread a book with no deadline. It sparked my desire to write that had dwindled some. On our way home from Alabama to Louisiana on New Year's Eve, the idea came to me to write about all the things I'm thankful for. I quickly went down a rabbit hole, and I challenged myself to come up with 365 things to be thankful for. This went from things that were obvious to be thankful for to harder topics. Some things are even a bit silly. I spent the remainder of the day writing these prompts on a sheet of notebook paper. I somehow managed to do this, cut them all up, crumple them, and put them in a large-mouth jar all before midnight. I decided I would draw a prompt daily from the jar (thus the book cover) and find a way to be thankful for it and express that through an essay or short story.

I am a person who daily challenges myself to think there must be some positive in all that happens: the good, the bad, the ugly, and all the in-between. I try to challenge others to do the same. I believe just going through stuff and not taking some lesson from it or growing as a person means you missed the point. I believe there is meaning to all this living. In saying that, I wrote prompts about people, places, events, traits, and things. All of those fall into categories of things I love, don't think often about, or don't like at all. I didn't want this to be easy for me. If it was going to be what it needed to be, it needed to be random, happy, painful, and a plethora of other adjectives.

To add, there are sensitive topics in this book. I already mentioned this in the "Author's Recommendation" section, but this is a final caution. Lastly, some names were changed. Some were not. If real names were used, I asked for and received permission. This book may appear to be a daily read, but it can easily be read as a normal chapter book. This is not what I'd classify as a devotional, though there are certainly components of a devotional in it.

At the time of this book, I am in my thirties. I am a Christian and I figure that will be obvious here, or at least it should be. I hope that doesn't discourage anyone from reading, because one thing I believe you'll see is we are probably more alike than you think. I, for one, find reading books authored by people of different beliefs interesting and educational.

I am married to a man named Phillip who is a preacher and is currently serving as a full-time pastor. We have three biological children, bonus daughters, and we are Alabama natives currently living our first year in another state: Louisiana. Being a native Alabamian, sassiness and being opinionated are a part of my genetic makeup. I am positive all that will be evident. I've got a lot of opinions in here, so heads up.

I am the only child of two only children. I lived in the same little town and same little house for almost 18 years. I am the first person in my immediate family to graduate from college and I hold a bachelor's degree. Is furthering my education in my future? Probably... I'm not sure when. I have a history of working in social work prior to our move. At the time of this book being written, I stay home with my youngest child and coach tennis at the local high school.

I want to make something clear. I have no hate in my heart for anyone I bring up in this book, or any of the future books. I've got love for all of you. Some of the stories are great, some not so much, but all of them happened and I quote them to the best of my memory. There's no changing the past. There is only learning for the future. There is beauty in forgiveness, and I've found it to be, frankly, drop-dead gorgeous. I've learned to forgive others; it is a daily practice. I am still trying to learn to forgive myself. Some days I "forget" God's gift of forgiveness other promises are for me, too.

Most of these stories are going to be from my own life. In a way, those stories serve as part of my testimony. This work isn't a chronologically accurate testimony, though. There are going to be a few stories from other people's lives and there are going to be a few stories I made up. If there are any stories I made up as examples, I will make those clear. I hope you'll laugh. I also hope your heart will be touched.

You also may be annoyed with the use of "thankful" and "grateful" throughout this book, but to be honest I ran out of ways to say it! Besides, recheck the title of this book. You knew what you were up for when you picked it! Bless your heart.

A wonderful preacher my husband knows, Mr. Richard Fox, recently said it best when he said, "Real life is hard. Real life causes real pain, and pain is hard." He also said, "I don't want to waste God's air for nothing." I wholeheartedly agree. Not my air; not my life. His. That is why this exists.

I won't lie. There is a small voice of fear in my mind that tells me this whole endeavor is stupid. It tells me this will be embarrassing, that there is no point in penning all this. I fight it with diligence. I have wrestled with my gut churning in anxiety. I have persevered despite this.

I hope this openness, honesty, and fully exposed work (and the works to follow) will remind others- and help me to remind myself- that when it comes to life, there is always good in it.

With love,
-Melinda

Prompts and Pages:

Day 1: Horses 1

Day 2: Delayed Shipping/Mail 4

Day 3: Hoarded Money 6

Day 4: Uppity People 9

Day 5: Baking 13

Day 6: Innocence 17

Day 7: Microwavable/Easy Meals 20

Day 8: Storms 22

Day 9: Confidence 24

Day 10: Thick, Curly Hair 26

Day 11: Daughters 28

Day 12: Flower Sales 30

Day 13: Desserts 34

Day 14: Candles 36

Day 15: Fairbanks, AK 38

Day 16: Employment 42

Day 17: Sunshine 45

Day 18: Being Included 47

Day 19: My Husband Learning New Things 50

Day 20: Disabilities 52

Day 21: Dogs/Beloved Pets 57

Day 22: Bitter People 60

Day 23: Seatbelts 63

Day 24: Burns 67

Day 25: Swings 69
Day 26: Backroads 72
Day 27: Kindness 74
Day 28: Electricity 78
Day 29: Servers (Waiters/Waitresses) 81
Day 30: Unexpected Blessings 84
Day 31: Harvey 87
Day 32: Old Photos 90
Day 33: Christian Books 93
Day 34: Art 96
Day 35: New Friends 99
Day 36: MK 101
Day 37: Self-Harm/Suicidal Thoughts 103
Day 38: Eggs 108
Day 39: Devotionals 110
Day 40: Mental Health Awareness 112
Day 41: Spouses 117
Day 42: Church 120
Day 43: Givers 124
Day 44: Good Grammar/Spelling 127
Day 45: Apologies Never Received 129
Day 46: Rain 132
Day 47: Christmas Lights 134
Day 48: Holy Spirit 136
Day 49: Mom 139
Day 50: Judas 142

Day 51: Hot Showers 144

Day 52: Tobacco/Nicotine 147

Day 53: Grandpa 151

Day 54: Prayer 155

Day 55: Non-Believers 157

Day 56: Country Living 159

Day 57: Shakettas 164

Day 58: God-Given Talents 166

Day 59: Knowing No One 169

Day 60: Hospice 171

Day 61: Date Nights 173

Day 62: Lost Sheep 175

Day 63: Counseling/Therapy 178

Day 64: Cheap Children's Clothes 182

Day 65: Nurses 185

Day 66: Cows 190

Day 67: Sobriety 193

Day 68: Losing 196

Day 69: Delayed Flights 198

Day 70: Eve 202

Day 71: Tantrums 207

Day 72: Courage 210

Day 73: Chad 213

Day 74: Control Freaks 220

Day 75: Comedians 223

Day 76: Waffle House 225

Day 77: Old Friends 227
Day 78: God's Voice 229
Day 79: Cringey Moments 231
Day 80: Bible Stories 235
Day 81: LEGOs 237
Day 82: Bonus Kids 239
Day 83: Barbers/Hairdressers 242
Day 84: Love 245
Day 85: Clean Water 248
Day 86: Ruiners 250
Day 87: Moochers 254
Day 88: Sunrises 256
Day 89: Daydreamers 258
Day 90: Smiles 260
Day 91: Broken Dishes 263

Day 1:
Horses

Ha! Horses. Of all things to pick on January 1st. So random.

I was never allowed to ride horses while I lived with my parents. I don't know the reason, really. It always changed. Sometimes it was "you might get hurt" or "there's no reason you should want to" or something similar. Their reasoning was unpredictable. You'd think growing up in the country and working at a tack and saddle shop within walking distance from my house, I would have been riding horses all the time. No. I lived in fear most days. If I was caught riding a horse, I was threatened to have my you-know-what tore up, etc. Anxiety was a constant in my life. So, I watched everyone else. I learned about tack, how horses can be a money pit (I still have no idea how people afford to have them, but for those that do, more power to you,) and different types of horses. I even watched horses be broken in the round pen beside my neighbors' barn. However, I never rode one or dared to sit on one out of fear of what would happen to me if it was found out.

It is because the consequences were believable. I'd seen too much violence and aggression during my childhood in my family and I knew what the very realistic possibilities were. I unfortunately remember a lot of things, but I'm grateful I don't remember some of the things other people recall about my life.

Fast forward to May 2010. I was playing college tennis. My tennis team made it to the national tournament in Arizona. Our coach took us to a ranch where it appeared their main business was guided trail rides. Anxiety blended with excitement in my heart as we walked up to the hitching post. I'd suffered from horrible allergies after a dust storm earlier that week and this was the first highlight I'd had since I'd been knocked out of the tennis tournament. My horse, Dusty, could certainly feel all my emotions. We were both a bit stiff and awkward.

    I was 18. I'd been out of my home for months now at college all because I was blessed with that way out. There was nothing anyone could do or say to me right here, right now. I got on with the little knowledge I had of horses and my team, the guide, and I rode for about an hour through desert land, cacti, and rock formations, soaking up the dry heat and taking in views I'd never have back home. I found it so fascinating how I grew up around areas of thickly grown pines and oaks and here it was completely different. I even saw what the trail guide called a wild horse. It was nothing like I'd ever seen. Dark brown and black in color, short, muscles rippling, living up to its description of "wild" in appearance. It ran away as soon as it knew it had been spotted.

    The whole adventure was so liberating. I didn't have to worry about threats! I didn't have to worry at all! I didn't know what to do with myself! I was still. I was genuinely happy. Even when my teammate's horse got too close to Dusty and bit him, causing him to rear up with me, I was calm. I dropped the reins as I'd been told to do by the guide should that happen. The guide turned around and immediately screamed at me to drop them when Dusty wasn't stopping. I threw my hands in the air and made a face as if to say, "They ARE dropped!" while I sat still in the saddle with my best poker face on. Dusty calmed down and the horse behind me from that point on kept a good distance between us.

    I thought back on all the good times I'd missed. My first boyfriend, Zeke, was great with horses and used to try to get me to ride with him regardless of what was told would happen to me. His rebellious streak was ten miles wide, I believe. I remember him being almost reckless. My rebellious side, probably more like a few feet across, wasn't quite developed enough yet to outweigh the potential consequences, so I always told him no. He was obviously annoyed with each "no" but was always kind to me about it. I don't think he realized just how scared I was, especially of my dad, and I don't think he understood how concerned I was about getting in trouble.

I have only ridden once since then. It was at my husband's pawpaw's barn in 2011. It didn't carry the same joy as that first ride, but it was a fine, good memory with someone I love. Would I ride again? Absolutely. Sometimes my imagination runs wild; I ride in my mind. In my imagination I am good at it. I am smiling, free for the time the daydream lasts.

I'm thankful for a horse named Dusty in Arizona. He was good to me. Horses are so intelligent and intuitive; he was certainly patient, and I am glad he was chosen for me. I'm thankful for how freeing it was to be able to do something I'd longed to do without fear of pain, fear of hurt. I'm thankful for it being the right time and place in my life for me to actually enjoy it. I don't believe I'd have enjoyed it while I lived at home. I'd have been a nervous wreck each time with the what ifs rattling in the back of my mind, making their way down into my heart and down into my gut like the ball in a pinball machine. I would rather do something and enjoy it than do it while being on the brink of tears the whole time.

I am reminded of 1 John 4:18 which says, "There is no fear in love; but perfect love casts out fear, because fear has punishment..." What joy I was robbed of because of this type of fear. I am convicted of times when I may have caused this type of fear, when I was not disciplining out of love but instilling anger in punishment. I am thankful for a forgiving God who *is* love, who I can cling to and find peace in.

But, like I said, I am thankful for horses, too.

Day 2:
Delayed Shipping/Mail

I woke up this morning with a to-do list. Yesterday was Sunday for me, so other than church not much else happens outside of normal routine cooking and housework unless it's an emergency or someone is sick. While going through my to-do list, which included listing appointments to schedule, sorting through kids' toys to get rid of, cleaning, and more, I began to remember the mail didn't run Saturday. The mail person had turned around at my mailbox without so much as opening my box. I had already received an email from USPS saying I had quite a bit of mail coming, including paperwork that appeared to be about an important upcoming appointment and surgery consult. No mail. Nothing. A bit frustrating.

This morning, I checked to see if the post office was open today. They weren't. I rolled my eyes and complained about Saturday when I didn't get the mail I needed. As I continued to gripe, I walked toward my jar. I keep it put up in a cabinet in my kitchen to make sure it is out of the way of grabby little hands. I unscrewed the lid, dug deep into the jar, and pulled out the crinkled paper that said, "Delayed Shipping".

God seemed to say, "I see your smart-aleck attitude. Write about *this*." Very funny, God... but I deserved that. I smiled and let out a faint laugh as I told God how hilarious He was.

To add, I also recently ordered a personalized Harry Potter wand for my niece as her Christmas present. It was placed in the mail on December 8th. I have watched it since then. It has been at Royal Mail in Sheffield, England since then. I'll be honest, I did not notice it was made in England or shipped from there. To make matters worse, the Royal

Mail employees have been on strike for weeks now. I also cannot reach the seller, but everyone else talks about great communication and excellent products on her review page. Yet another dilemma this morning.

If I'd had that piece of mail with me that I so wanted to see, I wouldn't have gotten other things accomplished I wanted to. You see that piece of mail I wanted was about my upcoming laparoscopy and hysteroscopy to check on a mass in my pelvis and polyps inside my uterus. I'd have sat down, gotten distracted by it, not cleaned like I wanted to, and quite frankly let my attention wander or be lazy. I would have let thoughts about all of it consume me and consume my Google search bar. I'd have thought about next Monday, the date of my consultation. My thoughts run away with me quickly; they always have. If I'd gotten the package from England, I'd have gotten even more frustrated and impatient because I wouldn't have been able to mail it to my niece today because the post office is closed.

I'm thankful for being able to focus on things that need my attention *today*, not my attention next Monday. I'm thankful for being forced to be in the moment and not in the tomorrows. I'm thankful for God reminding me my worries don't get me anywhere, for teaching me patience, and correcting my bad attitude daily.

Day 3:
Hoarded Money

Granny cleaned houses for homebound elderly people. Be advised, Granny was in her 70s while cleaning for these people. These people were her age and older; she was just in better shape and was always finding a way to make money. This cleaning also sometimes included cooking for people, making sure they had a hot meal before she left for the day.

During the summer, she'd drag me around with her to different houses every day. We'd be there for hours. I dreaded this most of the time. One house I particularly dreaded was Ms. Christie's.

Ms. Christie was only a year older than Granny, but in poor health and mentally unstable. Ms. Christie had lived a troubled life that not many people spoke about. It's to my understanding she married a man who'd abused her and got her pregnant. When the baby died soon after birth, it's said she lost her mind. Her husband sent her to Bryce Hospital in Tuscaloosa, AL. I suggest you do some reading on the horrors of this place as well as the spooky legends surrounding it. I believe every Alabamian over 30 years old either knows a good Bryce Hospital spooky story or at least knows what it was. I've got relatives who spent time there and I know others whose relatives have, too. I only know Ms. Christie was there because of the box of letters we inherited upon her death. They could be a story themselves. They start out with a woman with somewhat average, but pretty, handwriting sending letters to loved ones, telling them it all was a misunderstanding. She said she wanted to come home and that she wasn't crazy. As the letters go on and new medications, water therapies (basically waterboarding), and electroshock therapies are administered, her handwriting gets worse and worse. Her mind turns almost childish. At the end of almost all her letters, she reminds the reader, "I'm not crazy."

I say all that to explain who she was to me when I was young. Ms. Christie was a large, soft woman with crazy eyes that went in different directions. She had a voice that seemed to screech while remaining soft. She was so nice, but I was so scared of her because of her appearance and the smell of urine wafting from her bedside commode. She lived in an old cabin with a dusty front porch and rocking chairs. It came complete with an original wood-burning stove no longer in use. I think it was her childhood home. The whole place and Ms. Christie always creeped me out to the point I stayed in the car while Granny cleaned until she would force me inside to say hi and be friendly. It wasn't a "hot car" situation. I chose to be out there to draw, do puzzles, whatever I wanted, and was able to get out of the car whenever I needed to. Every time we'd get ready to leave, Ms. Christie would have a conversation with Granny about the known reality of death. Ms. Christie pointed to Granny as she spoke.

"Now, Earlene, when I die you make sure you get that couch."

The couch. It may have been one of the worst parts of the house. Yellow and floral, it was covered in some type of wipeable material. It was crunchy when you sat on it. It was somehow sweaty and dry at the same time. It was directly across from Ms. Christie's bed. It was the place I was made to sit when I had to go inside.

Granny cleaned this woman's house for years and years. Finally in 2007, Ms. Christie closed her eyes one last time and it's my hope that her sweet soul went to Heaven. I believe she did, or so says the evidence of how she lived her life. Ms. Christie's sister didn't want much of anything in the house, and lo and behold Granny inherited several things, including an old cedar trunk that sits in front of my king-size bed now. As instructed, she made sure to get that gross couch.

Mom and Granny lugged the heavy piece home on a small trailer. One of the cushions fell to the ground as they unloaded it and to our surprise, money fell out. Everywhere. It wasn't long before they were both digging into the couch and handing me wads of cash as they continued to search. My teenage eyes grew wide with each $20 bill or $100 bill they gave me.

The teenager in me saw thousands of dollars. I held so much cash in my hand, how could it not be thousands? It was probably more like $1,000, but it was still more money than I'd ever held.

Ms. Christie had quietly been shoving cash into this couch for who knows how many years as a means of saving it. She met someone, Granny, who cared for her and showed her more love by acts of service than anyone else had. Ms. Christie wanted to help Granny in the only way she knew she could. That couch was an icky safety deposit box no one knew existed.

I'm thankful for this hoarded money. I'm thankful Granny was able to get this financial blessing as a thank you for all the cleaning and meals she'd provided. I'm thankful Granny didn't ignore the gift she was given, otherwise that couch would be buried in the ground probably along with the house now. I'm thankful for the memories and the hindsight I have about how I should have been friendlier to Ms. Christie. I'm thankful for being able to forgive the fearful little girl who didn't understand.

It reminds me we shouldn't ignore the gifts God gives us. He may hand us something we don't want that turns into one of our biggest blessings down the road. That's what I believe, and I'm not crazy.

Neither was Ms. Christie.

Day 4:
Uppity People

I need y'all to understand how difficult this one was for me. As I said in the beginning of this book, I purposefully wrote down prompts that I knew would challenge me and prompts I did not like. "Uppity People" falls into that category. The past three days have been challenging to some degree, but they were all things I could get typed quickly. This one took me all day to figure out. Was I busy? Yes, and that alone made this one difficult. However, this one was mulled over all day.

To figure out why and how I could be thankful for uppity people took me journaling my thoughts. "Uppity" itself means things like pompous, full-of-oneself, presumptuous, arrogant, self-important, self-righteous. These are the people who probably have neck cramps from all their looking down on other people while their noses are turned upwards. Takes talent.

I wrote down examples of these people I've known in my life. I found myself knowing several over the years. Most of the examples I thought of were people who used their name for clout, made it known you were lesser than them, stared at people with condemnation, just to name a few qualities and actions.

I also found myself examining my own day-to-day thoughts and actions. These uppity people and I aren't necessarily all that different. I think you'll find you fit in, too. I think we all can be a bit "uppity" depending on the day and who we are talking about. I believe we all like to make ourselves feel better about our current situation, sometimes looking at other people's misfortune as some sort of measuring stick. We pretend we are ten feet tall against their three-foot yard stick, but truth be told we are just wearing a blindfold with our eyes shut so we won't have to catch a glimpse through the fabric.

Allow me to paint a picture for you.

It was the late 1990's. A 30-something farmer walked into his local grocery store around lunchtime to get some dog food. The man was greasy and sweaty. It was early fall in North Alabama and his jeans and shirt were both covered in dirt and hay. The only thing not covered in hay was the matted mess of hair under his worn-out cap and his eyes behind thick-lensed glasses. His boots were worn out and falling to pieces. As he carried the sack of dog food over his shoulder to his truck, a woman noticed him. The woman wore heels, had on clean, pressed dress pants, and a floral blouse fresh off a rack from a store where triple-digit prices were common (that's just the dollars, not the cents.) She scowled at him as he walked by her, eyeing him up and down. They, by chance, had parked next to one another. The farmer felt eyes on him. He looked up to see the woman staring. With a snooty tone and a grin set for a laugh, she commented. "*You* must be a farmer." This particular farmer on this particular day was not willing to take the comment lightly, so he quickly retaliated with a rude comment before getting in his truck to drive home.

Later that evening, the farmer sat in his old recliner with a notepad figuring up expenses. He was on his fourth Dr. Pepper and halfway through a bottle of Kentucky Gentleman by now. He heard loud noises from the rental house across the road. The man who lived there was known to sell drugs. The farmer immediately began complaining to his wife about the "dope head" across the road and all the commotion he and his friends caused. The farmer laughed as he commented, "That boy won't ever amount to anything, just some drug addict. At least I'm better than *that* guy."

Into the wee hours of the night and early morning, people were still awake at that rental house across the road. The man who lived there sat with a couple of friends talking about everything from hallucinations to work and life. Smoke floated from their mouths above the room as they talked together. The man who lived there began complaining about the immigrant who had begun working at his job. They worked at a plant together, but the man made it known how "disgusting" this immigrant was compared to himself. "His clothes are always dirty; he brings the same stuff for lunch every day. Has to ride with somebody to work because dude doesn't even have his own car!" The man stopped to retrieve a small baggie of white powder out of his pocket. Before he opened it, he finished his thoughts by saying, "He can't even learn English. I got my own crap going on, but I ain't as bad off as *that* guy."

The next day, the immigrant in question shows up with a co-worker to his job at the plant. His Wranglers are a bit snug, but they are what his wife could afford at the thrift store, and he is just happy she found some. Thanks are expressed for the continued rides to work. He walks in but does not clock in, as the supervisor is paying him under the table for now and paying him considerably less than the other employees. He quietly places his lunchbox in the breakroom before going to his assigned job. A few other guys who speak his language work closely by him and they take the freedom of their foreign tongue to speak insults about some of their coworkers. They snicker and laugh together quietly. His eyes glance around the building and he spots his supervisor. His supervisor is a wealthy man with marriage problems, including a list of multiple girlfriends. The gossip is well-known, but the supervisor puts on a good front. The immigrant man shakes his head and thinks to himself, "What a terrible man. He isn't faithful to his wife. He has more money than he knows what to do with. I bet he's never really worked a day in his life and has always been able to tell people what to do. Thank God I'm not as sorry as *that* guy."

The clock strikes 4:30 p.m. The supervisor packs up his things to leave for the day while shift workers count down the minutes for their workday to end. The supervisor places his briefcase and lunchbox in his dual-cab truck before heading home. Up pulls the supervisor to a gated driveway. He punches in the code and the gates open to a beautiful two-story home with a pool in the backyard. Three children run to meet him as he steps out of the truck. He greets them each with a brief hug before entering the home and making his way into the kitchen. His wife is not done with supper and has not got laundry folded and put away yet. The supervisor rolls his eyes and thinks to himself how he doesn't understand why he stays with her. The thought crosses his mind, "What does she *do* all day?" The rest of the night is filled with snide comments from the supervisor towards his wife, a long list of insults all seeming to insinuate he is too good for her and how she is nothing without him. She starts arguing with him. One comment he makes finally strikes a nerve that leaves her in tears the rest of the night. "I'm better than you will ever be. I may be as sorry as you say I am, but at least I'm not *you*. You're worthless."

The next morning, the supervisor's wife gets in her Mercedes to go to the local grocery store. She feels she needs more wine after last night's fight. She pulls into the parking lot only to see a beat-up farm truck she recognizes.

She rolls her eyes. "Oh great, it's that *farmer* again. My life may not be perfect but at least I'm not *him*."

I am humbly finding thankfulness for uppity people because I find myself being one of them and needing forgiveness for being judgmental. I am thankful for being able to recognize it in myself and not simply just write an entry on why uppity people upset me and how they've hurt my feelings before. I'd gain nothing from that, and neither would you. My hope is that you realize that on at least one occasion in your life, you have been an uppity person, too. I'd make a bet we all have.

I am thankful God is the ultimate judge. I am thankful He sees all our sins and shortcomings the same. None of us are better than the person next to, behind, or in front of us. We are born into this life the same way, messy and with nothing, and we will leave this life in the same manner. I'm thankful He is working on me, and I hope you know He is working on you.

I'm glad He reminds this uppity person of how much of a "lowly person" she truly is. I am thankful for the daily opportunities to do better and grow.

Day 5:
Baking

I grew up in a house built in the 1940's by my great-grandfather on Granny's side. The house probably could have been one of those "quaint" old country farmhouses people often daydream about, but it was not what I'd call "quaint" during the time I lived there. In fact, the home was not cared for very well. It was in the beginnings of disrepair. More often than not, fights ruled the house. I believe the floor was made of pins and needles. It was neither the cleanest nor tidiest, but probably one of the better areas of the house in that regard was the kitchen. The kitchen sat on the south end of the property. From the kitchen sink, one could look out the window down onto the driveway (the house sat atop a full basement, and I would consider it somewhat tall on that side of the house because of that.) One could see two trees with two dogs, Shorty and Red, each assigned to one respectively. Beyond that, there were a few acres of field, and then Granny and Paw's house.

In this home, there was rarely any peace to be found. One of the few memories I have there where I didn't feel afraid or worried was when I made biscuits with my mom. Mom made the fattest cathead biscuits I've ever seen to date. They're one of the few things I remember her baking and enjoying. She would make them from scratch with me on the little counterspace we had by the kitchen sink. I was small when we did this, probably between the ages of 3 and 8 years. Mom is 5'10" and always seemed to tower over me as she kneaded the biscuit dough together. I remember looking up and being able to see her tan elbows, sleeves rolled up above them, and her brown frizzy hair lingering around her shoulders as she rolled the dough out onto the flour-covered counter. She would help me onto something to see the countertop better for myself or she would wiggle me onto the counter's edge where I'd have a front-row seat. From this height, I could also see her collection of vintage copper cake pans, including the one decorated in zodiac signs. They were a shiny distraction from the task at hand. Mom would draw my attention back and use her biscuit-cutter or a jar lid to cut the circles out and we would place them on metal pan greased with Crisco.

She'd always purposefully save dough to the side for the two of us to play with. Artistic ability is an inherited skill on mom's side, I know, though trickles of it probably come from Dad's side as well. I don't know where my grandma inherited it, but she had the ability, passed it onto Mom, who passed it onto me, and it seems I've passed it onto my daughter, too.

Mom would teach me to make a ball in the palm of my hands by rolling them gently over the dough. Her long, labored fingers would work it perfectly while my small hands would want to crush the balls as I attempted to roll them. She'd ease my hands apart and work on the finesse it took to make a ball and not a pancake. We'd make a smaller ball and place it on one side of the larger ball before leaning it slightly over. She would teach me to pinch wings and a tail lightly with my fingers out of the larger ball, gently massage the smaller ball into the larger one to create a neck, and – my favorite part – smash part of the smaller ball with my fingers to create a beak. We used to call them little birds. Oh, how I loved that! I believe at least one time we let those birds join the biscuits on the pan, but most of the time they were just for fun. I close my eyes and fondly remember the giggles and the tweeting we'd do.

The oven would work its magic on Mom's biscuits and before long, they'd be ready to come out. The little circles had expanded and grown tall inside the oven; the layers of white flakey goodness sat stacked atop one another like handwritten love notes tucked away in a secret place. The tops shown gold through the shaded light flowing through the kitchen window. They were delicious, but I believe the rarity of them is what made them even better, not to mention the quiet moments Mom and I had together where nothing else mattered.

Over the years, I'd get into Mom's flour and sugar (sometimes with permission, often without permission, of course) among other kitchen items and make recipes I'd put in the microwave. They all tasted terrible, but as a kid I loved the fact that I could create anything I wanted with my hands. When I grew up and moved out, I continued to have a love for baking. After I had children of my own, I was able to share this with them. They still love to bake anything with me, arguing and playing rock paper scissors over who gets to do which step of the recipe. Their sense of pride over their creation and the time I get to spend with them makes me so happy and fills me with joy. Lately, I've been baking every Wednesday night for church. My husband has been doing a Bible Study on Wednesday nights with desserts and coffee, a small-group type of setting. It has allowed me to try new recipes and introduce people I've grown to care a lot about to some of my favorites.

When my husband and I were houseparents at a girls' group home, I got to bake with some of the girls there on occasion. One of these girls, who ended up being our bonus daughter, dreaded baking and would do anything she could to avoid it. It turns out her grandmother would bake with her and her sister when they lived with her and after her grandmother had basically stepped out of her life, our bonus daughter lost any fondness for baking.

During Christmas a few weeks ago, our bonus daughter came to stay with us. She wanted to bake cookies with my kids. She has come to a point in her life where she wants to reclaim hobbies she once enjoyed and create her own memories surrounding them. I assisted some, but I allowed her to use my great-grandmother's roller to roll out cookie dough. That was special to me, and I don't think enough people realize that a lot of kids in broken homes or with foster care backgrounds don't get to have- or ever use- their own family heirlooms. My kids got their black plastic stool and stood by her pressing out various Christmas shapes into the sweet gooey flatness. It made me glad to see her share that memory with my kids and be a positive experience. Turns out, I had printed her a cookbook for Christmas with family recipes, recipes she and I have made together, and even recipes from other houseparents. I hope she cherishes it as much as I cherished making it.

Today is my bonus daughter's 21st birthday, so for today to be finding reasons to be thankful for baking is fitting. (If pigs sprout wings and take off in flight one day, that'll probably be the day she reads this book.)

I am thankful for baking not only for the deliciousness that obviously comes with it, but the fond memories it has provided me. I am thankful for baking because it gave me a sweet memory with my mom that no one can take from me. Those memories with her are some of my favorite ones from my childhood. I'm thankful for the time baking allows my children and I to have together. I'm thankful for the redeeming it has begun to do in my bonus daughter as she works on rebuilding her life after all she's been through. I'm thankful for the ability to be able to provide something yummy for people. I hope they enjoy eating it as much as I enjoy baking it.

Finally, I'm thankful for little dough birds. When there is dough or playdoh anywhere near and I'm teaching other kids or playing with my own, I'm always going to make a bird for them. It usually ends up with nest, eggs, the works, and that's okay. It is always a great time and makes me smile just as much as them.

Thank you for the time spent with me. Thank you for the biscuits. Thank you, Mom.

Day 6:
Innocence

This one has been one of those let-me-ponder topics. I've found when pulling these from the jar, sometimes it is a quick, "Oh boy, do I know a story that could explain this!" Other times it is a jaw-opening moment where I believe a frequency of white noise may be escaping my mouth or there may be smoke sizzling from my ears. With this topic, I was referring to childlike innocence. When I wrote it, I remember writing it down with the full intent of being thankful for it, but it took me a bit to compose my thoughts and explain why.

Tonight, my husband and I took our three young children to an event called Jurassic Empire. It is a drive-thru diorama where one can enjoy animatronic dinosaurs, some life-size and but all life-like, and listen along to explanations of the dinosaurs and fun facts about them. At the end of the drive-thru, pictures could be taken for an extra $10 with a dinosaur children could sit on. The cost was $45 for all five of us together in a vehicle and it lasted for about an hour. We went at a great time where the full moon was in the sky, giving it an almost spooky feel, and the blue, red, and green lights placed below the dinosaurs lit them up in the coolest way.

I am pretty frugal (some would call it cheap, but I digress) so the thought of paying that money seemed a bit much to me, but was it worth it? Oh, absolutely. I watched my children (elementary and preschool ages) gawk, ooh, and ahh at all the large creatures as their bodies leaned out of the car windows to get a better look. Tripp (my youngest son) had squeals of delight and began making sounds like the dinosaurs. One man who worked for the diorama was walking around with a baby raptor puppet. He would let it come to the windows of the vehicles where kids could pet it. The puppet would open its mouth and its hide felt scaly. My kids petted the raptor's head. They smiled.

Anniston (my oldest child) asked the man if the baby raptor was real. He replied, "What do you think?" with a grin as he walked away. As we rode through the exhibit, I seemed to notice she was more fascinated with figuring out if any of what she was seeing was real. Ridge (my other son) seemed to simply enjoy learning all the scientific information as we drove along and recognized dinosaurs out of books he'd read and movies he'd seen. Tripp, as I said before, was busy trying to become a dinosaur and making chomping motions with his teeth. As I said, my daughter was very caught up in the "Is this real?" question. It didn't take away her ability to enjoy the moment, but it hit me that her innocence is starting to fade away. What I mean by this is that her sense of wonder, her sense of naivety, her ability to be caught up in her delight, seemed a bit duller as she asked questions trying to figure out the truth.

Now, is she still innocent? Absolutely! I'd argue she is my daydreamer and always has her head in the clouds. She is a big creative soul in a little body. She is still fairly innocent as far as her knowledge of worldly things. Tonight, however, I just happened to notice another side of her: the side that is trying to grow up on me. There is nothing wrong with her asking questions and getting to the bottom of what is going on. I want her to ask all the questions about all the things, but I hope she always asks me or her dad first. I hope we create that environment for all our kids. The way in which she was doing it showed me a side of her my mama heart was dreading. I know my oldest son is not far behind her; he is already my little old soul. I have a few more years left of this childlike wonder left in my littlest one. I have decided I'll make better efforts to enjoy it. I'll soak it up like dry ground soaks up rain, because one day all it will be is memories.

Watching innocence in children is so precious and can melt the hardest hearts. I am thankful for childlike innocence because it only lasts so long for most people. Some people are still able to tap back into that kind of innocence even after they're long into adulthood, and at times I envy those people because I lost that ability a long time ago. It is something we all come into this world with, but something that is so easily taken away by the things of the world and even sometimes, unfortunately, by other people who feel they have a right to it. I'm thankful for being in a position in my life where I can pause all the fast pace of the world and enjoy watching my children's innocence during times like tonight. The moon and multicolor lights dancing off the reflection of their eyes to a chorus of "wows" in my car made me smile and laugh and took concerns of life away just for a little while.

My kids are all in bed now. My youngest is no doubt dreaming about the dinosaurs he saw and tomorrow I'm sure he will be concocting ideas of how to play with his own dinosaurs to imitate what he saw. I wonder what it would be like if we were childlike in our faith like we are supposed to be, like if we were to really delve in deep on what verses like Matthew 18:3 mean. Would we go to bed dreaming of all the great thing God has done? All the things He is going to do in our lives. Would we wake up praying and thinking of ideas to serve God? Would we be excited? I believe if we did like we're supposed to, we'd wake up giddy and ready to take on the world with a refreshed and full heart.

I think we need to revisit our innocence and recapture what childlike faith is. I believe life would be a lot better if we did.

Day 7:
Microwavable/Easy Meals

This one is sort of funny to me. I think when someone is trying to think of 365 things to be thankful for, they start writing anything they can think of. Don't get me wrong, I'm thankful for food in general. I've got a long Baptist history, so obviously food is a winner. However, specifically microwavable food is an interesting one.

If I think back over the years, I can think of the time I believe I officially became thankful for microwavable food. It was early Fall 2009, and I was living in a dorm at the community college I was playing tennis for. These dorms had a lower floor for guys and an upper floor for girls. Except for a couple of people, we were all athletes. There were tennis players, volleyball players, baseball players, basketball players, and if memory serves me right softball players and cheerleaders lived there too. After classes and after practices were over, it was as if everyone would intermingle and the whole building became like one giant house. Often, unless someone just wanted the privacy, doors were left open for people to come visit.

I lucked out and had a suite with three other girls: two I had grown up with and graduated high school with and one I'd competed against in tennis. We had two girls each in two bedrooms, we shared a bathroom (we can all agree that four girls in one bathroom was a horrible experience on so many levels,) and the best part was we had a small kitchen with a dining room area. Our rooms had poorly painted gray blocks for walls. In college, you couldn't have a hot plate or any sort of oven, but... you could have a microwave. Although I was thankful for things I could heat up in the microwave, I was sick of the same stuff, and I desperately wanted chicken quesadillas while living on a ramen noodle budget. I posed the idea of quesadillas to a few people one night and told them I'd make it happen in the microwave. We pitched in funds together and I went to Walmart for flour tortillas, fiesta blend cheese, and frozen grilled chicken packs. Once I got back, I heated the frozen chicken in the microwave, then got out a plate and began layering cheese and chicken on a tortilla before folding it over and popping it in the microwave for another minute. Ding! Finished. Steaming, bland, quesadilla bliss (what, did y'all think I had money for seasonings?) I took a bite before it could cool off, I was so hungry. It was delicious. I gave a thumbs up during mid-chew.

After they trusted the success of the first one, those that had pitched in money began to await their own quesadillas. As they each received one on their paper plate, they'd find a place to sit in the dining area or prop against the wall. What a variety. Three or four different ethnicities in one place; there were girls, guys, and people heights of five feet tall all the way up to people who were pushing seven feet tall. There were some whose eyes would close as they took a bite as if to soak in the warmth and taste for just a little longer. I can only imagine it was the first "home-cooked meal" they'd had in months. Some of them were from as far away as New York just appreciative to have a scholarship somewhere, even a little community college in Alabama. How long had it been since any of them had someone besides the lunch ladies in the college cafeteria to cook for them. Most of the food I was eating was cheap food, fast food, or food bought buy my college boyfriend when we went on dates. Looking back on it, while brief and a somewhat unremarkable moment, it was probably important at the time, whether we realized it or not. It was as if we had a mini fellowship there in that kitchen.

I'm thankful for the simplicity and the ease with which microwavable meals can happen. As a mom now, I am even more grateful some days for this! I'm thankful for the ability to get creative and cook something other than a bowl of Velveeta Shells & Cheese, but those still serve their place. I'm thankful a bunch of misfit young adults found a way to put differences aside and "break bread" with one another.

Day 8:
Storms

Storms have a bad connotation. They mean everyone must come inside from play time. They keep outdoor work from getting completed most of the time. The right conditions can cause a storm to leave destruction and death in its path. However, I believe we can find reasons to be thankful for them.

I am really beginning to see God is for sure working in this. I've questioned it somewhat since beginning this work, writing from these prompts. I get a lot of "what-ifs" in my mind, such as what if people criticize, what if people think this is bad, what if I get a lot of push back for my opinions and experiences? I am glad today helped me to see past all of that and to see I am on the right path. This morning I opened my jar and pulled out the "storm" prompt. It just so happens that last night a small storm came through our area. The only reason I know is that the thunder woke me up just enough to know it was happening. Our youngest quietly crawled into bed with us at some time in the night. I woke enough just to see him pull the covers up and slide in between my husband and I, his typical spot. Rain could be heard hitting our roof as we drifted back to sleep. Violet, our two-year-old German Shepherd, at one point must have been startled by the thunder because she woke us up falling off the foot of our bed onto my cedar chest. Then, we had Sunday School this morning. We discussed verses out of Nehemiah and touched on fear for a bit, mentioning storms at one point. Just the two instances were enough for me to feel more confidence in what I'm doing with all of this.

I stopped for a moment during church and wrote in my notebook the question, "Why would someone be thankful for storms?" There were thoughts that immediately came to mind, and I jotted them down. I think first and foremost I cannot talk about literal storms without likening them to storms we have in our spiritual lives. Storms may be destructive, but they reveal where things are weak or need more strength. Just like with tough times that come through our lives, they reveal parts of us that need work. It reminds us of what reality is and not just our false perceptions of it. During storms, we cling to whatever makes us feel grounded and safe, just as my small son crawled closer to us when the storm seemed big and scary because he believes and trusts we will protect him. These things are put to the test after the storm ends, and we see what is left standing. Storms not only reveal what is going on in us, but they reveal how powerful and strong God is. God has promises/plans for us even in chaos when nothing seems "good". There's a well-known verse, Jeremiah 29:11, which reminds us of this. In saying all of this, storms also allow for rebuilding. When floods destroy or tornadoes tear down, it allows for the old to be wiped out and for new to be built back in its place. Storms bring growth, physically by rain and spiritually the same way. Lastly, I wrote that storms remind us of our humanity. We often give ourselves superpowers we don't actually have and live as though we are immortal, but storms remind us of just how miniscule and fragile we are in the grand scheme of it all.

I am thankful for storms because I believe I've learned just as much during storms as I have during the good weather in life, probably even more. Storms remind us to stay on our toes and to be prepared, to stay vigilant, whereas sometimes when weather is always good, we become complacent. I'm sad for things and people that have been taken because of the storms. There is certainly room for grief. However, as I mentioned, storms *do* have their place and there's reasons for them. Do I know the reasons? No. I am sometimes capable, though, of seeing the lessons learned from the experience. You can see the lessons, too, only if your mind is set to search for them.

I hope if you are not able to see it now, that one day you will. Storms are always going to come, but they do end. I stop to pray now for you to know this and believe it. Doing neither can cause a dark bitterness to consume your soul, and your soul is worth much more than that.

Day 9:
Confidence

The truth is, I opened my jar with a different prompt stuck to the lid this morning. I didn't feel like it was the prompt of the day, so I laid it to the side and dug for another one. The choices were "electricity" and "confidence". The minute I picked up confidence, it sparked a song in my head. The song is "Do It Again" by Elevation Worship. It's been stuck in my head most of the day. I chose the confidence prompt of those two solely because of that song.

The song reminds us God's promise still stands. It reminds us God is faithful and that we are always in His hands. We are reminded God has not failed us.

Today I had my doctor's appointment/surgery consult for the hysteroscopy and laparoscopy. The appointment went as well as to be expected. I have surgery scheduled for next Tuesday.

Confidence, by definition, is the feeling or belief that one can rely on someone or something. Another definition states confidence is the state of feeling certainty about something or a situation. Finally, another definition points to self-assurance. I have some confidence in my surgeon's ability to do her job. She certainly impressed me today as she quoted my medical history perfectly (which, regarding my childbearing history, is quite extensive and a bit crazy.) She has the credentials and is well-studied. However, I also know reality of human nature. She could have an unsteady hand that day for reasons out of her control. She could make the wrong decision while I'm under the knife. She could be distracted. I'd venture to say I have "loose" confidence in her abilities because I know she is as human as I am and imperfect.

Just like the song says, my real confidence lies is in God. He's brought me to this point for some reason and will bring me through it for whatever purpose He sees fit. I am confident he Has me right where He wants me. I'm confident He has allowed me to see the physician He desires me to see for whatever reason that may be. God is Holy and perfect in every way, and I can have full confidence in Him whereas confidence in man can fail or prove foolish. Confidence in God has nothing to do with self-assurance and everything to do with blessed assurance.

I am thankful for confidence in daily tasks, sure. Earthly confidence looks like walking in a room knowing your worth, walking into a competition sure you'll win, and many other things. I'm more thankful for Godly confidence because that is the only confidence I can really count on. It is without blemish and goes with me wherever I go, no matter what situation I may face.

Psalm 27:3 tells us, "Though an army should encamp against me, my heart shall not fear; though war should rise against me, even then I will be confident."

I've seen God move. I believe He will keep doing what He does. Everything else around me may fail, but my God never will.

Day 10: Thick, Curly Hair

I have a confession to make. I have thick, curly hair… that probably wasn't the juicy secret you wanted me to admit to. It isn't just the normal run-of-the-mill "thick" hair. It is hair that is deceptively thick. When it is combed out or brushed out, it looks normal, but pulling it up in a ponytail proves otherwise.

I was not always thankful for this. When I was very young, from kindergarten until fourth grade, my granny would French braid my long, thick, curly hair every single day. If she didn't, kids at school would mess with it, pull on it, or I would come home with it in a long and matted mess. Once I had a girl in my first grade P.E. class who ran up behind me and untied my hair as we were running our laps. My hair flapped in the wind behind me as she laughed and ran away with my ponytail holder in her hand.

I had the same routine every morning. Mom would drive me next door to Granny and Paw's house before she went to work. Granny would have me sit in a chair at the bar (it was a bar for food, not the kind of bar where they serve alcohol.) She would brush through those thick curls, making them grow like the Grinch's heart at Christmas time. They'd frizz out and she would tame them with hair spray and water as her knotty fingers gracefully braided the thick strands. I would scream and cry with every tangle she would hit and complain of the headaches as she made sure the braid was tight. Afterwards, either Granny would take me to school, or my neighbor would take me along with her son. Finally, in fourth grade, I decided I was sick of having long hair. On the day before I was to compete in the county spelling bee, Mom agreed to cut my hair. I had two feet of hair cut off that day and I felt like a new person.

For the next few years- especially during the pubescent years- I'd struggle to figure out how to manage this head of hair. There was a song by Sara Evans that says the straight-haired girls all want curls and the brunettes want to be blonde. I can certainly identify to some degree. When high school came along, I was flat-ironing the curls out of my hair as often as possible and using sun-in every chance I could in the summertime. It took my college roommate embracing her own curly hair to make me want to let mine do its thing from time to time. Now as an adult in her 30's, I have finally found the right curl cream to tame the frizz when I want to let it be curly and have found the right routine to do a good blowout on my hair. I finally figured out how to embrace it and be happy with it. I've come to a point I can pretty much do whatever I want with my hair, and I can enjoy it.

I'm thankful to have my hair. I've learned to love it not only because I know how to handle it now, but because my daughter inherited it from me, and I find hers a million times more beautiful than mine ever was or could be. Both my sons have thick hair; one has straight hair, and one has wavy hair. I'm thankful for all the time Granny put into braiding it for me, even though it was an act of torture most days. She was doing it as a labor of love for me that I could not truly appreciate back then. I regret not listening to her for my daughter's sake when it came to learning how to braid hair myself. Lastly, I am thankful for what I feel silly for calling my "hair journey", learning how to appreciate what I have and instead of trying to be something or someone that I am not.

Day 11: Daughters

Oh, what a topic. There are several topics I don't think I can do justice on, and this is one of them. There is no way I can put into words adequately how important daughters are and how thankful I am for mine.

I am more blessed than I deserve to have a biological daughter as well as young ladies I call bonus daughters. Some people get neither of those opportunities and I am no stranger to that; I know how special it is.

Daughters are a breath of fresh air. They are fiercely independent from the time they scribble and create colorful Crayola worlds on their own to the first time they change classes at school by themselves. They are an imagination full of dreams where they are the heroine, saving themselves and everyone they love in their thoughts- and unknowingly in reality- just by being themselves. They are a bag of every emotion known to mankind, shaken not stirred. They are full hearts and broken hearts at any given time in their lives, both needing an equal amount of love and desserts. We are wrapped around their fingers forever, spinning from both the wonder and the headaches they cause, while they are none-the-wiser, spinning circles of their own in playground dust.

In tears, I type "I love my daughters." Until they have their own experience with daughters, they'll never really get it. You'll fight tooth and nail to make them a better woman than you ever were. I am thankful for being a mother. I am certainly thankful for having my sons- which will be a whole other prompt- but I am thankful in a different yet similar way for my daughters. As a matter of fact, my biological daughter gets her own prompt just as my sons do.

God, thank you for my daughters. I am unfit to deserve such precious souls in my life, but you saw fit to let me enjoy some of this physical life with them. Thank you from the bottom of my heart.

Day 12: Flower Sales

From the time I began retaining memories all the way up until I moved out of my house, I can remember what I'll refer to as flower sales. In the Southeastern United States, there is a tradition called Decoration. Decoration happens once a year at cemeteries where people come together to decorate the headstones of their loved ones who have gone before them. Back even when I was a kid, it was a huge deal. Aunts, uncles, cousins, everyone in your family would come to gather at local cemeteries and churches. Often, churches would have "Dinner on the Grounds", where there'd be a potluck, and everyone would enjoy the late Spring/early Summer as they had every cheesy casserole and garden-picked vegetable imaginable. Everyone would reminisce on their loved ones and talk about exciting news of the living.

Mom and Granny learned quickly they could make money selling Decoration flowers. They would make saddles to go on top of headstones, vase fillers, stick-ins, pots, baskets, you name it.

Around late March or early April, they'd begin making these floral arrangements. They'd hit up sales at stores like Hobby Lobby and stock up on what they needed. Mom and Granny would sit for hours every night at what we referred to as "the shed", which was a small barn that had served many purposes over the years, anything from a shed for a tractor to a small house for my great-aunt and great-uncle decades before. Granny would take over the greenery, installing it into Styrofoam. Both the greenery and flowers were wrapped in green wire and green floral tape. Mom would take over designing most of the pieces. They would rope me in to come help wrap stems. I would spray some Deepwoods Off on my legs and arms in a futile attempt to ward off armies of mosquitoes, walk down to "the shed", flip over an empty five-gallon bucket for a seat, and begin cutting wire and wrapping it around the variety of stems for what seemed like forever. Granny encouraged me to wear gloves like she did, but I felt they just got in the way. She'd let out a "Well fine, then!" followed by a word that rhymes with "bit" and just let me work and cut my hands up. After so long, my butt would fall asleep from the rim of the bucket and my complaints would settle in. Wire would poke my fingers in the wrong way, and they'd bleed, giving me an excuse to go back up to the house for a Band-Aid. I would then mysteriously vanish and not return the rest of the evening. After a while, I believe they just got tired of hollering for me or walking back and forth to the house to find me for reprimanding, so they'd eventually let me go.

When it came time to sell the arrangements, Mom and Granny had acquired a routine set of customers. They went down every weekend in May to a place we called Rainbow Crossing. It was a four-way stop of two highways that had a heavy traffic presence. We sat in front of a gas station. The other side of the intersection at one point had a decent little country-style restaurant. Outside of that, there was not much of anything for a half a mile or so in either direction.

We'd arrive about 6 or 7 a.m. in our maroon Chevrolet Tiara van and small black enclosed trailer. We would leave sometime after lunch depending on what kind of money we were making. We'd easily make anywhere from as little as $200 to as much as $1,000 in one weekend from people stopping by. The deal was if I made a flower arrangement, I got to keep the money if it sold. I loathed having to make the arrangements all the time and all the critique that came with it, so I did not make that many on my own.

After Decoration was over, cemetery committees would call Mom and Granny to come get any leftover flowers that had blown off graves or that needed to be removed from the grass before mowing. I want to say this was usually a few weeks to a month after flowers had been put out. They would wake me up in the wee hours of the morning to come help them haul off trailer loads of flowers so the mowers could do their jobs. Oh, how hot and sticky those damp humid mornings were, not to mention sleepily tripping over footstones and stepping into fire ant beds. I got covered in more grass and ant bites than I care to remember. A lot of people found this whole process cruel and ugly. The thing is, there were signs posted in the cemeteries about rules for the Decoration flowers. There were obvious rules posted about what was allowed to be left at the cemetery and several warnings stating anything that had fallen off headstones, been blown away by storms, or that was still sitting on the ground, would be thrown away by a certain date. The flowers needed to be secured to the headstone because it was not the cemetery committee's responsibility to ensure the flowers stayed put. Mom would often suggest for customers to stake their baskets into the ground or secure their vase fillers in some way. Another suggestion was to duct tape the saddle of flowers to the top of the headstone. Sometimes people tend to get their feelings hurt even when there are clearly stated consequences for not following rules. My family never took anything that remained on the headstones, even though they got accused on several occasions. That always made me so angry because I knew for a fact that they'd never disrespect someone's grave in that way. Mom and Granny had even taught me to not walk across people's graves and try to walk between them the best I could, or at the foot of the graves, as to show respect for the dead. Maybe that's just an Appalachian thing? Anyway, Mom and Granny would use these flowers again for the next year by recycling them and organizing them into colors, styles, and greenery types. The flowers would be stored in the shed all year long through the brutal Alabama weather changes and be revisited the following year to check their conditions. The process of making flower arrangements would then begin again.

 Even after my parents divorced when I was 19, Mom continued the practice on her own. Granny made her own arrangements. They retained their own separate customers and gained new ones. Granny continued to make flowers occasionally even up until her death in 2021. Mom continues to sell flowers to this day to make extra cash.

 I think it helped me build people skills, and I've ended up using those skills in social work. I met people buying flowers for grandparents long gone, people buying flowers for their babies who only lived a few hours, and people buying flowers for their spouses. I'd listen to their stories as they shared, each one sprinkled with different types of love. I met people who'd known my family for decades who would share the good, the bad, and the ugly with me. It was quite an experience.

I am thankful for the work ethic I saw in Mom and Granny all those years. I am thankful for the time they put into making money to support me growing up. I'm thankful for the early mornings and the late evenings. I'm thankful for the variety of people I met during flower sales.

I'm thankful for a tradition that is, sadly, slowly disappearing. It is a huge part of my childhood that is quietly fading into history just as many other things already have.

Day 13: Desserts

This borders on the edge of the "baking" prompt I've already written on. Because of this, I have admittedly sat this off to the side for three days. I had to come up with reasons why I was thankful for desserts, not solely baking.

After some more ridiculously deep thought on why someone would be thankful for desserts, I remembered my birthday cakes. All my birthday cakes were made by Granny over the years and decorated by Mom. Granny even continued to bake birthday cakes for me up until around 2020 when, between her failing health and the COVID-19 Pandemic, buying cakes from the deli at Walmart became easier. Each year had a different theme. My first birthday was a teddy bear birthday party. Pictures taken on disposable cameras and developed at the local Walmart were placed in a thick photo album for me to have proof the party happened.

From that point on, Granny let me lick the bowl after she baked the cakes. She'd grease the pans in Crisco before mixing the boxed cake mix of choice in one of her Pyrex bowls. Granny would sometimes let me use the mixer. She'd have me stand on a small metal stool and put the mixer on the lowest setting for me. Once everything was said and done, I'd use a spoon and clean the bowl of any remaining cake mix.

After the cake had cooled, Mom would be charged with decorating it in just about any theme I wanted. I've had a Barbie birthday cake, a Mulan birthday cake, and countless others. Keep in mind, these aren't the fancy cakes you see today with multiple tiers and layers. These cakes were single-layer sheet cakes with homemade frosting. Mom would also decorate Paw's birthday cake because his birthday was the day after mine and we always celebrated together. Together every late August/early September, we'd enjoy our desserts and have photos taken of us holding our cakes.

Very rarely were desserts made in our family simply for the sake of having desserts. Once I got out of the house and began baking more on my own, desserts became a part of my life more often. Friends would bake desserts just because, and so would I. We didn't need a special occasion to make each other smile.

During our time at the girls' ranch, my husband would take our girls out for milkshake nights. I can't enjoy milkshakes because they tear my stomach up, but boy does he love a good milkshake. Shoot, he loves just about any dessert except chocolate cake. Randomly, he'd tell the girls and our two older kids they were all going out for milkshakes and all of them would rush to our 15-passenger van. They'd all make a mad dash to Sonic during the summertime when the milkshakes were half-off. It always brought so much joy. Before we came to the girls' ranch, we'd taken our foster parent classes and, through them, learned milkshakes can help calm people down because of the muscles in the face used to drink them. There's a whole science behind it, I promise. I like to think because of that knowledge and knowing the emotions the girls were dealing with on a regular basis, it all may have been a low-key motive for milkshake nights.

I am thankful for desserts because, for the obvious reason, they are delicious. I am thankful for desserts because of the togetherness they bring. Whether they are planned or are given by surprise, they make days brighter. They are shared with people we love for just a moment in time, typically over stories that bring laughter or tears.

I am thankful for special desserts, like my birthday cakes with Paw. He has been gone since 2012 and those memories are dear to me. I am thankful the girls from the girls' ranch fondly remember milkshake nights.

It appears to me life is short, but desserts make it sweeter.

Day 14:
Candles

Why did I write some of these? I mean, you try writing 365 things to be thankful for, I guess.

I used to not be much of a candle person when I was younger. I grew up a kerosene lantern person. When the power would go out at my house during storms, we had antique kerosene lanterns we'd light. I have a few to this day on display in my house, though I'm not sure I'd be comfortable using them with their age. I remember the distinct smell of kerosene as Mom would light the lanterns throughout our house so we could see better. Mom was never a fan of anything floral-scented or powerfully scented in any sort of way. It tore up her allergies, and she would dramatically make sure everyone knew that (sorry, Mom, it's true.)

When I got out on my own in college and into my first couple of apartments, I realized I liked "smell-good things". This may be one of the more feminine things about me. I was able to walk around in stores and smell candles I enjoyed, sometimes buying some. They were always good for when the power went out, but I could buy scents that made me happy. I'm a sucker for clean scents like linen smells, but I'm even more of a sucker for candles that smell like men's cologne. Sandalwood, cedarwood, tobacco scents, things labeled names like "cozy warm blanket", you get the idea. I also love coffee-scented candles. Suddenly, I have the urge to go light one...

Writing this I realize candles became something I could buy for myself to enjoy. I wasn't buying it for anyone else but me. Everything I do in life is typically for someone else... for my husband, for my kids; when I was at work it was for people I worked for and with, and so forth.

Any time I want to do something for myself, I feel guilty. Maybe that's a mother thing. Buying a candle here and there is something I can buy cheaply that I enjoy. It's just a little something that's solely for me.

I now have a whole drawer full of candles in my great-grandmother's China cabinet I inherited. I slowly pull it open and can select anything I want. In the spirit of preparedness during bad weather, I sit out several throughout our home just in case I need to light them. In the defense of a rough day, I'll pick through my favorites and let my youngest pick out his favorite candle. He'll pretend to smell it and tell me, "That's the one!" He chooses the candle I secretly was hoping he would. He thinks he's done such a big job. He'll watch me strike a match or use a lighter, creating a dancing flame to press towards the candle wick. To him, it probably looks like magic, or that's what his eyes tell me.

I am thankful for candles for all the things I mentioned, but I'm most thankful for the power they have. They can turn a pitch-black room into one with glimpses of color and shadows. It illuminates what was once unseen. It eliminates all the scary unknowns and reveals them for what they really are.

I recently read a book that described us as stained glass for God's light to show beautifully through for others to see. I believe God has the power to do that through us if we allow Him our souls and lives to work in. If you look at stained glass in a pitch-black room, you can't tell it to be any different than anything else. It is the light which makes it look different, that shows it for what it is. Imagine how beautiful that could be, watching the light God left in us show through our faces, our actions, our lives, so that others can who He is.

Day 15: Fairbanks, AK

My husband and I were in a strange spot for a while. This strange spot would last into May of 2022. I had found employment within a couple of months of being laid off from our houseparent positions during the beginning of the COVID-19 Pandemic. Phillip, however, did not. He applied for multiple positions in different types of job settings. He tried finding employment as a pastor, youth pastor, all the above and every door was slammed in his face. This led to him being a stay-at-home dad from March 2020 until May 2022.

During early 2021, I was standing at the kitchen sink washing dishes and loading the dishwasher. He was sitting in the living room. Most days during this time in our lives were just tiresome, absolutely tiresome. Between our three small children, our bonus daughter, and living paycheck to paycheck, I think tiresome covers it. Phillip casually asked me from the living room, "What would you think about being houseparents in Alaska?" I rolled my eyes at him. He had a grin on his face. At this point, I didn't even care what we did. I was willing to go wherever and do whatever job. I'd really enjoyed being a houseparent and Phillip had as well, but I wasn't sold on doing it again just yet. I just knew I was unhappy in Alabama and unhappy with the financial situation we were stuck in. I said, "Sure, why not. Apply." Within a day, the group home in Fairbanks, AK had responded to Phillip's application and was on the phone with him. As eloquently as I can put it, I could have crapped my pants.

We were apparently the perfect fit. We went through the first interview easily. We'd been through two years in a girls' group home setting, so we knew the ropes. This facility had all boys. They talked about the demographic of boys we'd be working with, how they were a basic level group home, and so forth. We talked about a lot of what-ifs and how if we were to move forward in the interview process if we'd get to visit there before we moved. Not long after this first interview, I began religiously watching *Life Below Zero*, watching YouTube documentaries on living in Alaska, and preparing every way I possibly could. I learned about the short lifespan of windshields in Alaska and came to my own conclusion that moose are the large annoying racoons of the Yukon. I imagined myself shooing moose away from our driveway and yelling, "Go on, git!"

As I was praying about this journey with Phillip, God worked on me a lot. We were living in the first home we'd ever purchased. We bought it in September 2020 when rates were great. It was a slice of heaven. A little less than one acre of land, it had the perfect sunrises and sunsets. It sat by itself surrounded by pastureland, which is something I've always wanted. The kids had a yard that was mostly fenced in where they could have as many adventures as they desired. It was in driving distance of a Dollar General but about thirty minutes from anything "important". It was quiet and lovely and just enough room for us and our little family.

Prior to this potential move to Alaska, Phillip had spoken with a church around Montgomery, AL just a month or two after we'd bought this house. I immediately became livid with God. I said, "God, seriously? You're gonna let me get in this dang house. And then you're gonna force me out of it. We've been laid off and homeless living with Phillip's parents and *then* you're gonna take our first home from us?" One thing I've learned is you can be aggravated with your circumstances and throw your little spiritual temper tantrums. God can take it, and I believe He'd rather you speak directly with Him about everything. I immediately heard the conviction in my heart and the Holy Spirit reprimanding me. Needless to say, God was working on how tightly I was holding onto worldly possessions even then. Now God was possibly going to move all of us to Alaska.

Around this time, Granny was coming to the end of her life here on Earth. I knew it. She was just going downhill and had been for a while. Dad would call me up letting me know I needed to come to her as soon as possible, and when I'd show up, she'd be wide awake and talking, feeling great again. I thought the end was impending so many times it felt like the grieving process was rewound repeatedly and the play button kept being pushed before it was through.

Just before her death in March 2021, we'd had our final interview with the social worker and president of the group home. They loved us. However, they wanted us to chat with some of the houseparents who were already there. Plus, we learned there was a strong chance we weren't going to be able to visit there before we moved. We'd just be selling our house and going straight up there as soon as possible.

I remember calling one of the houseparents who'd been there a while. She was very polite, open, and honest with me. She talked about how she was from the "Lower 48" (which is evidently what Alaskans refer to mainland as) and her parents ended up passing while she was gone. We talked about how that was hard for her and the toll it took. I ended up sharing my own personal struggle with Granny. It is then I realized God had placed this lady in my path possibly for just that very reason.

Throughout this whole process, Phillip and I were both praying fervently. I had genuinely let go of the desire to keep the house I'd worked so hard for. I had also given over to God the worry about being gone if Granny died. Granny had done quite a bit of my raising and was more like a parent to me. One night Phillip and I agreed we just weren't getting any peace about neither the job nor the move. We prayed together about the whole thing. We were supposed to get a call back from the group home at some point to discuss the decision, what they wanted, and what we wanted. That call would never come. They just dropped off the face of the earth. A couple weeks after this occurred, Granny would shut her eyes for one last sleep and go to Heaven. I was able to see her and talk to her in her final days. She made sure I promised I'd take care of my babies, I told her I loved her, and she told me she loved me, too.

It took another year of heartache and disappointment from one interview to another for Phillip. Financial struggles continued to abound, but God worked in that and created a heart of peace in both of us. Eventually in May 2022, Phillip would be hired as a pastor in Louisiana. By that point, God had worked on both of us and allowed us to not be so tied down to the house, to comfort, to what we *knew*. I am thankful for Fairbanks, AK because it taught us to hold on loosely and be willing to go whenever and wherever He said to go. Had Louisiana came any sooner, I would have probably fought tooth and nail to keep that little piece of paradise I called home. I had no desire to move out of Alabama when we first bought our new home, but over time God changed that and loosened my ties. Some of those ways hurt, like loss of loved ones or simply the feelings of uselessness or feeling unwanted. We were feeling purposeless at home. My heart would not have been ready to accept the change and I would have fought against the greatness God had planned for us. Sometimes we would rather hold onto these little petty things rather than trust God to give us the great and unexpected wonders He has in store for us.

Finally, if I'm being real, I'm thankful God put us somewhere warm. I am naturally a cold person and love the sunshine, so all that cold stuff wouldn't have gee-hawed with me. God knows His children. He kept this Southern woman in a hot and humid climate.

And all God's people said, "Amen."

Day 16: Employment

I'm clearly thankful for employment. Employment allows my husband and I to financially provide for our family. Employment, in our fields, means we are able to minister and work with people. My husband is a preacher and has been a youth pastor, houseparent, and pastor, as well as filled in for preachers at other churches. I have a Bachelor's of Interdisciplinary Studies with an emphasis in Sociology and Behavioral Science. I was supposed to have a BSW (Social Work), but life changed that, and I was able to graduate with all social work courses minus one and do a twenty-page thesis to graduate before our first child was born.

Outside of the gaps of employment where I was able to stay home with my children, I've held some sort of employment since I was 15 years old. I worked at a tack and saddle shop way back then as what I'd call an eBay sales manager. I would photograph saddles and tack to post on eBay for the manager/neighbor/friend's mom. She paid me in cash. I worked at Burger King in addition to that the summer before my senior year of high school. When I was playing tennis in college, no one would hire me, so the way I made money was unlocking and hustling old cell phones as well as doing homework for the basketball players. For one week, I worked at The Shoe Department during Christmas as a temporary employee. It was the absolute worst job I've ever had, and I have been threatened by dangerous people on numerous occasions during my time in social work. I've worked at Bojangles' Famous Chicken 'n Biscuits. I've been an ACT Prep Tutor, worked in school systems as a summer camp counselor and after school aide. I was employed at a mental health facility as a summer camp counselor, been an employee of two different state Child Protective Services, a houseparent at a group home, a sexual assault victim advocate, and currently I am a high school tennis coach and substitute teacher. Who knows, I could have missed something in there.

I think employment has typically come easy for me, so there were times in my life God had to humble me and reveal some things to me. One of these times came during college. In the summer of 2010, I had left the college I'd played tennis at to move to Florence, AL. My boyfriend at the time, who I had been with for going on two years at that point, went to UNA and because of that, I wanted to go there. I'd visited UNA before with a childhood friend and liked it, so I didn't bother to look around anymore. I had already discussed with the tennis coach there the possibility of me playing without a scholarship, but I could not realistically do that and work a full-time job, not to mention both sets of my grandparents were helping me pay for school. My parents had refused to apply for a Pell Grant for me I'm sure over tax issues since they still claimed me as a dependent, and apparently had not paid taxes in some time. I moved to Florence in late May/early June 2010 with a roommate (who I'd become friends with through my then boyfriend) and thought, "This is a college town, surely I can find work quickly." Absolutely not. I applied at all kinds of places for all kinds of jobs. I was turned down for minimum wage employment (back then it had just been bumped up to $7.25 per hour) for two straight months. I began selling off quite a bit of my clothes and eating very little. I drank enough water to cause Wilson Dam to open. There was a place in Sheffield, AL (look up Alabama Shoals Tri-Cities and you'll learn a lot about the area in proximity to Florence) in a Foodland parking lot where people had yard sales on the weekends. It was kind of a mini flea market. I'd take all my junk there and lay it out to make a few bucks. I'd also bring my fiddle and leave my case open, playing old gospel songs and bluegrass music I knew by heart to potentially make a few bucks. I had a few people tip me, but man it was hard times. I lost 30 pounds that summer from walking and working out at the apartment to keep my mind off being broke, not to mention I was mostly eating canned goods and small meals I could afford. If I'm being honest, my boyfriend was living at home for the summer and any time he would drive up and we'd hang out I was often more thankful he'd take me on a date and feed me than I was getting to see him. That relationship is a whole story in and of itself…

phew, that was a mess. The one time I had a "job" that summer was when a former tennis teammate told me about a day job in Huntsville, AL. I, along with my roommate's boyfriend who was also in dire need of money, went to Huntsville to work outside a voting booth. I can't remember who the candidate was or what the position was. We just wore pins and held up signs. I remember it was so hot and we were out there for a while, all for $100 apiece.

It wasn't until August 2010 I had an interview with Cracker Barrel as a waitress. They told me they'd call the next day to let me know if I'd gotten the job. I looked across the street and thought to myself, "Why not apply at that place? You've got to find *something*." Prior to that, I'd never even seen that restaurant or gotten food from there. I drove over and applied at Bojangles' Famous Chicken 'n Biscuits as a cashier, or whatever they wanted me to do. The manager told me he'd call the next day to let me know. The following day I waited with my phone in hand on a call from either Cracker Barrel or Bojangles'. Bojangles' called and offered me the job. Little did I know that would change the direct trajectory of my life, but for the time being I was just jumping for joy over having a job.

That struggle to find employment gave me a whole new appreciation for when people are struggling to find work. It gave me the type of patience I would need later in life when my husband and I were having financial struggles. I am thankful for employment because it taught me a lesson I needed, especially back then. I was at a point where my convictions were fighting with my worldly desires. God showed me quickly not to rely on my own abilities but to rely on His timing and where He wanted me to work. God revealed to me I needed more than just a job to make it. I needed Him. God can give and He can take away, whatever is necessary for you to get whatever point He is trying to make for you.

Day 17: Sunshine

I drew this out of the jar around 1:30 am. Why so early? I had to stop eating at 4:00 am because I had surgery at 12:30 pm. Who on earth schedules a surgery for that time? Not to mention I didn't get to have surgery until 6:19 pm that evening. I believe the term to be used here is "hangry"?

I sat without sunshine in the dark of my living room eating breakfast foods, drinking coffee, and watching investigative documentaries about unsolved murders. Around 3:45 am, my youngest son came waddling from my bedroom looking for me. He's been sleeping with us a lot lately. He starts out in his bed but typically ends up with us. As time has gone on, I've become laxer with it. I read somewhere they won't be sharing a bed with you by the time they're in high school, so don't worry about it so much. I took that to heart with him. I wish I'd have taken that to heart with the older two. His nappy bedhead turned as he walked past the couch, and I whispered his name. He grinned, walked back toward the couch, and he climbed up in my lap. I sat there with him while he groggily watched the commercials and commented about trucks, fruits, whatever he saw, until about 5:00 a.m. when I brought him back to bed with me.

Before my surgery, I went up to the tennis courts to unlock them for my tennis team to use later that day since I wouldn't be there. It had rained the day before and there were a couple of puddles on the courts. I sent them a group text letting them know they'd probably need to squeegee off the courts and I asked them to please behave for their substitute since their P.E. teacher wasn't there to watch them, either.

Even though it had rained the day before, it was going to be a beautiful day for tennis. The sun peaked through the pine trees and shown over the courts. It was about 70 degrees already at 10:30 am. The breeze was cool and perfect. Light sprinkled across the courts revealing their green and white as well as revealing their age and cracks. I thought in my head how funny it was that I got to see such a gorgeous day just before I was going to be shut up in a hospital for hours. I thought to myself, "Man! What a day to miss tennis. This is the PERFECT day for it!"

The rest of my day would be waiting in a windowless hospital room for a surgery that was six hours behind schedule. However, my children got to enjoy the sunshine! My youngest was babysat by one of our church members/deacons (who's grandson I happen to babysit). They went and checked deer feeders together and I received pictures from their trail cam showing how excited my son looked. Then when my other two kids got out of school, the wife (a teacher) brought them home and they all five went fishing together. I got to see a picture from that as well. The pictures showcased the sunny day, and I could close my eyes and imagine being with them.

I'm thankful for sunshine because it allows for good times. It allows for work to get done. It allows us to enjoy the outdoors. As I said before, I don't do cold, so I always welcome the warm sun. I'm thankful for sunshine because of all the good memories made in it.

I hope you are thankful for sunshine. You can think of a dozen reasons to be thankful for it, I'm sure. It allows for plants to grow, tennis to be played, puddles to dry up... however, I'm partially convinced it causes kids to grow up too fast. Every time mine go out in the sun and come back inside it seems they aren't as little anymore. They sure don't seem to keep.

Day 18:
Being Included

It will probably sound a bit melodramatic of me to say this, but this prompt would be easier if it said *not* being included. I have more familiarity with being left out or being the weird kid in the group and that would be a lot easier to write on. Y'all, I had to really sit down and examine this. Why would I be thankful for being included? I had to ask Phillip for his opinion. I popped my head out of the shower the other night and asked him the question. He thought for a few seconds and commented that when people feel included, they feel as though they're a part of something important or a part of a family and that can be a good thing.

I've mulled over and over in my head of times where I felt included. Most times when I did feel included, it seemed like it was forced inclusion. Some of those incidents may have been forced, others were probably just in my head and in my insecurities. Openly I can say two of the times I've felt the most included and felt as though I was wanted as a part of a group were when I worked at Center of Hope in Lawrenceburg, TN as a sexual assault victim advocate and when I was a member of the Sunday School Class at First Baptist Church Colbert Heights in Tuscumbia, AL. I felt like I was wanted, and I was valued at both places. I feel this way at the church we are at now, Fellowship Baptist Church. Just from looking at those patterns, maybe allowing yourself to feel included is part of the equation, too.

Recently, a man named J.T. Perkins came to mind. He is "Google-able". He was a champion fiddle player from Alabama and when I was very small, I had the pleasure of meeting him. Granny had worked with his wife at a Wrangler plant for years. Paw had known J.T. a long time.

Prior to meeting J.T., I was captivated by a fiddle player at Opryland in Nashville, TN. I was 6 years old. He had black hair and wore simple country western style clothing. Up on stage he created a sound I'd never heard in person before, and I immediately fell in love with it. All I talked about for days after was how I wanted to play the fiddle just like that guy. As soon as they could call and schedule a time, Granny and Paw took me over to J.T.'s house and filled me on the legendary fiddle player.

It was an older, humble home. I sat in a straight-backed chair with Paw sitting between J.T. and I. I was very bashful, and a bit overcome by all the greatness I'd been told about on the way over. J.T. sensed my shyness and asked me if I knew the song "Turkey in the Straw". I grinned and nodded. He picked up one of the many fiddle cases he had, unsnapped it, and popped it open. A smell I describe as smokey and fragrant filled the air. It's a smell fiddle players will recognize. He rosined his bow, the rosin glimmering amber in the sunlight coming through the Perkins' window, and he began to play "Turkey in the Straw" for me as if his fingers had written the song. The fiddle sang the words while he simply instructed which song to sing.

The plan was for me to take lessons from J.T. Perkins. That plan didn't last long because he passed away in 1998. I was so disappointed. Paw had bought a fiddle for me already in just my size. It was almost my birthday, too.

Here comes the part about feeling included. J.T.'s funeral was something for the books. I can't tell you how many people came, but if a whole county could possibly attend a funeral, I think that would be close enough. It was a beautiful day in August. It was hot, I do remember that. My Dolly Parton-style dress with all the frills and lace had me sweating like a turning rotisserie chicken. I itched and complained, naturally, and Granny would continually threaten me with a butt whooping. Granny and Paw drove me to the cemetery after the service at the funeral home so we could pay our respects. There were so many people I didn't recognize. Quite a few of them had one thing in common: they were fiddle players. J.T.'s casket was carried to his gravesite. His wife and relatives sat in chairs beside the open grave. At once, you could hear the snaps of fiddle cases being opened almost in unison. Awkward plucks were heard as the instruments were awakened from their sleep and placed under the chins of the musicians. Bows had been pre-rosined and were positioned in their correct place. Together, they all played... well, songs I don't even remember now. I imagine "Amazing Grace" was played. I want to say maybe "Ashoken Farewell" was played also. It was breathtakingly beautiful. I think the trees heard it and gasped; a soft breeze said so. The summer sun seemed to tickle the leaves as it rushed through for a listen. The old church building probably creaked as it leaned in to hear better. After the songs were over, everyone said their goodbyes and packed up to learn how to live a life without their old friend.

I believe being included is a lot like this. People can't be there at every beckoned call. However, the right ones will be there exactly when you need them. Maybe not in person, but in spirit and prayer. At some point in his life, J.T. had touched these people in some way by his friendship and comradery. They put everything aside in their daily life and pressed pause so they could come play and send their friend off in style. I'm sure there were some that would have given anything to be there, but circumstances happen, and life is hard. I'm willing to bet they cracked open their case and played in honor of him as soon as they were able. Being included means you aren't forgotten. All these years, I saw being included as getting invited to all the "cool" stuff, asked to be in all the pictures, just being invited. Now I see that being included, for me, is synonymous with being thought of.

I'm thankful for being included in this way. I don't have to have the "experiences". People don't owe their time to me in that way. I'm simply grateful to be thought of from time to time, and I like to believe I am.

Day 19:
My Husband Learning New Things

I recently began babysitting for one of our church members. Phillip and I could not come to peace in our hearts about a price. We knew what we "should" charge and what would "make sense", but we simply couldn't ask for it. The father plays guitar and teaches at the local high school. His wife is who I took over coaching tennis for because she wanted time off to be with her new baby. After some prayer, we all agreed Phillip would take guitar lessons from him in exchange for me babysitting. At first, Phillip discussed me taking lessons since I have a background in playing fiddle and mandolin and dabbling with the banjo. I tend to be naturally gifted with stringed instruments and playing by ear; it's just one of those things. He also discussed at least one of our kids getting to take lessons, but we weren't sure their attention spans are there yet. I- mostly jokingly- told him he should take lessons and I'd learn whatever he brought home when I decided I wanted to.

Phillip is one of those people who could be good at so many things. I have always believed that. When he puts his mind to something, he can do it well. In my heart of hearts, I feel at some point maybe someone discouraged him or made him feel inadequate, so he just never passionately pursued many hobbies or interests. He denies this. Perhaps he is just easily bored or discontented with things. I believe maybe at times he was given a side comment that he was "too this", "too that", or not quite what someone was looking for… maybe. Maybe he is one of those people who, if they can't do it great the first few times, is deterred from doing it. Perhaps the longer we're together the more I'll understand. I've seen him do so many things at random points in our time together and be good at them only to see those hobbies drift away as if they'd never happened. Once he fixed my childhood wagon all on his own after the pieces that held the sides on came off. Another time when he was a stay-at-home dad, he made homemade chocolate and peanut butter cups that were delicious, just because he saw the stuff in the pantry to make them. He compliments me sometimes telling me I can do anything I set my mind to. I only wish he'd believe that about himself. Maybe the older we get, the more we "grow up", he'll get there.

While we were in Alabama recently for his cousin's wedding, we stopped at a pawn shop and bought a guitar for him. He'd been borrowing a guitar from his guitar teacher up until this point. It was a bit beat up, but it would certainly do the job. Since November, he has practiced this guitar almost every day. He has learned chords and songs and techniques. I've watched him play during his lunch break. I've watched him get out of the shower, put his sleep shorts on after drying off just enough to be considered dry, and sit on our bed strumming songs he's learned. I'll watch him with his back facing me as he concentrates on the music. He asks me if I recognize the song and most of the time I do. He doesn't know how many times I've smiled watching him do this. I get a case of girly giggles watching him sometimes. When and if he reads this, he'll probably be embarrassed that I wrote that.

I'm thankful for being able to watch this grown man learn something new and have the desire to do so. I've wanted this for so long for him, just for him to find something that is solely his. I'm thankful he has this expression in music he can enjoy and share with others. He has brought his guitar back home to Alabama the last few times we've gone back and has played songs for his parents and family members. I hope they appreciate how big of a deal this is for him. He recently had it at church one night and played a song for some of the people there. I'm so thankful to see my husband gain confidence I've never seen him have before. I thank God for the opportunity and how He has orchestrated all this out.

Day 20: Disabilities

I'm kicking myself for writing this one; however, if I'm going to use this as a type of therapy for me, I need to do it right. The reason I say I'm kicking myself is because I'm embarrassed for how I've acted and felt in the past regarding disabilities. The more I think about and process it all, though, I think I only felt that way because I didn't understand it.

The first memory I have of someone with any sort of disability was when I was from when I was in second grade. I'm going to use the name Martha for her. I don't believe I ever fully knew what her struggles were. She seemed a bit childish for our age, had difficulty maintaining her emotions, and looked a bit different than other kids. For whatever reason, I got it in my head that if I was just super nice to her and got her to play with me, it would make her like the "rest of us". Very noble of me, huh? Please catch the sarcasm there. I don't know who I thought I was to be on a mission to bring someone out of their "shell", I mean for goodness' sake, I was the kid who peed her pants on the playground at recess and didn't tell anyone because I didn't want to get in trouble with my teacher. I was also the kid in second grade who drew a full-on nude photo of Rose from *Titanic* because my friends dared me to (and to think Mrs. Cooley threw that away, it was pretty good!)

The more I tried to hang out with Martha, the more I realized being friendly and playful wasn't doing what I thought it would. It wasn't changing her at all. I remember thinking to myself, "I'll get her a present! Maybe then she'll not be so shy or strange!"

Close to where I grew up was a place called Hulaco General Store. It is no longer open. Legend has it a Dollar General ate it up like kudzu. One day when Mom and I were buying corn for our ducks, I happened to look up and see a metal wind-up duck that could waddle. I insistently wanted Mom to get that as a gift from me to Martha. Mom bought the duck and let me take it home but ended up explaining to me in the best way she could that Martha was just different than me and may never be able to play the same way I did, have friends in the same way I did, or do other things. Mom explained Martha would need extra help probably for a long time, if not for her whole life. I still didn't really get it and was somewhat in denial of it all, until one day Martha called me a bad word when I asked if she wanted to play with me. Alas, my little noble quest ended almost as quickly as it had begun. I wasn't getting cussed out by a fellow second grader anymore.

There was another young lady I went to school with from the time I was in kindergarten until I graduated high school. She was in the special education class and was practically non-verbal. If I remember correctly, she wore diapers. Everyone was sweet with her, and I never met a soul who treated her wrongly in school. The most "outcast" of kids would wave at her and even the most "popular" would high five her in the hallway if she held up her hand to request it. Even so, the truth is she made *me* uncomfortable. It wasn't because of anything she had done or because I didn't like her, it was because I just didn't know how to react or what to say. I would often try to avoid her at school if I could just so I wouldn't make a mistake or say something wrong. Anxiety overtook me when I would see her, and I'd hope she wouldn't speak to me. If she waved, I'd smile and wave while my heart raced out of my chest. I had a terrible fear of somehow hurting her feelings by doing something in a way she didn't like. Don't get me wrong, I am a firm believer that hurt people hurt people, and I did and said my fair share of not-so-nice stuff when I was younger. But, when it came to most instances, I would have died inside if I knew I'd hurt someone.

I would have a few other incidents in my life where I felt similar. One was when I was about 16 years old and selling flowers. I was casually sitting in our van with my feet propped up on the dash. I'd been listening to my CD player, probably crooning along in my head to some George Strait or Terri Clark. Another family was parked close to us having a yard sale. Their adult son who had Down Syndrome had walked over to me and told me he liked our flowers. I shyly told him thank you. He came back with the comment, "They're pretty, but they're not as pretty as you." I choked out another thank you as he walked back to his family. I was mortified. Again, looking back on it, it wasn't because there was anything wrong with what he said or did. I was mortified because of that same anxiety I already mentioned and a lack of knowledge on how to speak to people who weren't "like me". Years went by and God allowed me to work a job at Riverbend Center for Mental Health as a summer camp counselor during 2011. I was able to get firsthand experience with children from all walks of life who were dealing with learning disabilities and different disorders. It was new for me, but it allowed me to play with these kids and get to know them for the fun, beautiful souls they were. My time there allowed me to teach them how to handle emotions, friendships, basic hygiene skills, and it allowed them to teach me a thing or two as well.

God dealt with me when He gave us our first child. Now, did Anniston have a diagnosable disability necessarily? No. To this day she has been classified into "unspecified learning disorder". She's also got a slightly low IQ according to the test she was given. Anniston had chronic ear infections and strep in her first years of life which led her to need early intervention at least once sometimes twice a week, and speech therapy. Additionally, she had an undiagnosed lip tie and tongue tie. I just thought I was a "bad mom" who couldn't get her kid to latch right during breastfeeding (again, please catch the sarcasm, y'all aren't bad moms and neither am I.) She also struggled with following directions to the point of being incredibly defiant for her teachers (not so much with us). Her attention span was- and still sometimes is- short, and she especially struggled with making friends. I remember one of Phillip's former co-workers from the bank he worked at telling me once if I would just read to Anniston more, she wouldn't have a speech problem. It took everything in me not to slap the taste out of her mouth. How dare she assume I didn't read books daily to my daughter, repeat phrases, everything under the sun. Further along down the road, it came to our attention Anniston had essentially quit trying to speak correctly when she got to preschool because what was the point? No one would understand her, anyway, and none of the kids really wanted to play with her. They were just told to "be nice" and she was often not chosen for anything. She was left out of a lot.

    I've never known heartache like trying to fight for my child to be treated like a person, just like a regular human being. I remember specifically one of my favorite pediatricians we saw told me she had OCD tendencies and talked about how smart she was. If I remember correctly, we were still in preschool moving up to kindergarten. During the next IEP meeting, the IEP team wanted to test Anniston for Autism. I just wasn't sold that was her issue, so I suggested we could test her for OCD since her pediatrician- you know, the doctor- had already brought it up a week or two prior. It was shut down immediately, saying they didn't have the ability to test her for OCD (and didn't want to), but *did* have the ability to test her for Autism and wanted to do that. They would not hear anything I said. It became instantly clear where their priorities- and their funding- stood. I'll be honest, I showed my tail to some degree in that room, and I thank God He found a way for her to get out of that school.

Today, Anniston is a normal kid when it comes to functionality. She'll be 10 years old in a few months. Outside of her pausing to say her words sometimes or being a bit repetitive, you'd never know she had the struggles she's had. She is a bit immature for her age, I'll admit that, but that is the least of my concerns. I'm happy for her to stay a kid. I do joke she has the attention span of a gerbil, but boy is this kid talented. She can touch anything with a pen or a brush and it's as if it turns to gold in her hands. She's got better handwriting than some adults I know. She is loving and kind. She has average grades, she has messy backpacks and desks, she is the kid who is totally content playing on her own and being completely independent. She is my baby.

I am thankful for my ignorance about disabilities and how God directly impacted my life to correct and educate me. God worked on my anxiety as well as any judgments I've had in the past. He's forgiven me and allowed me to forgive myself so that I don't live in shame. He caused me to reflect on everything and everyone I've known before and opened my heart in a way it may never have been opened. I am thankful for "disabilities" because they really aren't a lack of abilities, they are just different ones. They pose challenges like many other things in life do, each different. Through all this living, God has helped me grow. I'm thankful for the parent I was forced to be because of Anniston's experiences. Her life has changed mine in ways she may never fully understand and without her trials, I may not have been the mom or the person I am now.

Day 21: Dogs/Beloved Pets

Pets can come in all types. I grew up on what I'd describe as a farm. It certainly wasn't some huge operation or anything, and we didn't really raise anything to sell on a large scale. We had dogs, cats, ducks, geese, cattle, and for a very brief time we had black pot-bellied pigs. My parents figured out quickly they did not have the time for pigs. I loved having a lot of animals as a kid. I could often be found domesticating stray barn cats and sneaking them inside even though I was allergic to them. I'd somehow talk mama ducks into letting me pet them while they sat on their nests. Geese and I didn't have the best relationship and anyone who has been around geese for any length of time can attest as to why. I got along fine with most other animals and in a sort of lame but good way, they gave me someone to talk to since I was an only child. When my parents would argue or things would get too loud inside, I could go out and love on all the feathers and fur I wanted, and all they wanted was love and attention, too.

    I'm thankful for all the loyal pets I've had over the years, but for me there's just something to be said about a good dog. I have very fuzzy memories- both figuratively and literally- of dogs all the way back to when I was three. I remember two puppies named Red and Spot running up to me and licking my face while their little tails wagged fervently. When I close my eyes and see this, I smile. I can hear the little-girl version of myself laughing.

    The first dog who I remember being a big part of my life was a Doberman named Sam. She was easily pushing 11 years old by the time I came along. She was built thick, protective. I know of one person who caught her wrath when they were trying to be funny by scaring me. Sam was very patient with me. I've been told a story about when I was being weaned off the bottle that I would walk around asking for my "bobble". Paw told me, "Ol' Sam got it." I waddled over to the screen door politely questioning Sam as to where the "bobble" was. She would wag her stub when I'd ask her, just happy to be a part of a conversation with her favorite and only kid. I have lots of pictures of Sam standing guard over me when I was a baby and small child. One picture it even looks like she is grinning as she sits beside my dad and I on Halloween.

    I remember the days leading up to Sam dying. I was 5 years old. Before now, she'd been okay with me chasing her around the yard and always kept a calm demeanor. I remember one day she turned around and snapped at me when I was chasing her. She didn't bite me but growled and made it very clear she didn't want me to play with her. I didn't understand; I cried. Shortly after that, she went missing. I learned she'd gone off to an area behind the "shed" that had once been a stable. I remember asking to see her since she'd been located and not being allowed to go back there. It had been explained to me she'd "went off by herself to die." Sure enough, that's what she'd done. Sam was a very old dog, and it was her time to go. She just wanted her own space to close her eyes where her little human wouldn't have to watch what was to come. While she was being buried, I found comfort in playing with baby ducks my family had just bought and sharing a bag of raw leaf spinach with them while I cried.

    I had so many dogs growing up, I could name them all and each one would have its own story. Julie was a Chihuahua I'd gotten from a yard sale when I was 8 years old. She, too, would live a long life and would be the only inside dog I was ever allowed to have at home. She was white with some off-white coloring down her back and looked a lot like the dog from the old Taco Bell commercials. When I first got her, I'd sit her in the middle of my chest and cup my hands under her hind legs while she fell asleep listening to my heartbeat. I'd watch her in awe, amazed that she loved me and would stay so still for me. I felt so lucky to get to experience this little dog growing up. I enjoyed taking lots of pictures of her when I got into photography in the 4-H Club, and she was absolutely spoiled rotten. Her most important job, though, was lying in bed with me on nights when it was bad at home. She'd curl up under my comforter at the foot of my bed. On nights like that I'd either fall asleep crying while she kept me company or I'd finally just close my eyes when it sounded like all the fighting was over. I wish I'd appreciated Julie more in my teenage years than I did. I blame part of that on my environment and part of that on caring more about friends and boys than my most faithful friend. I'd write I wish I was a better teenager, but teenagers (as a whole) aren't the greatest, anyway. That's something else I often must forgive myself for.

Today, our family doesn't keep many pets, contrary to what I grew up with. Phillip had a dog named Sasha he'd got just before we started dating. She was a Beagle/Jack Russell mix and the best fetch player you could ever ask for. She'd run herself ragged playing fetch with a tennis ball. She was there through our dating, marriage, all three kids, all the girls at the girls' ranch, and all our numerous moves. In late 2020, we bought a German Shepherd puppy named Violet. I knew Sasha was coming to the end of her life and I wanted the kids to have their own dog to grow up with. As predicted, Sasha made it to August 2021 and had to be put to sleep because of numerous tumors in her chest. I know it broke Phillip's heart. She was obviously *his* dog and she just put up with the rest of us.

Violet loves our kiddos and I believe she'd go to battle for any of them, but she is indeed my dog. She listens to me over anyone else. She won't let me go to the bathroom on my own. She must be with me or close to me. I think dogs choose people, and if anyone ever needed proof of that, just look at the foot of my bed now as I write this and tell me who is faithfully laying there while I heal from surgery.

Until we got Violet, I didn't even realize I wanted that companionship again. I'd gone years without having my own dog to take care of. I'd reluctantly put up with my college boyfriend's dog, even more reluctantly after the dog chewed up one of my yearbooks. Sasha certainly wasn't my dog and I jokingly say she considered me the "other woman". Getting Violet and having the bond we have has honestly been incredibly therapeutic for me. She was something I certainly didn't know I was missing in my life.

Loyal pets don't ask questions. They just love you. At times, that is all we need. We have a lot to learn.

Day 22:
Bitter People

I have a confession. I didn't write about this on this date. I have found writing these the same day I pick them from the jar isn't always feasible. I picked the topic on the right day, but I did not write about it. My incision in my belly button had opened five days post-op and I had to have it chemically cauterized at the local urgent care. My favorite nurse practitioner there fixed me up. If it says anything about how I felt on this day, his first words when he saw my incision were, "Oooh, soupy." I focused the rest of the day on, I don't know… not letting my belly button fall apart.

I'm glad I was distracted from writing on this day because Mom and I were on the phone the following day for a while. She brought up a childhood friend's grandfather she'd seen recently. We talked about how sweet he was and that he was doing well.

I commented to my mom about my childhood friend and how I don't really speak to her anymore. I hadn't talked to her in years outside of a comment or two on social media posts. Life does that. It pulls people apart naturally sometimes, especially when 90% of the people you grew up with left your hometown like you did. I go to her social media page and see how she's doing occasionally, but the truth is I unfollowed her a long time ago because of how bitter her posts were. I love my friends, and if they ever need me, I'm always a phone call or message away. However, I also must take care of myself, and if that means not seeing daily posts that are angry or hateful, so be it.

I can take my fair share of people posting angry stuff. It's okay to be angry. She is just one of those people who was angry when we were kids, too. There is no telling what all she went through I don't know about, and I am no stranger to childhood traumas and abuse. I'll admit I was an angry kid. There were several occasions when I lashed out physically at other people or said mean things I regret when I was sad or upset. The difference is she was just someone who had no tact and didn't care to make people cry out of being purely hateful and downright rude. I think she set out to hurt people's feelings. I remember specifically a time in high school she made a girl in our class cry for no real reason and just laughed directly in the girls' face, and it was over something the girl had no control over. The girl was someone neither of us particularly cared for at the time, and I am sure the girl had said some messy things about us before, but what my friend said was on the verge of heartlessness. From the time we graduated until now, she's exhibited a lot of bitterness in what she says online, and some obvious religion/church hurt (then again, who hasn't had a little bit of that at some point? I sure have.) I had to make the conscious choice to unfollow her but remain friends because I do like checking to see how her and her little family are doing. I truly hope they're doing fantastic. I love watching people I've grown up with being successful and fruitful.

 I'm thankful for people like her. I'm not thankful for their bitterness itself, but I'm thankful for what they teach me. Their characteristics help me recognize seeds of bitterness in my own heart. They help me to visualize what I could look like to other people, and it makes me mortified to know I could be turning people away. I'm naturally not much of a people person, it is something I've learned to be. Because I'm a Christian and want to serve God, I want to be someone who draws people near and not someone who pushes them away.

 Bitterness is an easily planted seed that doesn't take much sun or water to grow. It grows in the coldest and darkest of places in our souls. I pray for you as I type this, that if you have these weeds choking the garden in your heart that you have the strength and work ethic to pluck them, to tend to your garden. I must tend to my garden daily, not just when I feel like it. I know it is the same for you too because we're human, and guess what? Stuff happens. We live in a sinful and imperfect world, and that is just how it is. I pray for this friend of mine that she'll be healed from her hurt and receive the peace she needs.

I'm thankful for bitter people because they remind me of who I've been and warn me of who I could become. I pray you recognize those areas in yourself, put your gardening gloves on, and get to pullin'.

Day 23:
Seatbelts

I've been in what I call "fender benders" before, or what one could even say were "fender tappers" because there was nothing to show for it. There's been two car accidents in my life worth speaking of, one with me as a passenger while I was very pregnant with Tripp (I was okay as was Tripp and the driver), and the other when I was driving. Both instances I was wearing a seatbelt.

I grew up not wearing a seatbelt with anyone in my family. It was never a rule and never enforced. The only time I wore one was when Granny or Paw decided randomly that I should, or if I was riding with a friend or friend's parents. I'd gotten very good at the "pull-it-over" I called it. Mom only got pulled over once with me that I remember. We were on our way back from selling ducks at the Lacon Flea Market. We were riding in her 90's model black Chevy pickup. We passed a cop, and she told me to "pull-it-over". We got pulled over that time and were given a warning, or for all I remember it may have just been a firm talking to.

When I started driving, I began wearing my seatbelt every time I got in the car. I don't know if it was just standing social convention, not wanting a ticket, or why, to be honest, especially since I'd grown up not wearing one most of the time. It's been commonplace for me. To this day I don't understand how people just "forget" because it is the first thing I do when I get in a vehicle and the first thing that I have my kids do. I can't control much, but that is one thing I can do.

I was 17 and it was February of 2009. It was my senior year and I had just signed my tennis scholarship. I'd been dating my boyfriend, Chad, since the prior October. Whenever I reference my college boyfriend, he is who I'm talking about. He will also have his own prompt somewhere down the line. I'd gone off on a bit of my worldly era in life. I'd describe it as that point in my life where I was saved, but I didn't know what that meant as far as following what God wanted me to do and how He wanted me to live and build relationships. I never drank, smoke, or did any sort of drugs in high school. That's right, not once. I was the kid you probably wanted your kid to be friends with, in that sense. I'd lived through so much alcoholism among other things at home I wanted nothing to do with it. Could I cuss the shingles off a roof? You better believe it. I'd been practicing cuss words since I was old enough to hear Dad get mad at farm equipment. As far as any other trouble, I was really a great kid. However, I liked guys... like, a lot... and I'd found a guy who liked me back so that was good enough. My best friend and I had decided to take some, well, inappropriate pictures to give to our boyfriends for Valentine's Day. Not awfully inappropriate, certainly stuff I'd rate PG13, though. We'd decided after I got my vaccines that day at the local health department (I had to get updated on all my vaccines before college and I'd also gotten the shot that supposedly prevents cervical cancer) I would drive over to her house. I'd bought some lingerie in secret already for the occasion as had she. I just laughed to myself because this was a time when digital cameras were the best way to do dumb stuff like this and now people just whip out their phone and do things they shouldn't. Y'all were buying your kids digital cameras and had no idea what we were doing with them, huh? Praise God for maturity and better decision-making!

  I had not considered that I may be dizzy after the vaccines. Teenagers are not notorious for listening to side effect lists and warnings. I told mom I was going to my best friend's house, and I'd be home later. I drove down the road adjacent to the one she lived on and remember feeling kind of distracted/out of it. I was listening to country music on the radio in my little dark green 1998 Dodge Stratus. I could be found listening to mostly country on any given day with some rock, emo music, or rap thrown in occasionally. As I rounded a curve, I went off the edge of the road just a tad. I heard Toby Keith sing "Beer for my..." as I overcorrected and started to spin out of control. At the time "horses" would have come up in that verse of the song, my car took out several yards of a fence and part of a tree. I was gripping the steering wheel for dear life. I remember being frozen in time as I spun and the only thing in my mind I could hear was, "You're about to die." It sounded like the voice of a flight attendant, or even Matthew McConaughey, all calm and matter-of-factly. What took only a few seconds seemed to take forever all at the same time.

My car finally came to a stop when it landed crooked in the ditch bank. My air bag had not gone off, and as soon as that thought came to my mind- BAM! It did. It hit me square in the face. I tried to put my car in park, and it wouldn't quite make it past reverse, but I was able to turn the key off. I felt a tightness in my right hip and saw that it was my seatbelt. I unbuckled it. It had done its job. I'd have surely gone through the windshield had I not had it on with as much force as I'd stopped with. I had no cuts, no broken anything, but I don't think I'd have noticed in the moment if I had. My adrenaline was through the roof.

I unbuckled and got out of the car to see the owners of the fence standing there. They hadn't had time to ask me if I was okay before this tall thin man in Coke bottle glasses, who I will affectionately refer to as "the Yankee", walked up to me from his yard after he had watched the whole wreck unfold and said something like, "These curvy country roads will get ya dontcha know. You were going real fast, ya know." I just looked at him stunned and kind of mad. "No crap, really? I'm okay, though, thanks for asking." I said in a smart-aleck tone. My tennis racquet was hanging in a tree as my backpack and tennis bag had busted my back glass. My junk was everywhere; that was loads of fun to pick up.

Long story short, my car was totaled. The cops were called to the wreck. I was not checked out by EMTs; I kept telling everyone I was fine. Besides, we didn't have the money to foot that bill and I didn't have health insurance or any insurance on my car other than liability. Mom was called. She had been at the grocery store getting cat food. Chad was called and as soon as he could he came to check on me. I called my best friend whose house was only a couple minutes up the road, and she refused to come sit with me while I waited on my mom. What that was about, I'm not sure I'll ever know. I'd have come to her.

The surprise of my life came when I told my dad what had happened. I had a panic attack and a complete mental breakdown when I realized I'd have to tell him. I was a red-faced, crying mess whose racing heartbeat could probably be heard yards away. I begged and pleaded for any way around it because I truly believed he was going to hurt me when he found out I had totaled my car. We just didn't have money to fork out for another one. He ended up laughing about the whole thing and telling me we could get another car, but he couldn't get another daughter. He was unpredictable. I couldn't read the man.

I am thankful for my decision to wear a seatbelt especially that day. I was unbearably sore the following morning. I remember trying to get out of bed and I felt like my chest had been cemented to my mattress as I tried to get up. It was if someone was sitting on me. I felt like absolute dirt for the next few days. As a matter of fact, I played a tennis match the following day. I lost the match and was stiff as a board. For the next week, I'd look down to see a bruise across my hips and a bruise across my chest, both from the seatbelt. I'm thankful I had it on that day. If I hadn't had it on, there was a good chance I would not have been able to keep playing tennis or I easily could have died.

I'd like to sit here and tell you that incident was the way God kept me from doing stupid stuff that day. Well, I didn't do the stupid stuff *that* day, but later. He just interrupted my timing in the moment for reasons only He knows. If God hadn't allowed this to happen at this time, though, I wouldn't have had the miracles that came afterward. I ended up having to foot all my money I'd worked hard and saved up from working to fix the fence I'd wrecked. That money was supposed to have been for my dorm. It was the way I could move out of my house. I prayed to a God who has no reason to forgive me for all my stupidity and, through people who loved me, He blessed me with enough graduation money right to the cent to pay for my college dorm. It became one of my first lessons in relying on Him and not on myself, even though it would take me a while to consistently do it.

In life and on the road, please buckle up.

Day 24:
Burns

My first thought was to sing Johnny Cash lyrics in my head when I pulled this one out of the jar. The fact is, I did as I typed that sentence… and this one…

I haven't experienced a lot of burns in my life. The only one I have a scar from is on my left forearm just above my wrist. In 2015, I baked a cake for something at church. I had my oven mitts on, but I'd slid the cake just a little further back on the lower rack (for whatever reason I guess I thought the bottom rack was a good idea.) I bumped my arm up against the top rack and remember immediately saying, "Ouch!" I thought no more of it as I closed the oven door and put my cake down on the stove. My arm continued to tingle annoyingly, and I finally looked down at it. My skin had bubbled off my arm, and it was easily the worst burn I'd ever had. Quickly, I turned on the sink and ran cold water over my arm. I then went to the bathroom and put toothpaste on it. It soothed it a lot, but there was no wrapping it, there was no putting bandages on it. It just hurt to touch it. To this day, I still have a scar about three inches long and about a half inch across at the widest point.

My great-grandmother on Grandpa's side suffered severe burns as a small child. Her name was Mary Moore Locke, and she was born in Alabama in the early 1900's. The irony of this story is burns deal with heat, but she was born on one of the coldest winter nights they'd had all season. The family's dog had crawled under the bed to keep warm, only to be found frozen to death after my great-grandmother's delivery.

I've been told she fell into the fire in the family's living room. Her family quickly pulled her out, but she had serious burns on the front of her body, all the way from her neck and torso and down the fronts of her legs. She'd struggle for quite some time after that to regain movement and give her wounds time to heal. Her family would watch out and care for her the best way they knew how. For anyone who has dealt with a burn in any way, you know the skin is terribly sensitive. It bubbles and blisters, often bursts after the blisters form, and then the skin is paper thin as it heals back. The slightest rough movement can cause it to bleed or open again, only for the healing process to start over. For the next few years of her life, she'd have to stay out of the sunshine as often as she could. She'd watchfully keep her scars covered. As she got older and dealt with other ailments and illnesses (along with the death of her husband leaving her with four young children to raise alone), she'd sometimes ask her oldest child- my grandpa- to help her with her hair and getting her ready to go to town. My grandpa got to see her scars up close and personally as he'd learn to brush and pin her thick black hair and even put on some of her makeup for her when she was having rough days. He hasn't spoken about it much, but I'm sure they were precious moments with the only parent he had left.

    I think we can be thankful for burns for a couple of reasons. They remind us we aren't fireproof. We are prone to injuries and not immortal, and I think the way we live our lives sometimes reflects we believe otherwise. Burns allow other people to care for us and be a blessing. Often, we deny people a blessing for themselves as well as us by having the "I've got it" mentality. If my great-grandmother had been so stubborn to a fault, she could have reinjured herself. However, she allowed my grandpa to step up and help her do things she *could* have done on her own but chose in the moment to teach him and allow him to assist her. I am thankful God allows us to be servants for Him and exhibit to others what His love is like.

Day 25: Swings

I love swings. I've always loved swings. Playground swings are great and all, but the big porch and backyard swings that fit two or three people... Those are gems.

My family had a swing for most of my life. The swing I primarily used was at Granny and Paw's house. It was in the backyard nestled on the land between the back porch and large garden. The swing saw a couple of coats of paint through the years, but I remember it being dark colors mostly. It was chained between two pressure-treated logs driven into the ground. The swing is still there on the property today, having survived the first house burning down in 2011 and the rebuild of a new one.

When I was growing up, swings were a place of peace to me. There was so much fighting and tension when I was growing up, mostly centered around my dad. I don't recall much fighting going on when people were in the swing. Everyone was relaxed when they were on the swing. When I was little, my legs were short and couldn't reach the ground. I usually sat with Paw on the swing, and he'd slowly move it back and forth for the two of us in a slow, calm rhythm. Black orthopedic sneakers sat shifting forward and backward on the dark rubber mat placed under the swing while my tan, blonde hairy legs swung freely back and forth. Most days, Paw would have his pocketknife out whittling a stick. His whittling captivated me because he had what everyone called "the shakes", a condition he'd had since childhood. I'd often ask him, "Paw, whatchoo makin'?" He'd reply, "Nothin', just a whittlin'." I'd pester him with a million questions about why he'd whittle just to whittle and not make anything, and I'd ask him if he was making something for *me*. There was nothing productive being made, just time being passed. Other times he'd crack open pecans he'd picked in the yard, and we'd enjoy them together. If it was ever just me on the swing, I'd lay down and let it sway back and forth while I gazed up through the thick tree limbs at the leaves creating a green stained glass for the sun. I'd look past and try to decide what shape the clouds were. Either with Paw or by myself, I could be found in the summertime enjoying a chunk of rich red watermelon. The juice would dry quickly on my small lips and fingers in the hot sun and the dust from the swing would congregate to all those sticky areas. That always called for one of my grownups griping at my stickiness and telling me to get a wet paper towel to clean up.

 I grew up and bought a house one day. At this house, I hung up a swing I'd purchased from a co-worker for twenty dollars. It was covered in country white chipped paint and only held one of my children and I at the same time comfortably. If one of my kids was sitting in it with me, it was guaranteed the other two would be close by chasing Violet around the yard. The swing was weather worn and on its last leg. I like to think our house was a sort of "swing retirement home" for this piece. I started out with it on the back porch until I decided to try it in the tree on the west side of our house. It hung just high enough above the ground where I could sit at a comfortable level to rock at. This was the best spot on the property. The watercolor sunsets God had painted with purples and oranges from His palette made the hay in the pasture next to us glisten like glittering gold treasures. When the wind would blow, the field would dance and every now and then a herd of deer would jump through it. I had drilled a hook into the tree for a solar lamp or a citronella candle to rest so I could come out there at night when I needed a breather from day-to-day life. It was the perfect spot to drink my coffee and reflect on my blessings while I snuggled in a cozy blanket. I could talk to God right there and it was as if He was sitting right beside me. By the time we were ready to move, we had to tear it down and put it on the burn pile. Age had gotten the better of it and a hole had worn through the plywood seat. I believe I can say for me it's the most missed item of our Alabama house.

I'm thankful for swings because in my life, they've been a safe spot. They've been a place where I can relevel my heart when hardships have caused its beat to run too fast. God can reach me anywhere, but there's something about swings, whether it be alone or with people I love... they just hold a special place in my heart.

I'm thankful for those rocking moments with Paw. They became such a signature part of our relationship that after his death in 2012, it was as if I could feel him sitting on the bench beside me at college after I completed my finals. He passed just before my finals to complete my bachelor's degree and while I was about 4 ½ months pregnant with Anniston. I sat on the bench next to the University of North Alabama's amphitheater on that cool December day and I looked to my right as I sighed in relief, knowing all the work was finished. I envisioned my warm, sweet Paw sitting beside me as if to congratulate and comfort me.

In a land of imagination where I wonder what Heaven is like, I wonder if there is a place we can swing together there while we worship and sing to God. Heaven is such a mystery, and I think we have a difficult time imagining what that perfect place will be like because all our eyes have seen are imperfection and things we'd say are "close" to perfect.

Perhaps he's sitting there getting well-deserved rest, knowing all his work is finished, too. Maybe he heard my good news today about my benign biopsies and smiled on my behalf. Perhaps sometimes he sits down, takes up a stick, and whittles while he waits on me. Farther along, we'll know all about it.

Day 26: Backroads

I grew up in one of the most blessed lands geographically in the United States. The part of North Alabama I am from happens to be part of the Appalachian Plateaus. I have jokingly referred to it as the Appalachian Toes rather than the Foothills. Being at the tail end of the Appalachia doesn't take away from the quality of the scenery by any means. The dirt is rich. The hills ripple through the earth up a growing trail along the Southeast into Tennessee, North Georgia, the Carolinas, and onward. Maybe on one of the days of creation, God stood at the northernmost point of the Appalachia and slung battle ropes with His mighty hands and watched them reverberate into the ground. Their shakes tapered off at the southern ends and created my home. As He did so, He already knew the good and the bad they'd be subjected to, and He did it anyway. The leaves on the millions of trees change beautifully in the Fall creating reds, oranges, and yellows that I believe cause the angels roll their eyes with envy. I believe if the mountains could sing, they'd sing a soft native song of the long-gone peoples who cared for them, and at other times hum a deep sound of a bow pulled across a fiddle harmonizing with a plucked banjo. If they could talk, they'd have every emotion you and I do. They'd cry over the unnecessary deaths over centuries of wrongs, they'd raise their voices roaringly over the injustices, they'd shout joy over new beginnings of people and nature. Yet, they sit silently just listening, only reflecting the echoes of the present, retaining all the secrets.

The way to travel these hills to get the most from them is primarily through backroads. The backroads go every which way but straight, paved and unpaved, hugging the sides of the mountains like tight-fitted jeans on a grown, curvy woman. These roads were carved out by our ancestors as they rode wagons and horseback and walked their way through steep terrain, grassy valleys, and lowly hollers. Today, they are often driven by older folks enjoying a Sunday drive, log trucks taking more trees away to make room for homes no one can afford, and by angsty, moody teenagers needing a moment's peace from tough reality.

That is why I love backroads. I learned to drive on them. I became comfortable with the sharp lefts and rights, the tall ditch banks, the hard shoulders, and gained too much confidence with them way too quickly. When I got my own car and my driver's license, backroads were a way of escape when my home got too loud and aggressive. They'd take me anywhere I wanted to go, whether that was a physical destination or just a destination in my mind the road could never get me to. I'd roll my windows down in the warm weather and let the wind whistle through my car. My arm would lay out the window freckling in the sunshine while I let my hand make waves through the air stream. I'd daydream about stuff I wanted and didn't need. I'd methodically plan my escape and future on a list I primarily kept in my head. I'd cry over questions God wasn't answering on *my* time and He'd gently but firmly remind me of the stuff He had already done for me.

Unfortunately, each ride had to end, and I'd be forced to go back home. The backroads allowed me to have time to myself where no one could hear me or watch me. Backroads were a place to disappear from the mainstream. I wouldn't be questioned. I wouldn't be judged by anyone. I could sing and talk as loudly as I wanted to. God and I could converse, just the two of us. No one could tell me how to speak, how to feel, what to think. For this, I am grateful. The older I get, sometimes it seems the harder these places and moments are to come by. Their value is priceless in a world where the volume of each day is always increasing.

Day 27: Kindness

I don't think I can do prompts like this justice. The amount of kindness that has been shown to me in my life cannot adequately be collected into a few sentences. Kindness has been shown to me out of habit, out of pity, out of respect and despite what I had or hadn't done to deserve it. I've chosen a few examples of kindness for you from my life out of the uncountable amount there are.

In 2013, Phillip had taken on a youth pastor position at a church in Mount Hope, AL. We were living with his parents after Anniston was born and driving 45 minutes to an hour out of our way every Sunday and Wednesday for 8 months waiting on the house we were going to rent to be move-in ready. We were young, had only been married for a year, new parents, and our only income at the time was Phillip's youth pastor position. We were starting to stress over the amount of gas it was going to take to get to this church. The math wasn't "mathing" and the gas sure wouldn't be "gassing". During all this, I found a part-time position at the school that required me to drive this distance every weekday for just three hours a day. A couple at our church about our grandparents' age saw the need and offered us their cabin in between church on Sundays so we wouldn't have to drive all the way back to Phillip's parents' house. It was a beautiful, gated spot with a pond out front. The tin roof made it perfect for rainy days rocking on the front porch while Anniston slept. We could eat lunch there, nap, let Phillip work on his messages, whatever we needed to do. The couple also agreed to babysit Anniston for me while I went to work at the school every day… for free. They, as well as additional members of their extended family, took care of my sweet baby girl for no charge at all until the school year was over.

On another occasion probably around 2017, Phillip, Anniston, Ridge, and I were all at the local Foodland getting groceries after church one Wednesday night. We were exhausted. I had been working a job that was mentally and emotionally draining, let alone time-consuming. I'd been feeling stretched thin and had little to no patience for my children or my husband. Phillip was serving as a youth pastor at a different church. Relationships with the pastor and a few of the church members were somewhat tense at the time and it was weighing on his mind. Anniston and our son Ridge were 4 years old and 3 years old. I found one of the buggies with the fancy car-designed seat on the front and buckled them in it to see if it would give us a bit of relief from their attitudes. They enjoyed it but were obviously tired and ready to go home. We were financially strapped at the time. We got a buggy full of groceries and I know we were both wondering how we were going to make this food work until I got paid again. We got in the checkout line behind a lady who'd change our lives. She noticed our kids. She complimented us on our beautiful children, and we thanked her. She paused bagging her own buggy to tell us she felt God leading her to buy our groceries and asked us if that would be okay. To say we were stunned is the understatement of the century. I think my mouth hung open. We asked if she was sure she wanted to do that, because we felt like it was a lot. She immediately said yes, no questions asked. This lady paid for well over $100 in groceries for us and it left me in tears and Phillip on the verge. We thanked her earnestly. I believe I put out a Facebook post hoping it might reach her, but I never heard anything from it.

In 2018, I was in Walmart with one of my girls from the girls' ranch. She was starting her first job soon and we were there to purchase her some non-slip work shoes. Our girls were allowed to get jobs once they reached a certain "level", and she would be working fast food. The employees of that Walmart came to know my husband and I fairly well since we went in there to buy groceries weekly. My girl and I got in line to check out with her shoes and a familiar cashier began speaking to me. We were talking about the girl starting her first job and explained that was why she was getting the shoes. A man behind us heard the story and heard about what the girls' ranch was for, their mission. The man instructed the cashier to put the shoes on his ticket. The man sweetly told us he would be honored to pay for the shoes and told my girl he was proud of her for going to work. The man paid for the work shoes, and I know my girl hasn't forgotten it.

I know by now someone is cynically thinking something like, "Yeah it must be easy to be so 'kind' when you've got stuff to give or money to buy things." That's right. I see you.

Allow me to share one last moment with you. When I was in seventh grade, I hated myself. Absolutely disgusted with my body. I was teased for being "big". I wore a size 12 in women's clothes already. I'd lost weight from the year before and gotten taller. I'd started playing tennis and that had helped me gain some confidence, but I was still made fun of often. For whatever reason, I thought it would be an adventure to be in the school beauty pageant. It was called The Sweetheart Pageant, and it was for all the junior high kids (sixth through eighth grade) around Valentine's Day. Mom took me to Cato's to pick out an outfit to wear. I was disgusted at the time by how feminine dresses were and how they awkwardly laid against my early curves. I loathed that I wasn't skinny. I settled for a nice light pink shirt and black skirt. Instead of trying to brush my hair out, we'd decided to let it be naturally curly. Mom helped me scrunch it with mousse and curl cream to get it large and in charge. Mom helped do my makeup as well.

The night of the pageant came, and each girl was given a boy from eighth grade to be their escort. The boys would be at random, you didn't know who you'd get. The boys donned rented tuxes from a local store for the occasion. They were all the "popular" boys, the ones who played sports or had good pedigrees in our hometown. One of the boys was someone I had P.E. and Spanish with. There was a small group of us in Spanish class, and somehow, we'd all managed to get along despite being so different. He ended up being my escort. He was about my height, tan, blonde, and had a nice smile most girls my age thought was dreamy. He came up on my left side as we approached the curtain to walk out. He held his arm out for me and I looped mine around it. I could tell I was about to cry out of nervousness. My face was flushed. I thought to myself how stupid I was for doing something like this, I was too ugly and big. Unbeknownst to me, I was shaking a little. He noticed and reached over to put his other hand on my arm. He quietly told me it was okay, not to be scared. I heard my name get called. We walked across the hardwood floor of the auditorium stage to the decorated arch. Before he walked away, he whispered to me as he passed. "Good luck" he said in a friendly voice. He patted my arm once more. No, I didn't place or win anything in that pageant. That was quite alright with me. I won a sweet memory I'd retain for years.

    I don't know if you ever talk yourself out of doing something kind for someone because you don't have the stuff, the money, the abilities, the time, but what I can tell you is this: you just need the heart for it. You don't have to dress kindness up. You don't have to type out a resume for it. It speaks for itself. I remember the words that boy said to me in the moment I needed them just as clearly and importantly as I remember the free babysitting, the groceries paid in full, the shoes bought for my girl. All kindness takes is a gesture. I am thankful for kindness because it is so simple. People make it complicated when it isn't. I am thankful because it reminds me during my sorrows or hardships when it is easy to be snippy, to be self-centered, that I am to be kind despite whatever those things are in my life.

    "So then, as we have opportunity, let's do what is good toward all men, and especially toward those who are of the household of faith." - Galatians 6:10. Notice it doesn't give us a list of conditions or exceptions. Notice it doesn't say as we have the money, as we have the stuff to hand out freely… it says as we have *opportunity*.

    Choose kindness today. It'll create an impact that will outlast your lifetime.

Day 28:
Electricity

Sometime in the very early 20th century in rural North Alabama, a photographer named AJ Moore was traveling to the state's Northwestern corners, towards the Shoals as it's called. This was prior to the TVA coming to the South and bringing power to the people. Most folks in this day and time still used lanterns and candlelight, wood stoves and open fires, coal, steam, you name it. A young man in his prime, AJ had the energy for such a trip. Trips like this could take a day or two. He was on horseback and navigating terrain carrying his photography gear, some money, probably some water, bread, and jerky of some sort. He only carried his sidearm. Probably the most dangerous thing that lurked in the mountains were robbers at this time. Greedy men could easily hide in the hillside waiting on unsuspecting victims to pass through. During this time, horse thievery was unfortunately very common; the consequence when caught was a public hanging.

AJ and his horse stopped for the night in a valley after they'd traveled for the day. The next day he planned to finish his journey. AJ laid down only to hear some rustling in the bushes and trees. Imagine it. All was quiet except the noises of nature: crickets, frogs, bats, maybe some soft howling off in the distance from some hunters and their dogs out looking for coons. Stars may have peeked out between thin clouds covering the night. Per AJ's account of the night, the moon wasn't out. It was very dark other than the small fire he had kept going. What appeared in front of him caught his attention. He saw two glowing green dots, not but a short distance away. He thought to himself, "What kind of critter have I come across now?" The two dots seemed to watch him, unblinking. They appeared to belong to a large animal judging by their size. Thoughts ran wild in his mind while he readied his sidearm. Could it be a bear? Maybe just a coyote? But if there is one coyote, there's more? A cougar? AJ swallowed his nerves and decided the best thing for him to do was to shoot in the direction before whatever it was got the best of him. Hopefully he'd make contact.

BANG! He pulled the trigger. He screamed out of adrenaline as he did so, and fear overtook him. To his shock, the glowing green eyes turned to glowing green floating matter that trickled down to the earth. When AJ regained his composure after a moment, he realized what he had shot was foxfire, a bioluminescent fungus sometimes found in the woods. There's probably some moral to the story here, but the point I'll make is this: I bet he probably would've appreciated some light being shed on the situation by being able to flip a switch of some kind.

Today in 2023, we are spoiled rotten. How our forefathers harnessed the power of electricity into energy has really made things quite a cakewalk for us compared to those who came before us. We use electricity to make just about anything possible in the present day. We can cook meals; we are able to keep warm or cool depending on the weather. I can type this on my husband's laptop while it is hooked up to a charger. Electricity allows you to get your Whopper at Burger King in a decent amount of time. Electricity supports the computer at your bank so that their system can update your account balance. You don't know how thankful you are for power until it goes out. We tend to throw quite a hissy fit when there's no power. We can't watch our favorite shows, we can't charge our phones, we can't even make a piece of toast. We can't turn on the bathroom lights when mother nature calls, and when it strikes in the middle of the night and you're fumbling through your house for the commode, things can turn very ugly very quickly.

I'm thankful for electricity, because quite honestly, I appreciate the convenience. I take it for granted. There are so many parts of the world where people operate contently without electricity and to me that is admirable, given I've never gone an extended period in my life without it. This prompt is one that caused me to reflect on just how much of my life is spent using electricity and it gives me more of a respect for those that keep it on for us and for those that went without it all those years ago.

What do you find yourself thankful for only once it is gone? I hope you make time to pause and reflect on that.

Day 29:
Servers (Waiters/Waitresses)

My mom was a waitress when I was very small. I was so small that all the memories of her working as a waitress are blurry. I can remember the restaurant in our hometown. The restaurant had been there for a while even when I was born, so I'd argue it's a building going on 40 years old, if not older now. I want to say it was southern food back when she worked there, kind of like a meat-and-three style restaurant. It's been a pizza place, BBQ joint, and last I heard it is a Mexican restaurant. I vaguely remember going with my Granny and Paw out to eat there one night while she was working. Mom glided through tables carrying plates on both arms. I remember her black apron swaying side to side as she moved. With her height, her pens in her apron pockets seemed to sway close to my face tempting me to grab one and start scribbling on a napkin. I remember complaining my French fries didn't have ketchup with them. I didn't act out all that much as a kid, or so I've been told, so I'm guessing I wanted attention or didn't want to be there to begin with. She took a moment, straightened me out with some one-on-one tough attention, and brought me back to the table.

I've known a few other people who worked as servers in my lifetime. My roommate when I moved to Florence worked as waitress at Waffle House. I remember her coming home to her apartment (prior to me moving in with her I'd stay at her first apartment on the weekends) and talking about her tip money. I'd never paid much attention to how much servers made until I met her. I didn't realize how much they relied on tip money to make their bills or have money to eat on. Another person, my bonus daughter, was a server at several different restaurants.

Between their two experiences, I learned a lot about how servers were treated. Both young ladies were sexually harassed in ways the customers could have easily been charged with crimes, but in fear of losing their jobs nothing was typically said. They were cussed out on several occasions over things that were beyond their control. They've been threatened. Both would come home completely exhausted on multiple occasions. I saw my roommate fall asleep in her work uniform more than once. I've seen nights where they barely made money to cover gas to come home and I've seen nights they raked in $200-$300 in tip money. They'd tell me of the great tippers and the unprepared or impolite who stiffed them. Every now and then- catch that frequency- they'd tell me about customers who'd take time to get to know them, their situation, and even pray for them, additionally sometimes leaving them enormous tips because they were led to.

I was never a server. I always got fast food jobs where I worked front line and dining room as a cashier. Bojangles' was the closest I'd come to that since we cleaned off the tables and got to know our customers on a relatively personal level. I have, however, been served as a customer more times than I'd care to try and count. I would say on 99% of my outings, I've been friendly and polite with my server. On the other 1%, they could probably tell I was becoming impatient or frustrated but I've not been flat-out rude to my recollection.

Servers put up with more out of people than they should have to. The most common theme I've heard from servers is they hate Sunday crowds. They complain people come from church to eat lunch and are often poor tippers, short-tempered, leave huge messes, just to list a few. To think how many servers have missed out on having the Gospel shared with them or experiencing what Christ's love is like all because somebody needed to fix the "rumbly in their tumbly" like an aggressive rage-filled Winnie the Pooh.

Most servers I have met have been kind and just trying to do their jobs. Whether or not I'd agree they've all done it "well" or not isn't the issue. They've got things going on in their personal life that could be affecting their work ethic that day. Their mind could be in a million different places. Chances are most people don't give their job 100% every single day, anyway. I try to make a point to tidy up as I'm leaving a restaurant- especially since I have three small children who aren't the most delicate eaters- simply because these people are equals and not lesser than I, and we should all set out to make each other's lives just a little easier.

I'm thankful for servers because they remind me what a servant heart looks like. Yes, they're getting paid to perform their duties, but think about it. As followers of Christ, we are supposed to be following the ultimate unblemished example of the best servant the world has ever known. Ephesians 6:7 tells us to serve with a good attitude, serving as if you are serving God and not people. Servers, in a way, have a job after God's own heart, whether they realize and/or accept it or not. I'm thankful they remind me of the character I am supposed to be having as a Christian on days when the world seems to get the better of me.

I pray you consider the next time you're going out to eat at a restaurant, you'll pray about who your server will be. You'll pray during your blessing of your meal about the way you should minister to them. You've got a once in a lifetime chance with potentially a total stranger to exhibit what Christlike is. Maybe you'll let them know you appreciate the job they're doing and to keep up the good work. Maybe you'll feel so led to pray with them right there or pray for them in your car. Maybe you'll tip them like they've never been tipped before. Maybe you can invite them to church. The possibilities are endless.

"Let us consider how to provoke one another to love and good works..." -Hebrews 10:24

Day 30:
Unexpected Blessings

It was November 2013 in Moulton, AL. Phillip, Anniston, and I were finally getting to move into our rental home to be closer to our church in Mount Hope. We'd been living with Phillip's parents since Anniston was a month old. We were in a small space that was getting smaller day by day, a phenomenon which seems to happen when multiple adults live in one home. We were moving on faith. We were moving believing God would handle it. We did not have the money for first month's rent like the landlord wanted. We were missing money for several move-in necessities. If our bank account had walls, they'd be squeaky clean with the number of times we'd had to dip our hands into it only to scrape the bottom. We didn't say much to many people about the situation, only Phillip's family mostly. We trusted it would be alright and we'd somehow figure it out, even if it meant talking to the landlord about everything. The day we moved in, Phillip was given checks by several different people. When he was done counting the money, it was the exact amount we needed for the first month's rent and our expenses.

Our household finally was struck by COVID-19 in late October 2020. Anniston was exposed at school and three other kids in her class plus her teacher were now positive for COVID-19. Anniston's symptoms were that of a common cold. The boys didn't catch it. I believe I caught it regardless of what my negative test said. I had sinus-related issues and dizziness with a lack of smell and taste. Phillip caught COVID-19 and he felt horrible. He had aches and pains all through his legs, his stomach was all messed up, the works. Amid this, Phillip's Aunt Janet informed me via Facebook Messenger she and his other aunt, Peg, were sending us meals to help while we were all quarantined. Shortly after, we began receiving meal upon meal from Hello Fresh that I was able to prepare for us and our kids. We were set for weeks.

Phillip and I were loading our large U-Haul truck by ourselves in the middle of June 2022 preparing to move to Louisiana. Phillip's parents and Nana were keeping the kids so they'd be out of our way. We'd been working all day and if you've ever been to the Southeast in June, you know it's a scorcher. I'm grateful for the shade we had from our front yard trees that day and the fact we still had power on at our house. I'd had a light breakfast that morning, but Phillip and I both were otherwise fueled by coffee from the start of the day. We chugged water throughout the day because, you know, didn't want to risk dehydration. We didn't have much food left in the house because we'd boxed up what we didn't need and had been eating everything we could to clean the fridge out. We were also very tight on cash. I'd left my job a few days before now and Phillip hadn't worked. The church in Louisiana had graciously paid for our gas and U-Haul to move. Multiple trips up and down the metal ramp of the U-Haul were beginning to weigh on us. One of Ridge's friends' parents messaged me and said they wanted to bring us lunch. It was 1:00 pm, and for anyone that knows me, if I have not had lunch by then I may meet Jesus soon. They drove the short drive from their house and not only brought us lunch but brought us a whole tote of snacks so we could have something to munch on for what would be a 12 hour-long trip. I still have the tote and have used it for every trip back to Alabama we've made.

Something happened recently close to where we are from that has stayed on my heart the past few days. For the sake of not knowing the family personally and only hearing the stories posted by a relative, I will leave out names and try to leave some anonymity. A young teenage boy and his grandfather were out fishing on the river. It's been raining a lot everywhere in the South and the area they were in likewise had been hit hard. The dam was fully open; all the spillways were pumping water out hundreds of thousands of gallons of water per second. I don't know the details of what happened to the fishermen. I don't know what caused their boat to go under. What I do know is both were thrown into the chilling 48-degree water. I've been told the teenage boy clung to a tackle box to try and stay afloat. He lost sight of his grandfather during all the chaos and unfortunately, at the time I write this, the grandfather is still missing. I look back at myself at that age and how terrifying this would have been; out in that big water where you can see land on both sides, yet it is so far away. To be fighting currents with whatever strength you could muster in the cold while your teeth shook like a rattlesnake tail, it must have been a nightmare on earth. Hopelessness began to soak into his soul like the water into his clothes. The boy screamed, and I can only imagine in that moment he didn't know what to expect. Then, the unexpected happened. Over the water came a boat with two fishermen who were traveling fast in the boy's direction. The two fishermen were able to pull the boy from the water and he was brought to safety.

 I listened online this evening to the testimony of one of the rescuing fishermen. He says the first thing the young man did in their boat was get down on his knees and pray for his grandfather. The young man reportedly was saved two weeks before this accident. It brought me to tears. Unbeknownst to the rescuers, that young man became an unexpected blessing for them, too.

 I am thankful for unexpected blessings. They come in all sizes when it comes to how we measure things in the world. They come as small as people who surprise us by paying it forward in the drive-thru line. They come as large as being pulled from the dark waters of a river. They come as you are the rescuer in a moment of crisis, just like this one. Unexpected blessings come at points in our lives when we need a reminder God never leaves us and has never left us. For some reason, we tend to forget.

Day 31:
Harvey

I prefaced this book by saying I chose prompts I did not necessarily like just like I chose prompts that I do. I also mentioned I'd change some names here and there and this is one of them. I had the bright idea to dig to the bottom of my jar this morning to see what would happen. Sigh. I guess this is what I get for purposefully trying to choose from a different part of the jar. I'm not sure I could have rolled my eyes harder when I pulled this out. I definitely didn't pull it out with a grateful heart, and I've had to ponder on this one all day.

I met Harvey when I was working fast food, around the time I met Phillip. He walked in, or should I say his voice walked in before he did. He was so loud. Tall and lanky, he strutted his way to the kitchen to begin his first day of work. He flirted with me and every other female before he could complete his first breath behind the frontline. This guy talked more than he worked; he was a distraction to say the least. When he *did* do something, he messed up things most would consider foolproof. He disappeared after less than 48 hours of employment; I was told he was fired. That says something. I've seen a variety of managers at that restaurant beg people who struggled to boil water to stay and work.

I thought my chance encounter with this person was over. I began dating Phillip and while we were driving one day, Phillip said he wanted to stop by his friend's house. We pulled up at a small, humble home in an area of town I had not visited before. My heart sank as Harvey came clambering out of the house. He saw me in the cab and began to wave and say something about how he knew me. I made a feeble attempt to hide in the floorboard of Phillip's 1993 Ford Ranger. What was I thinking? Hiding didn't pan out for me. At least I deserve an A for effort, right?

Because of Phillip, I agreed to give him a chance. I was told he wasn't that bad once you get to know him. During one of the first times I hung out with Harvey, Phillip and I went on a double date together with Harvey and his then girlfriend. On the date, he looked at my size 11 wide feet and, as animated as possible, he let out a "WOW! You've got some big ol' feet, girl!" in public. I thought to myself, "Yes, thank you, I'm aware." On another occasion during another double date, I had a scratchy throat. The four of us stopped to eat at Wendy's for supper and I was coughing while I ate my chili. Harvey is what I'd call a professional musician/singer/entertainer. He's rather good, some would say great. Harvey took it upon himself to inform me I was coughing incorrectly, would hurt my vocal cords if I continued, and began coughing "correctly" as loud as he possibly could in the middle of Wendy's. I was absolutely mortified. People turned around to see this man purposefully coughing with confused looks on their faces.

Some of you are thinking, "Melinda, you need to grow some tougher skin, perhaps?" Maybe so, guess it depends on how you slice it. When it came time for mine and Phillip's wedding, Phillip asked him to be one of his groomsmen. The only thing we asked of our wedding party was bridesmaids pay for their dresses and groomsmen rent their tux (cost at the time around $100 or less depending on where you went.) The tuxes didn't even have to match, they just needed to be black. He could have found something secondhand for cheaper; I wouldn't have cared. Harvey gave Phillip a rather rude talking-to about how that should be *our* responsibility. Harvey refused to be in our wedding because of something so unimportant. That hurt Phillip's feelings badly at the time. I was angry for Phillip. There'd be other times in our lives where it seemed Phillip caught the short end of the friendship between the two of them, and I've selfishly prayed on several occasions they'd part ways and be done.

Phillip is still good friends with Harvey. They both enjoy a lot of the same things. Harvey will call him and want to talk sports. Harvey will also call him and want to talk church because he, too, is in ministry. The way Harvey talks to Phillip and the way Harvey dismisses some of the Godly advice Phillip tries to give him- keeping in mind the advice is typically asked for- I think Phillip should be declared a saint for sticking by him. I could not. He is like mustard to me. A little mustard on a sandwich is pleasant, just as being around Harvey for a few minutes is doable. However, I wouldn't dump a whole bottle of mustard on a sandwich…

There are things beyond my control. One of those things is Phillip's friendship with Harvey and how Harvey treats Phillip. I've struggled so hard to find reasons to be thankful for Harvey or anyone like him. Don't get me wrong, he was good enough to come by the hospital when Ridge had pneumonia. He prayed with us over Ridge. I am thankful for his talents because he sure is talented. He can play and sing music beautifully, and I enjoy it when he is singing for the right reasons. I am thankful for Harvey because, although he is not my favorite or anywhere close, I am reminded I am not everyone's cup of tea, either. I'm sure someone could say much worse things about me without having to work half as hard. I am thankful Phillip and Harvey's relationship gives my husband a ministerial workout, so to speak. It teaches him to be respectful and loving even when I'm sure it is hard. As much as it pains me, the way my husband is sanctified more through dealing with someone like this, I'm grateful for.

I am reminded the God loves everybody, and that means God loves Harvey, too. He loves Harvey just as much as He loves me. I'm reminded Harvey and I are equals in the eyes of God and Harvey is just as beautiful a creation as anyone. I'm reminded to love my neighbor as God has loved me, regardless of how difficult it may be sometimes.

Lastly, I'm thankful God sent Jesus to die for Harvey just like God sent Jesus to die for me. We both needed it.

Day 32: Old Photos

Before I begin, I think I should define what I mean by "old photos". I'm not necessarily talking about old tin types from the 1800's passed down through a family, but I think those are really cool. I'm talking about any and all photos pertaining to your life up until this point.

For mine and Phillip's wedding, I wanted a slideshow of us as we were growing up and some photos of us together over the past year. I also wanted to put up some photos in an area of the church of our family members and our ancestors, since I'm a genealogy nut. I easily located pictures of Phillip at his parents' house I wanted to use. A lot of photos from my teen years I was able to access online as well as Paw's family and Grandma and Grandpa's families. To get my childhood photos, however, I would need to go to Granny and Paw's house.

Granny and Paw had a whole shelf on their wooden entertainment center dedicated to multiple "leather-bound" photo albums. They were the albums that had sticky paper covered by the plastic layer which allowed your photos to be sandwiched safely in place. There were albums of me, my neighbor Luke (Granny called him her grandson), and what I call the Tipton photo album with most of Granny's family in it, including her grandparents and their families. Around Christmas 2011, Phillip and I made the trip to their house to see them for the holidays, but it was also the perfect time for me to borrow these photo albums so I could scan in pictures for my wedding. I knew exactly where they were in the house because I used to sit on the couch and look through them often. I knew exactly what was in each one because I'd combed their pages and asked questions over and over again about each photo.

Little did I know only a few days later I would get a phone call from my dad telling me that Granny and Paw's house was up in flames and burning to the ground. I was told Granny got out safely and Paw was not home when it happened. Their home was a total loss. Although I had lost all my childhood home videos (which I have often been saddened over), by the grace of God I was able to get those childhood photos and the Tipton photo album before the home was destroyed. They stay safely in one of my favorite pieces, an old trunk lined with newspaper clippings from the early 1860's salvaged from the Nashville Flea Market.

I am obviously thankful for that set of photos because I was able to save them before they melted into oblivion. I'm so glad I made the decision to get them when I did. I am thankful for old photos for other reasons, too. I know one day my memory will fail me. I am not a stranger to that, and I am not someone who distorts reality into somehow believing I'm invincible to age. I am thankful I have a variety of old photos, whether associated with good memories or bad. Each photo allows me to reminisce or process depending on what the photo sends my mind back to. I learned not that long ago that avoidance does me no good.

I'm thankful for these old photos because I get to see characteristics of my children. I get to see myself and think, "Ah, he really does have my nose!" or "There's no denying my daughter looks like me." There's something about being a parent and getting to do this that is just so enjoyable. The same goes for my husband's pictures. I love seeing his dimples show up in my boys.

I'm thankful for the old photos from middle school, high school, and college because they allow me to take a step back and remember who I was. They give me a chance to remember why I was that person. It keeps me humble when I work with youth, teens, and young adults. I was always one wrong choice away from being in a bad situation as we all were. God saw fit to smack some sense into me, rather forcefully at times, and guard me with special care during others.

Old photos are evidence we've participated. They're evidence we've had cheesy grins; we've laughed, we've cried. They're evidence and a reminder one day we will be a picture someone smiles at after we're gone, so I hope.

Old photos are evidence we've lived. They're evidence we came, we saw, and we got the t-shirt.

Day 33: Christian Books

Contrary to the small number of books I read during high school and college, I do like to read. I've enjoyed it ever since I was a little kid. I read a variety back then: scary stories, mysteries set in all centuries, science fiction, fictional teen novels, a little of everything. I mean, I'm writing a series of books of short stories, right? You'd hope I'd enjoy literature to some degree, otherwise this would be a long ride… which I hope it hasn't been that bad of a ride for you… anyway, back to the prompt of the day…

I fell off the regular-reading wagon until probably around 2019. I began reading more when my counselor recommended a book to me. Had anyone else recommended a book, I more than likely wasn't going to read it because I wasn't going to make time to read it. Actually, a few people had recommended books to me, and I felt bad telling them no, so I ended up with some books collecting dust on my shelf I'd never desire to touch. However, 2019 is when I finally came to a point where I accepted I needed help. No, not help reading, mental health help. At the time it felt like I was accepting "defeat" in a way, but I was at a point where I knew my life was at risk. If my life was at risk, my family was at risk, too. The family part convinced me to get over myself and do what I needed to do, to quit saying "I'm fine" and shoving it all under the rug.

My pastor helped me find someone who was a Christian counselor. There was nothing against other counselors when it came to that situation, it was just that I wanted someone with a shared belief system to help meet my mental health and emotional needs. My counselor recommended the book *Uninvited* by Lysa TerKeurst. I don't remember how long it took me to read it, but I don't believe it took very long. It caused me to want to pick up reading that would help my mental health state and help me grow closer to God, using the books as supplements to my Bible reading.

In March of 2020, the COVID-19 Pandemic caused my husband and I to be laid off from the girls' ranch, as I have previously mentioned in this book. The numbers simply didn't work, and the girls' ranch needed to be downsized. Our three kids counted in numbers when it came to the girls, so it was either kick out three girls who probably didn't have a safe home situation to go home to or get rid of us. That part didn't hurt our feelings; it was a no-brainer. In one fell swoop, my husband and I both lost our jobs and lost our home our kids had lived in and loved for two years. Within a month we were moved into my in-laws' house about 45 minutes away, close to where Phillip grew up. Technically homeless and jobless, we began attempting to get our bearings straight again.

At the time, I'd been doing low carb/dirty keto for the past three years, only stopping for my pregnancy with Tripp. I'd dropped the weight and been able to keep it off even postpartum. I was getting bored and that meant I knew I'd want to eat… and eat. With no job and going stir-crazy waiting on job applications to go across the right desk, I took to walking the suburb-style neighborhood where my in-laws lived. I would load one-year-old Tripp in his stroller, and we'd walk distances and times which I'd predetermine before we set out on our journey. Tripp loved the walks. He'd babble on about everything he saw while I stared through the mesh of his stroller's lid down at his strawberry blonde curls. I enjoyed the walks for myself, too, except for my issues with music. I love music. Back when I worked out, I listened to music all the time. Music is a part of my every day, for that matter. I don't know why, but the music on mine and Tripp's walks was getting on my last nerve. My counselor identified that I was dealing with multiple stressors off the Top 10 Stressor List at the time, so no wonder I was edgy. Looking back, maybe it was God's way of wanting me to focus since I had nothing but time to commune with Him. He knew I'd daydream and go off in la-

la land if I was listening to music. I'm guilty of that with worship music at times, too.

I decided to try audiobooks. I'd been trying to go through the Bible in a year through the audio option of the Bible App after our pastor had shared the plan with us, so I had gotten somewhat used to being read aloud to. I'd also downloaded Christian Audio a while before that and had been snagging the monthly free downloads. The ones I'd listened to so far this year had been okay, so why not try it again, right? Audiobooks became my new plan rather than music for a while.

I specifically remember Kyle Idleman's book *Don't Give Up: Faith that Gives You the Confidence to Keep Believing and the Courage to Keep Going*. It was so fitting! It came as an audiobook at a time in my life where I was angry with our situation, angry at the girls' ranch and trying to find some way to rationalize it all. My anxiety and overthinking were getting to me, thinking there must have been something underlying where they didn't like us or had been plotting to get rid of us and put us in this situation. I was angry we hadn't found work yet. I was just so frustrated with every little thing. Mr. Idleman's book refreshed me and helped renew my prayer and study time where it had fallen somewhat to the wayside in between cooking supper almost every single night for all seven of us, doing classwork with my kids trying to finish up the school year, and trying to stay healthy and COVID-19-free.

I am thankful for specifically Christian books because they convict me. They are regular folks, Christian authors who are imperfect like me, trying to lift each other up. These kinds of books explain scripture in ways I haven't thought of, or they give me a reason to study harder and validate or invalidate what they're saying. These books teach me things and give me perspectives I haven't considered, helping me understand other people in ways I haven't before. They remind me I am not alone, and others feel the same emotions I do. I don't feel so isolated when I read them. They give me a pep in my step in this way, too, so that I can keep on going, no matter the struggle… so that I don't give up.

Day 34: Art

I'm pretty good at art. I feel awkward writing that just like I do any talent I have, but it is true. Sometimes you run across people who are naturally gifted in areas and art just so happens to be mine.

As I have mentioned in one of my earlier prompts, I believe my skill is inherited. My grandma could paint anything or draw anything she wanted. Her sister has told me she and my grandma were very different growing up. While she was busy going out with her friends and boys, Grandma was busy working on her art at their house or reading books and studying. My grandma created several pieces of art over the years that are still on display at hers and my grandpa's house. Grandpa recently gave me one of her pieces and I display it in my China cabinet, where I display basically everything but China. It is a small wood piece a little larger than the size of my palm. She painted a beautifully made strawberry plant with blossoms on it and wrote "G. Locke '83" on the bottom as her signature. It is sealed with a clear glossy stain for preservation. It is a special gift, especially since she has been gone for three years now.

Mom was doing art projects from an early age. In high school, she took art classes and furthered her knowledge of the craft, including oil painting. When I was growing up, she had a few of her paintings and other pieces hung throughout the house. One was a scene of oranges and browns. It was woods with a creek/stream running through it. Mom also had an area on our back porch where she'd paint when I was very small. The room had an easel in it. I remember the daylight from the window giving a glimpse of her paints and brushes on the table. I only remember going in there a few times before the hoarding and clutter on the back porch made the room impossible to get to.

The hoarding of junk on the back porch blocking her room can be seen as foreshadowing of life that would come our way. The junk on the back porch was exactly that: junk. It was stuff no one had the desire to put away. It was stuff someone could easily liken to the state of the mental health situation going on in our house. The dozens of cats we had would make their way onto this enclosed porch in the wintertime and have their babies amidst the junk. We'd have to dig through the mounds of stuff to find them. You can use your imagination for how this smelled and looked. I have one photo of this back porch when I was in second grade, not in my personal belongings but I believe Mom has it somewhere. I was sitting on a turned-over five-gallon bucket- a place where mom would usually smoke cigarettes and read books- holding my Siamese colored cat, Sabrina. I say this to say I don't believe I ever went inside her art room after I started grade school. I have no idea what is still left in there now if anything.

The only time I remember my mom doing art anymore (other than fulfilling my "draw this for me" requests as if I had my own personal coloring book creator) was to help me with school projects or do it for money. The Decoration flowers she made were only way she was able to express art, but again it was for profit. Mom also was commissioned by several people to make what we called Christmas Cards for the city park. They were large plywood boards that were set up for Christmas in the Park sponsored by local businesses and individuals. They had different scenes. I remember her allowing me to help when I was about 10 years old. She'd sketched out everything on the boards and we were set up in the tractor shed at Granny and Paw's house. One was a scene where the wisemen were following the star to meet Jesus. Dark midnight blue and white were used as the only two colors, creating a crisp clean contrast. I remember being allowed to help paint the wisemen's faces and bodies and learning how to move the brush just right to get the desired effect. Outside of that, I don't recall mom using her art skills anymore purely for enjoyment while I was living at home. Constantly working but remaining low income, the unstable marriage, the never-ending stress of not knowing what days and nights at home would bring shut away any spare time she had to express her artistic side; it was just like the back porch clutter, hiding away like it never existed.

As for my own experience with art, I was drawing from the time I could pick up a crayon and doing it well. It sounds cocky for me to say this, and I certainly don't mean for it to come off that way, I just didn't have to try that hard at most of it. I just watched mom. I saw something and I drew it; I thought of something, and I put it on paper. I learned a lot about shading and different techniques by the time I was in fourth grade, and I won a lot of art and photography contests as I grew up. I got into junior high, and my friends and others began to try their hand at art and the older we got, the more my interests went in other directions and my friends' talents grew. As a matter of fact, two of my childhood best friends do art professionally now and do a fantastic job at it. One has been a cake decorator/baker and a tattoo artist, and one is an adjunct professor of art at a university. I have tried my hand at doing some art for profit- and I have done well in spurts- but by typing this I see why now I cannot stand to do it as a business. Art is a release for me and something I enjoy doing, and I feel like the minute I consistently do it for profit, it loses its ability to relax me. It all makes sense now. I can crank out a picture or two every so often, but I don't think I have it in me- or at least not currently- to make a type of business out of it.

I am thankful for art because it is an escape for me. When life is too much, I can pick up paints and create whatever I want as a method to calm down. I can create gifts for people. I am now playing the role of personal coloring book creator, and although sometimes it can be annoying depending on the day, it is certainly a blessing to get to do it for them. I ought to be happier to do it.

I am thankful God chose this gift to pass down to me, if for anything for Anniston's sake. I'm able to watch Anniston take up fourth-generation art abilities and do just as her foremothers have. I hope she is ten times the artists my mom and I am, and my grandma was.

Genesis 1 tells us about God being the Creator, the great Artist, if you will. Verse 26 explains us the human folks are created in His image. I like to view artistic ability as evidence that it is true.

Day 35:
New Friends

A few days ago, I saw someone I'd gone to school with post a photo on their Facebook page with the following quote from C.S. Lewis: "Friendship is born at the moment when one man says to another, 'What! You too? I thought that no one but myself!'" I've admittedly not read enough of C.S. Lewis, but it sounds like *The Four Loves* should be on my need-to-read list.

Old friends reference people who have known you for some time. I've got several old friends. Most of those friends, because of my moving around and theirs, are mostly kept up with via social media. Those friends are people I met in the bathroom in second grade because we were sitting in stalls beside one another. One of us asked if the other wanted to be friends, and the other said sure; we'd remain friends for years afterward. Other old friends are like those who you shared a baby crib with at your granny's house. You grew up visiting one another until you eventually parted ways in life, but still would help each other at a moment's notice. They know the trouble you got into. They know the stupid comments you've made, the immature jokes. Some of these people get to see you on the other side of things, some do not; for those that don't, the person you were to them is the person they'll remember rather than the person you are. Sometimes old friends don't get to know who you grew into. Sometimes, if you keep up with one another through the blessing and curse social media is, you can get a glimpse of who your old friends are now and smile, knowing they made it.

New friends have a privilege like no other, though. Decades go by before you meet these people. God scans over your lifespan before other people know it exists and He mulls it over in the palm of His hand. I like to imagine He does this as He sits amongst the galaxy, balanced in time, stars glowing around, your timeline shown on His palm like multiple reels of a film on the wall. He examines the day He created your soul. He examines every minute from the first earthly breath you'll take, to all the embarrassing secrets you'll try to hide as a preteen. He looks upon your responses to all the stuff going on in your life, already knowing you'd respond in the way you did. He observes your future only He knows. God decides at just the right time, just the right moment, you need a new friend. He already predetermined who He'd put where (how fascinating that is since He is omnipresent and can do that!) He pulls your lives together to intersect for a length of time no man knows and watches the blessings it brings.

The new friends He gives us meet us at a moment in life where they don't know all the nitty-gritty. They don't know the time you peed your pants on the playground, the rude punk you were sometimes. They don't know other people's opinions of you. But, even if they learn all those things, they seem to keep no record. They meet the person who is a result of all of it. They meet the person who has overcome them. Maybe they've overcome the same thing, or maybe they've yet to deal with it and need you there. New friends meet you in a place where neither of you knew you needed a new friend, and they become someone who you think of every day.

I am thankful for new friends, especially being here in a new state with my family. I'm thankful I've found people I can trust for my family to be around and haven't had any sense of worry. I'm thankful for the support system they have brought, and I hope my husband and I can be new friends for them, too. Who knows, perhaps these new friends will turn into old friends one day.

Day 36: MK

I went back and forth on whether I wanted to use her real name, but this is my bonus daughter. I have lots of young ladies who are like daughters to me, this is the one I couldn't seem to get rid of. Just kidding, I love you, MK.

She is 6 feet tall. She has fair skin. Perhaps God had a cream canvas and thought He should spray a brush dabbed in dark brown over some of it, creating all her moles and freckles. Her eyes are a color I have not seen often, almost a seafoam bluish green. They contrast beautifully with her dark brown hair. On several occasions, people have confused us as biological mother and daughter or even sisters. Both flatter me because I am honored to be considered even somewhat similar looking to her.

Having a child that isn't biologically yours, one that you missed out on most of their childhood, can be difficult. She came to the girls' ranch at age 16 and has been a part of our lives ever since. When girls come to the girls' ranch, it wasn't for fun and games. They came because of difficult home life situations or because they were in state custody. I see her desires and I see her hurts, a lot of which I recognize in myself, but her traumas are not mine. The way she has and has not processed those traumas are not ways I have or haven't. She has a whole history prior to me I've tried to learn as much about as I can. I've met her dad on a few occasions. I've got her mom on social media as well as one of her former stepmoms. I know her history strictly from her description of it, and I've been a part of her recently written history for the past five years. I hope she knows I have tried to be a voice of reason she seems to have lacked before. I hope she knows she can tell me anything, even if it disappoints me, and I'll never turn her away. I hope she knows she doesn't have to earn being loved by me.

I thank God for MK. I have joked with Phillip that I hope God isn't preparing us ahead of time for some of the stress our biological kids are going to put us under by giving us some of MK's shenanigans as practice. However, if that is true, I thank God for the prep work. I'm thankful for her sense of humor. I'm thankful for her talents. She's a great makeup artist and cosmetologist. I thoroughly enjoyed getting to watch her play volleyball in high school. I'm thankful for the times I've been able to take care of her physically and emotionally, even when the emotional times were taxing on me as well. I'm thankful my biological kids call her their big sister. They brag about her and love her. One of my favorite photos of her is when she helped Ridge pull his tooth and then took him to McDonald's afterwards.

MK, if by chance you do decide to read books (since you don't read the books I've recommended to you! Hint, hint!) I hope you know I love you. I'm not going anywhere, and neither is Phillip. I know you're just like one of my own kids because my heart hurts for you when life is hard just like it does for my three little ones.

You've got us.

Day 37:
Self-Harm/Suicidal Thoughts

Some of you will read the title and it will immediately send you to either fight, flight, freeze, or fawn. Some will read that and get angry because how dare I try and find a reason to be thankful for this. Some of you will read it and immediately become awkward or incredibly concerned for me, as well as concerned for what is to come in this series of books. I've lost some of you just in those sentences. If you feel this is something you cannot read about, I suggest you stop here and possibly go on to the next prompt. It won't hurt my feelings. I will stop here to say that there are not many prompts in this book quite like this, so it won't be as if you'll have to expect this on every page. I hope you believe me and have seen evidence thus far to prove that point.

I was diagnosed with PTSD in late 2019. I would not have this diagnosis unless I had finally reluctantly agreed to go to counseling. At the time this occurred, I frequently had noticeable suicidal thoughts over the course of my adulthood. I say "noticeable" because up until this point, I didn't recognize what I was feeling. I just knew at times I'd feel panic. I'd be overwhelmed and angry. I'd become overly sensitive to sounds and hear what sounded like my own voice relentlessly telling me how stupid or useless I was. I'd have to escape by going for a drive or for a walk to just get away from everyone for reasons I didn't understand.

I remember in 2017 admitting to Phillip I wondered sometimes if I would be better off dead. I wondered if life would be better if I just wasn't in it, if people would be happier without me. I was standing in the shower. Like a lot of married couples, we talk from the shower. I'd had a rough day at work (child welfare at the time) and I called him into the bathroom to talk to him about what was wrong. I'd been an emotional mess and short-tempered. Feelings like this make communication difficult. I swallowed my pride and told him I was having suicidal thoughts, but I wasn't suicidal. I didn't *want* to kill myself, but I had intrusive thoughts about it. I *knew* there was a difference. He asked me how often it was. I told him sometimes. I had never kept up with the frequency.

Looking back on it, I remember having thoughts like this in early childhood. Once when I was very small, probably 5 or 6 years old, my parents were arguing in the walkway that divided our kitchen and dining room. They were cussing and screaming at each other. Dad was threatening to kill Mom. Somewhere in the midst, I was brought up and Dad was telling Mom how stupid and worthless I was. I don't know if he said those things because he hated me or to make sure he hurt both my mom and me. To this day, I haven't been able to figure out belittling your own children to hurt your partner or spouse. I'd recently watched *Pocahontas* and admired her for risking her life for John Smith on top of the mountain when Chief Powhatan was going to kill him. Her famous line was, "If you kill him, you'll have to kill me, too." I roll my eyes now as I realize my grabbing a butter knife off the kitchen counter was a bit of a waste of time. I did have a flair for the dramatic in that way. What was that going to do?

I stood scared to death beside my parents and quoted to them some form of what Pocahontas had said in the movie- probably something to do with if you hurt each other, you'll have to hurt me too- and I held the knife with the pointed end towards my stomach. At the age I was, I was very serious. I was over the constant mental anguish, the constant abuse, the being forced to choose which parent to love, the conditions of my home. I remember my parents barely giving me a passing glance, making me feel unwanted and affirming how unimportant I already felt in the world. The arguing continued as if their daughter hadn't taken what would be considered a "weapon" and held it to her own body. This incident was one of many times I'd feel this way. Most other times were the times when I'd hide under my blanket crying while they fought, begging to God to kill me so I wouldn't have to live like this anymore. I'd beg Him to die. I believe I can now identify these as the beginnings of suicidal thoughts.

I never self-harmed before I was 28 years old. I'd seen people do it. I had friends who had done it. There were movies that depicted it. As a matter of fact, I was kind of judgmental about it. I never considered getting to that point, but there was a day in 2019 which would change that.

We were living at the girls' ranch. Someone there had made comments to my husband which, in my mind, was a sort of betrayal that pitched me as being a bad mother. Being a good mother is something I do believe I am. I am not a perfect one, but from the time I was small, I vowed one day when I had a family, my kids would never endure what I had to endure, and I would be the best mother I knew how to be. Something happened in my brain when I learned about the conversation they had. I know now to call it a trigger. I don't know what it triggered. Maybe a sense of failure plus the feeling of betrayal by this person? All day long, I was stuck in my head. I stood outside that night after all the girls had gone to bed for a long time trying to regain control of my thoughts. I finally went back into the house. I immediately went to the bathroom. My mind was swirling, the quietest sounds were booming in my ears. My heart was racing. I could not get any relief. Without thinking much about it, I found a dull pair of tweezers I sometimes used to pluck my eyebrows and stabbed myself in the thigh and made two small superficial cuts on the inside of my left elbow. They were places I didn't think anyone would really notice. The hole in my thigh was small and not deep enough that I needed medical attention. The cuts were just enough to bleed some. It was as if I had just enough self-control to not do more.

Endorphins did what endorphins do and although there was a temporary release, I cried harder. I didn't say much at all, if anything, to Phillip before getting in bed and turning away from him. A while later I told him what I'd done and the thoughts I was having that night. We discussed my serious need for counseling and the fact I didn't know what was wrong with me. As you previously read in the prompt I titled "Christian Books", our pastor at the time assisted in connecting me with a Christian counselor in the area. She did one session with me and immediately identified the PTSD. I agreed to start EMDR Therapy and participated for several months.

Illness is a peculiar thing. Unless you see or feel symptoms, you don't know anything is wrong. Some people live their whole life without symptoms of terrible diseases or illnesses only to learn later they'd been missing those symptoms the whole time, either ignoring them or chalking them up as "normal". I've seen it happen countless times to people with cancer or autoimmune disorders. It reminds me of myself. My symptoms to me were just "me", just the way things were, a byproduct of growing up in dysfunction or just being weird, and I was in denial of them getting worse and coming to the surface. Looking back on it, I can see self-harm was happening way back as a child and teenager with other actions I was taking, from crash dieting to unhealthy obsessions and more. They were all something I could control that ended up causing me distress, but none of them had done the trick.

I'm thankful my thoughts got worse as I got older because I may have never dealt with them. I would have probably skated along. I may have never accepted something was wrong and got help. I may have flown under the radar and not begun a journey of healing I so desperately needed. My kids would have eventually caught onto me, and it would have done the very thing to them I'd never wanted: it would have hurt them. I would have continued to hurt Phillip in the same way.

Now, I did *not* say I'm glad I have these thoughts. I'm not thrilled to have this thorn in my side; these thoughts are certainly intrusive and can show up at the slightest trigger. Praise God I have tools I need to get back where I need to be and praise God for being able to express to Phillip now when I'm triggered and need to get out of a situation. Quiet time with God does wonders now. I love going to a body of water like a pond or lake to just sit and pray, study scripture, breathe again and escape the "noise". Driving is my second favorite coping technique I've utilized since I was turned loose with a driver's license.

I am writing this just days after a PTSD attack. I haven't had one in some time. Months, actually. This one I recognized immediately, though what triggered it was strange and I haven't quite figured out what memory or emotion it is tied to. I even sat down and wrote it all out so I could try and process it, but it still hasn't come to me. Maybe it will. In the meantime, I continue to thank God for this lonely weakness if it brings glory to Him and His strength.

I survive for Phillip. I survive for my kids. Most importantly, I survive for God because my life is in His timing and not my own.

Day 38: Eggs

I must admit I chuckled at this one. I mean, what a "duh" kind of moment here. Eggs taste good... well, most of the time. Eggs are packed with protein and, as long as you don't have cholesterol issues, are overall fairly healthy for you. I'll only eat scrambled eggs or deviled eggs. The folks that like fried eggs or eggs over easy (Phillip), I might need to put you down on my prayer list.

Back before eggs were the cost of a down payment on a house, I ate them all the time. Mom liked omelets and would make scrambled eggs for me in the same way she did her omelets. That is how I initially learned to cook scrambled eggs. They looked almost like the shape of a pancake, nice and flat. I now have my own method and don't have to make only omelet-style eggs. However, the first time I remember someone making scrambled eggs for me outside of my mom or my granny was one for the books.

We'd gone down to Mobile, AL to visit Granny's cousin Vera. South Alabama is just a whole different ballgame than North Alabama. Vera was a North-to-South transplant, but she'd been down there a while. I believe I was in fourth or fifth grade on this trip. Granny had warned me Vera "couldn't cook worth a flip" (Granny was not one to withhold her opinion) and I tended to heed Granny's warnings when it came to food. Having grown up with Granny's kind of cooking, my taste buds were accustomed to certain flavors. Vera fixed us breakfast one morning. She put a bowl of fluffy eggs on her small kitchen table around 10:00 am. I was used to breakfast early in the morning. Granny was usually up super early and already had breakfast done or was finishing it by the time I was ready for school. By 10:00 am, I had already gnawed off part of my own leg and was making glances at Vera's little black poodle named Gigi.

I didn't know the eggs were eggs until Vera sweetly pointed them out to me, letting me know I could have some. I said, "Oh... thank you." I looked questioningly at them and looked around for the salt and pepper. There was none on the kitchen table, there was none on the stove, and I saw none on the counter anywhere. At this point I felt too awkward to ask for any, and I saw no black flakes on the eggs showing there may be seasoning already in them. Granny looked at me and under her breath told me to get some of the **** eggs before she, well, use your imagination. I used the spoon to scoop some over onto my plate. I took a bite in fear of a whooping. Imagine eating damp fog, but still having to chew. There was no flavor except if you could eat the smell of sulfur. I've never really been hungry after eating eggs, but somehow, I was still starving after eating those. On this day, I grew thankful for my mom's omelet-style flat eggs because at least she used butter.

I'm thankful for eggs because they're a go-to breakfast for me and through that one not-so-great experience with them, I learned how important it is to cook them well! Even though the food wasn't very good, I am thankful for a lady who was willing to try to provide for us the only way she knew how.

I'm glad we have seasonings. Remember, salt and pepper are your friends.

Day 39: Devotionals

A good devotional is going to find you, I believe. It'll find you at just the right time spiritually in your life. It's going to grab your attention and it will almost immediately have something to do with your current situation in life. There will be days in a devotional like this where God is obvious, and the word coincidence is lackluster. Coincidence, to me, is the word for people who aren't convinced of God just yet and don't know how else to explain life's mysterious happenings.

Somewhere out there, someone was influenced and inspired by what God revealed to them. At a certain place, at a certain time. They jotted it down either in the form of a lesson or a story, in whatever ability God gave them to do so. Either they or someone who they shared the moment with thought someone else could use encouragement and inspiration. It was edited by people who are good at editing, proofread by the proofreaders. It was then published by the publisher. Once this was complete, it was passed onto stores, websites, and any apparatus an eBook can be read from. In God's delicate yet deliberate way of doing things, it ended up in your hands. The author's experience aligned perfectly with yours at the time when your mother died, the time you found out you had cancer, the time your house burned down, the time you lost the third job in a year because your kids had been repetitively sick. The words in said devotional were just what you needed to keep going, to know you were not alone in your struggles; the words showed you through scripture and meditation on God's word someone else went through it and made it to the other side.

I'm thankful for devotionals because for one, God's timing is perfect even during the tough stuff. I'm thankful for them because they'll show you scripture and explanations you may have never considered. I'm thankful because they remind us that nothing new happens under the sun for humanity overall (Ecclesiastes 1:9) and everything we go through, our God knew we'd experience just as countless others have, too.

To devote is to give time, thought, and resources to something you deem worthy. I hope you think about what you are really devoted to versus what you should be devoted to. I pray you figure out what properly placed devotion looks like in your life. When you do, it'll be a game changer.

Day 40:
Mental Health Awareness

I'm still astounded by the way God has allowed these prompts to coincide with one another at times. The little break was probably needed from the prompt regarding self-harm up until now.

In late 2021 and early 2022, I was once again working in child welfare. I was working in a services role providing support for families. It was probably my favorite social services job outside of being a houseparent at the group home. I had a particular case in which a boy who would turn 18 in just a couple months was seeing a counselor who came to school for their sessions. It was one of those "open and shut" or "easy" cases. I just needed to make sure he was seeing his counselor until he turned 18 and we could close our case. I'll call him Mitch. Mitch was smart. He was an awkward comedian and had an interest in old films. He was mature for his age. His plan was to join the military and get out of his house. I can't blame him. My goal was to get out of my house, too, so I understood where his head was. His parents weren't together; his sister planned to stay with their mom. The case itself had started out with a rather uncommon allegation, nothing that affected the safety of the kids' lives per se, but their quality of life. Mitch remained living with his dad and worked a part-time job after school and on the weekends. Mitch took all the shifts he could get to stay gone from home. It was just sort of a mess that had somehow worked itself out to be a little less messy than it had started.

His dad had a history of mental health issues and alleged temper problems. I'd been warned he was a bit testy at times and had a short fuse. The first time I'd visited, I could see that about him, but overall, he was cooperative and friendly to me. He was never rude to me. I'd dealt with much worse than what this man had to offer when it came to attitude. He, like everyone else in the family, was just ready for the court case to be over with and to move on with their lives without child services' involvement. I recognized that. I can only imagine how over child welfare I'd be if I were in their shoes.

I received an email one day from the boy's counselor. She was concerned because Mitch had disclosed something concerning that had happened over the weekend. Per the counselor, the dad (who from this point forward I'll call Terry) told Mitch not to come to his room for anything, that he wanted to be alone. Mitch explained that a lady Terry was talking to had called their relationship off and it had put Terry in a mood. Mitch said he was playing a video game in the living room and his phone went off. It was a text from Terry that didn't make sense, as if he were drunk. Mitch became concerned and went to check on his dad. Terry had made his way to the bathroom, crying, and seemingly drunk as Mitch suspected. Mitch discovered quickly Terry had taken a knife and cut his arm. Mitch said there was blood all over the bathroom. It just so happened someone had been staying with them that weekend and Mitch woke them up to come to the bathroom and help. They called for an ambulance and Terry was taken to the ER. Terry was later released and sent home. After reviewing the report, my supervisor asked me to go check on Mitch and Terry. I texted Terry and asked if it was a good time for a drop in home visit. He said to come on by, that Mitch would be home for just a little while before it was time for him to leave for work. Terry was usually open to me visiting any time and it seemed now was no different.

I drove up to the house. It was a small older home just off the town square. It sat on a lot less than a quarter of an acre amidst other small homes. I always tried to pull in the driveway, but there wasn't much room. I walked up to the front porch and Mitch met me at the door. I was able to talk to him alone in the living room first. I talked to Mitch about the concerns regarding his dad over the weekend. Typical of his nature,

Mitch downplayed how he felt in the moment everything happened. Mitch liked to seem tough and unbothered. However, Mitch did state he didn't feel things were as bad as the report made it seem. Overall, given Mitch's age and the more details I learned about the situation, Mitch seemed fine. He asked if he could go ahead and go to work while I talked to Terry. I told him that was fine and to have a good night at work.

Once Mitch left, Terry came out from the back of the house, and we sat on the front porch to talk. I could tell he was nervous to talk to me this time but was putting on a friendly face. Terry had been raised in a very strict military home, or so I'd learned over small talk during previous visits. Emotions were to be hidden and poker faces were the norm. After some chit chat about how Mitch was doing in school, I asked Terry to tell me about their weekend because I'd heard some stuff I was concerned with. Terry said he'd become emotional after a woman stood him up for a date. Terry said it wasn't just that, but the child services' involvement, his financial situation (he'd been out of work for a few weeks after losing his job due to COVID-19,) and other issues contributed to his mental state over the weekend. Terry admitted he got drunk and hid in his room away from Mitch. Terry quickly changed the subject and said he was fine. God had created a great time for us to be outside that day. Although it was still considered wintertime, the sun was out, and it was just comfortable enough to be outside without shivering. If things went south, I was in a good place to get to my car and leave, of course. Things were going fine, though. The openness of the porch and the fresh air did the conversation well. I sat beside Terry in a rocking chair while he sat in his; we rocked out of rhythm before syncing up.

"I was told you'd gone to the ER this weekend, Terry. That you'd cut yourself?"

Terry was quiet and stopped rocking for a moment. I slowed to a stop as well to try and match him.

"Terry, I couldn't help but notice the cuts on your right arm since your sleeves are rolled up. I know they don't look all that deep, but I'd rather you talk to me about it. You're not going to get any judgment from me for it."

I think Terry had forgotten to hide his arm. As I said that, he looked down at his arm. He leaned it over close to me so I could see the cuts better. "Yeah, I mean… I've done it before. See? They're not even that deep. There's just a lot of them. And they're not even the direction that would kill me, ya know?" I agreed the cuts were very superficial. Scary moments and lots of blood can make things look worse than they are, and sometimes stories are misconstrued to sound worse than they are, too.

Terry went on to tell me he'd been cutting like that since he was a teenager (he was about 10 years older than me, maybe a bit less.) Terry said it wasn't all the time, it was only when he felt helpless, or when everything seemed to compound like the realization of his stressors over the weekend. In that moment, I was able to identify with Terry a bit and explain that although I'd only self-harmed once, I knew the emotions surrounding it. I talked to him about the therapy I'd done and how helpful it had been. Terry spent about an hour talking to me about his concerns and issues. He told me he'd apologized to Mitch for scaring him and putting him in that situation, and that Mitch had never seen him like that before. Terry talked about how proud of Mitch he was.

I rerouted the subject back to Terry's mental health and asked if he'd be open to counseling. He was very turned off by the subject as he'd not had a good counselor before. I told him I knew how hard it was to get in with someone good, especially in the area we were in. Everyone was booked. I told him I could help him find someone if he was interested. After we talked some more, he seemed curious about some of the places I'd suggested. I later would get Terry the contact information for those places. However, given the type of case it was, I couldn't force Terry to go to counseling and the court wouldn't, either. The way the court viewed it, Mitch was about to be 18 and out of high school. The daughter was no longer in the home. Where was the need in forcing this parent to complete any services now?

Terry thanked me for listening. He told me he'd never been understood when it came to those situations. I offered for Terry to reach out to me if he was struggling as long as I was still working in child welfare. He appreciated the offer.

Later, Mitch graduated and joined the military as he'd planned. Terry is doing alright now. Last I heard, he'd found work again. I closed my case and the case regarding his daughter closed as well when she went to live with her mother permanently.

I'm thankful for the stigmas beginning to lift off mental health. It allows for conversations like this to happen, unashamed and unafraid. If I'd been the same person I was before, I may have been frightened to talk to Terry about this. If I'd been more concerned about my reputation or how he would talk about me than his well-being, we may never have talked like we did. If I hadn't been willing to be vulnerable, a good opportunity would have been missed because I was too proud to share my own weaknesses. I'm also thankful for Terry concurring with me. It's kind of nice to know I'm not alone in my mental health struggles.

I think we all are one step away from getting to that spot. I believe that is why it is so important we be kind. If we were more honest with ourselves, maybe we could be more honest with others.

Carry one another's burdens. Share them. Love your neighbor as yourself. Be the person you wish you'd had.

Day 41: Spouses

I won't talk about the "bad" spouses here. We've all known those. I want to talk about the good ones, because there aren't many left, and I believe it's time we identify what a good spouse looks like by shedding light on some examples.

My grandma was tongue-tied and lip-tied as a child. I did not know this until I was an adult and I found out Anniston was dealing with the same thing. Grandma and Grandpa called me on the phone one day and told me about it. Grandma was constantly bullied growing up because of her speech. She was called words like "stupid" and "retarded". Grandma was shocked to say the least when Grandpa asked her out on a date the first time. After they were married, Grandpa and Grandma moved to Chicago, IL for a brief time. While up there, Grandpa found a dentist to look at Grandma. She'd had rheumatic fever and it had done a number on her teeth. They were thin and fragile. While the dentist was checking her teeth, he commented on the lip and tongue ties. The dentist informed Grandpa he could fix it. Grandpa said he'd pay whatever he needed to, and the operation was on. A couple of snips and I imagine some cauterization, and everything was complete. Grandma learned how to say words she'd struggled with since childhood. Grandpa helped her learn to talk with her newfound abilities. To hear Grandpa talk about this is to hear pride in his voice. Grandpa said he brought Grandma back down to Alabama dressed to the nines and in a brand-new car. When she opened her mouth to greet her family, I imagine jaws dropped. She was eloquent and was able to express her intelligence. No one was going to call her "stupid" anymore. Grandpa said he made sure her family knew how good she was doing, and he would have sacrificed anything he had to make life better for her. Later in late 2019, Grandma would have a fall that would leave her in the hospital. She was learning how to write and talk again, and Grandpa was more than willing to bring her home and do whatever he needed to do for her, to be her full-time caregiver. Unfortunately, he was not awarded the opportunity and she passed from a stroke within a month of the accident in January 2020. If she'd not had the stroke, I know he would have spent hour after hour teaching her how to be her greatest self again.

There was a couple we met at a church Phillip served at. We met them in 2015. After Phillip had left the youth pastor position, we found out the wife, Jamie, was diagnosed with ALS. She passed away last year as a result. The couple had been together for years and had raised two children together, one of which with special needs. The husband, David, posted to social media at one point to ask for time off from other teachers since he was in education. He had to care for Jamie and make sure his kids were cared for. Jamie was an avid piano player before her diagnosis, and she didn't want to stop. She wanted to play worship music. A solution was found. David held up her head as she played the piano, this way she could read the music as she played her favorite hymns and worship songs. David did everything in his power to give his wife a better life up until her last moments. Jamie passed away while David was in the hospital with their daughter who'd suffered a head injury, and he could not be with her as she left for Heaven. I can say confidently a mother's love understands. I have a feeling she forgave him for that. Life was hard and death was no different. Prior to me publishing this, I got David's blessing to share their story. It just so happens I asked on the anniversary of Jamie's death. That wasn't planned. David said, "It was a blessing to try to take care of her and be with her. Watching how she carried on through that, I will never be the same." David, I'm sure she found blessings in it all, too. She loved you and her kids passionately.

Granny and Paw met at a church social as young adults. Paw proposed to her at a burger joint in Guntersville, AL. They married soon after. They were married for decades. On November 30, 2012, Paw had to go to the hospital. He'd been on dialysis and had not been doing well. He eventually got home that night to rest after hours of poking, prodding, and doctoring. Paw was sitting in his chair in the living room. It was a lift chair and had become his bed as well as his primary sitting space. Granny had gone to bed and left him in the chair to sleep. Not long after this, Granny heard a loud crash. She got up to see Paw had fallen. He said he was going to the bathroom and fell. Granny told him she'd call my dad to come help him up. It was around midnight by now. Paw insisted he didn't want my dad to get mad, and to just put a pillow under his head and he'd sleep by the couch. Granny did just that. Paw laid on the floor by the couch on a floor runner with a pillow to rest his head on. Granny laid on the couch beside him, leaning her head where she could see him, and they could conversate. She never told me what they talked about, but she laid there and talked to him as long as they both could stay awake. At some point, Granny's exhaustion gave way, and she nodded off to sleep. Granny woke up the following morning around 5:30 a.m. or 6:00 a.m. on December 1st to find Paw had gone to Heaven while they slept side by side. Granny told me the rest of her life if she'd known Paw was going to die, she'd have stayed up and talked to him all night long for as long as he could have talked.

I am thankful for spouses like this because they are examples of what love is. It is long-lasting. It is a true act of servanthood. The other person puts the spouse before themselves, and if done correctly it works. If done correctly, it is an example of Christ's sacrificial love we read about in scripture. These types of spouses go to the greatest lengths possible to make life as good as possible for the other person. I am thankful I learned what a bad spouse was and how to recognize a good one. I believe I found a good one in my husband, and I hope he can say the same about me.

Day 42: Church

I have fallen a bit behind in these. I've loyally drawn out a piece of paper every day, though, and I'll keep on doing that. I jot down in my planner whatever I pick so I can keep up. However, I have had a lot of irons in the fire leaving me with little time lately to sit down and write. I type that and realize that is an excuse: you have time for what you make time for. Do I really, deeply think about these prompts when I choose them? Yes, I sure do. I mull over and pray about what I need to write each and every time. When I pulled this prompt out, I jotted down some ideas immediately of what I would want to say. A few days later, I remembered I had written about it already. I dug through my writings on social media and found it. Rather than it being called "Church", I called it "Sundays" when I wrote it. It encompasses everything I'd want to say well. It is what I wanted to write and say at Granny's funeral in March 2021, but I couldn't find the words to say at the time. I modified it a bit here compared to my original writing, but the point is the same.

Granny and Paw took me to their church starting at a very young age. On school days, I would wear a variety of play clothes. I was never one to stay clean and I wore plenty of holes in my clothes as a kid. I remember Sundays, though. I remember being squeezed into dainty pantyhose some Sundays (I loathed and still loathe pantyhose) and on other Sundays my lacy socks were folded down just right over shiny, buckled shoes. I clicked them together every chance I got, despite multiple commands of "stop messing up your shoes" I received. The dresses were naturally frilly and the poofiest of poofy. My hair, on any given day, would have been French braided or "plaited" to keep it from being messy at school, as I've mentioned already in this book. On Sundays, however, it would be brushed out, blow-dried, and a shiny reddish-brown; the brushed-out wave would kink up as soon as the Alabama humidity hit it. My soft hair would be plastered down with Aqua Net, in a feeble attempt to keep it under control. Much like me, that was a futile effort in and of itself. Sundays were different.

Granny and Paw moved at different speeds. By the time Paw was making it to the breakfast table on Sunday mornings, Granny had already picked through what I used to think of as "cotton ball" textured hair and attacked it with the same Aqua Net used to battle my own. She had her dress with a matching suit jacket picked out, shoulder pads neatly placed. Jewelry would adorn every traditional place on her body; sometimes her earrings were heavy enough to question the integrity of her earlobes. She would save her pumps and her makeup for last. Granny was already hovering over the stove finishing breakfast. The bar was already covered in white and green Corelle dishes lined with paper towels to catch drippings and grease. Out from skillets and pans would plop bacon, sausage, and eggs. Sausage gravy would be left in the pot and placed on a potholder with the other food. You could see steam carrying fragrances all over the house. Lastly, she would pull hot biscuits out of the oven and put them on their own plate. I liked my "sausage and biscuit" plain and always ate them one by one. I sat at the head of the "table", or the bar as I've called it. To my right, Paw enjoyed grape jelly on his biscuit and always gulped it down with a glass of buttermilk. I still don't understand how he stomached that. I don't remember Granny ever eating much of her own cooking, sitting down to my left only for a short time to drink some coffee or some Coke or Pepsi with a miniscule breakfast compared to ours. It was Sunday. She needed to finish getting ready for church. Other things could wait.

Once Paw had finished his breakfast, he would sneak off to the "blue bathroom." This bathroom was the main bathroom and the one located down their hallway beside the bedrooms. It was powder blue and covered in tile. Paw was very firm that he didn't want to be seen without a shirt on, or even in just his undershirt, so I always found it extra sneaky to sit on the couch and angle myself just right to watch him shave. There was no real point to it other than I wasn't getting caught. He would leave the bathroom door open. The hallway mirror revealed his reflection and I could sometimes catch a glimpse of him. Sometimes he would catch me and ever so slightly give me a firm, "Hey!" and I would giggle and hide. I would continue to watch him lather up shaving cream on his face and shave his round cheeks. I can still close my eyes and feel his stubble on my face when he hugged me and the smell of Barbasol and aftershave, the feel of his hand squeezing my shoulder and the slight lift of his cheek when he smiled. He would slick back his thick, black salt and peppered hair before getting his shirt from behind him to put on and button back up. Any other day, you may find him in a similar outfit, but on days like today he may be caught wearing a tie or a suit jacket. His shoes would be black and shiny. Today was Sunday.

Before I knew how clocks worked, I knew we were cutting it close to being late for church because the CBS Sunday Morning show would have a smiling sun easing across the seven-channeled television and a trumpet would be playing in the background. If this came on, you could bet Granny was getting ill and telling Paw and I to hurry it up and to turn the TV and lights off. We would load up in the car. They had a couple of different cars and pickups when I was growing up, but we normally rode to church in an old Lincoln or a Buick. I sat all by myself in the back seat, per usual, saying a little white lie that I was buckled up. We would back out of the driveway with Paw in the driver's seat so Granny could finish putting on her makeup. Sunlight would dance in past trees over Paw's shiny hair. They would talk about church and grown-up things. Granny would offer me a choice of red lipstick or pink and help me put it on once we got into the church parking lot. It made me feel like a big girl. She would also have two types of chewing gum, Juicy Fruit and Doublemint. Most days, being the child I was, Juicy Fruit was the only way to go. But, sometimes, Doublemint was chosen for a bit of "razzle dazzle". After all, it was Sundays. Those were just different and needed a different flavor. We listened to AM 1380 WRAB on the way to church, and although that was the only station ever on in the car, Sundays were different with gospel songs and hymnal music playing rather than the local obituaries and "Helping Hand" being said first thing. Sundays needed Sunday music.

These memories are precious now. They are what I have. I did not come to meet Jesus at Granny and Paw's church and it wasn't until I was 13 that I did. The church I was saved at- and its youth program-were a strong foundation of who I am today and forever grateful for my youth pastor there. It took me a few more years to really sit down and get to know the Jesus that had saved me. That stopped neither Granny nor Paw from making that investment, from putting in that time on me. If they could have drug me every Sunday to that church, they would've. Often, I went kicking and screaming. Often, I got into some type of trouble by crawling under pews, including but not limited to the time my friend/brother Luke and I found a dried-up dead frog under a back pew and alarmed most of the church with our response (I, for one, paid dearly for that one. I can't speak on his behalf.)

I say all that to say this. Invest in your kids, your grandbabies, all of them. No matter how far you've gone or how far they've gone, I hope you're the one who shows them Sundays, who shows them church. When you're gone, I hope they can say, "Wow, I am so glad for Sundays and church with them." There are times assuredly my Granny and Paw heard my mouth, saw my dumb choices, and maybe thought they'd wasted their time. They may have feared how I'd turn out. I sure hope not, but it wouldn't surprise me. But their investment was not left without a return at the end of the day. I attribute that to them putting in effort, loving me, and introducing me to Sundays and to church.

Anyone can introduce them to a dollar. Anyone can introduce them to a ballfield. Not to say those things aren't memorable, meaningful, or good, but I hope my kids remember my husband and I for Sundays, church, and for trying to be Christlike examples to them. I hope they remember talks about Heaven, about Jesus, about salvation and our relationship with Jesus, about loving one another the best we can. If only, if only, I can leave them with that.

Day 43: Givers

I'm about to blow your mind with the definition of the word "giver". It means "a person who gives something." I can feel your excitement and the revelation you just had. Please, sit down; don't make a scene. I'll list a couple of examples.

I had a great-uncle. Keep in mind, I had a bunch of great-uncles. This one was different. His name was Beecher Geer. Uncle Beecher was married to my great-aunt Claries (pronounced Claire-iss), my grandpa's little sister. Uncle Beecher was tall and skinny. He had the metabolism of a superhuman, and I've heard legends that he could eat an entire chocolate cake in one sitting and not gain an ounce. He had thick Coke-bottle glasses, white scruff on his chin holding up a wide smile, and snowy white hair to match. Most times I saw him he was found wearing a ballcap. He had a friendly happy-go-lucky personality and was genuinely sweet. He frequented the Lacon Flea Market I've mentioned. A lot of times when Mom and I were there selling ducks or geese or yard sale items, he would be there. We'd run into Beecher and he'd make sure to give us something. There was no telling what it would be. Once he gave me a radio because he heard me mention I wanted one. He sought out an old radio and went out of his way to make sure I got it. I cannot count how many times the man did this for my mom and me. His five children could probably give several accounts of the same type of spirit he had. Strangers all-around may have never known the man, but they knew his generosity and willingness to give to others, because a lot of strangers received gifts from Beecher. He wore that trait proudly, never taking it off. If he thought of you, you'd see the evidence in your hands sooner or later.

I've worked with countless children during my time in social work. One thing that always astounded me was how wonderful kids were in the worst of circumstances. I was sitting at my desk when I was working one of my child welfare positions. One of my co-workers brought three little girls in with her. They'd been surrendered by their aunt and uncle. I learned that the girls said their uncle had molested them. The aunt said they were liars and sent them on their way to foster care. I can't remember where the parents were now, either dead or simply dead to the girls.

I tried to have an office fit for kids. My older two children had picked out lots of toys to put in a plastic container on the bottom of my bookshelf. I had a school desk I'd refurbished to have a chalkboard top equipped with chalk and an eraser. I had coloring books and crayons. The oldest girl came into my office while my co-worker dealt with their paperwork. My co-worker was hopeful she'd find a foster home for all three so they wouldn't be separated. The oldest girl was coloring at the desk and looked up at my wall where I had pictures of my kids clipped to an old frame. She asked me how old my daughter was. Anniston was about 4 years old, I responded. If memory serves me correctly, this girl was around 8 years old. You could see the lightbulb go off in her intelligent, bright eyes and she hurriedly left the room.

She brought back with her a cardboard box full of clothes. It had been sat down haphazardly in the hallway. It was the belongings the aunt had left with them. All they had to their names were some clothes in the box, no shoes but what they had on their feet.

"Some of these don't fit me or my sisters anymore. I bet your little girl can wear them!"

Stunned and speechless, I couldn't find the words to stop her and tell her it was okay, that she didn't have to. She began digging gleefully through clothes and laying them in my lap. Most were in good shape, some in play condition. The girl insisted her two sisters were much too small for the clothes and their aunt had been making them wear the clothes anyway. I had seen the other two girls and I knew for a fact they didn't fit the sizes, otherwise I would have immediately stopped the situation. The girl told me she knew how hard it was to find clothes that fit, and she just knew my little girl would love them. She was a grown woman in a little girl's body, and she should have never had to be. She was a mother and didn't even know it. However, she took the burden and ran with it, turning it to a positive. I took the clothes and gave her a hug. I assured her what a great kid she was. If I'd told this sweet angel no, that would have been a gut punch to a shot-through-the-heart kind of day. The girls were able to get other clothing from the foster care closet to meet their needs.

I don't think I have to write why I'm thankful for these people. I believe it's obvious. Their gifts are priceless. What is even more priceless is their existence, their reminder to us to be better and do better. Cherish the givers in your life and learn to be more like them.

Day 44:
Good Grammar/Spelling

I was famous... well, for a few days. In fourth grade, I somehow managed to become the school spelling bee champion. I took my title very seriously. I studied in the hallway with my classmates as they called out words to me. I was going to compete in the county spelling bee. I feel like the phrase "Yeehaw!" is appropriate here. I became a stickler for spelling during this time in my life.

I didn't have much else going for me in my life. I was overweight in fourth grade. I had extremely long hair. I was socially awkward and had a crush on a boy who ate paper. My prospects and my future weren't exactly looking fantastic. The county spelling bee was the occasion when Mom cut two feet of hair off my head. Styling my new shorter-but-still-long hair with the same horrible bangs going across my forehead, I was ready to take on the world... or at least the other spelling competitors in Marshall County.

Things were going alright. I'd gone a couple of rounds. Unfortunately, due to a woman with a thicker accent than myself, I misspelled the word "benign". It was misspelled because I, at the ripe age of 9 years old, thought she was saying "Bonine" as if it were a last name. I had no clue what she was talking about. I gave it my best guess up on that big stage in that old auditorium. I heard, "Sorry. That is incorrect. You may sit down." I felt like the empire I built had crumbled between my fingers and scattered into dust. As a has-been, I still proudly hold the title of 10th Place in the Marshall County Spelling Bee.

I learned in my social work courses in college how important it was to remember a person's name. You never know when you'll meet someone who has only ever been called crude names in their lifetime and never their real name. I took this to mean it was also important to spell their names. I've always tried my best to remember that to make sure people knew I cared about them. I wanted them to know they were important. On the other side of that coin, I learned when you're running someone's background and doing detective work on the job, you want to make sure you're looking up John Doe rather than Jon Doe or Kathy Smith rather than Cathy Smith. You never know what felonies John had on his record that Jon did not, or if Kathy is innocent and Cathy is the one with multiple substantiated child abuse/neglect reports. It is very important to get the right information!

My husband's middle name is spelled wrong. His mom spelled it the way she thought it sounded. Talmadge (after his great-grandfather) turned into Talmeridge. I remember laughing when I first saw it because I figured out immediately what had happened since one of my great-grandfathers has the same name. All laughing aside, it is where we get our middle child's name from: Ridge. So, in a way, I guess I can be thankful for misspelled words, right?

I'm thankful for people who take the time to correct their grammar and correct spelling. It just shows a level of detail I appreciate from people. It means they didn't get in a hurry. It means they spent time on something just for you. Though the content may not be personal, the effort certainly is.

That's also why writers get people to proof and edit their work. In saying that, I want to take another moment here to thank everyone who proofread this work. I truly and wholeheartedly appreciate the time you took to read my ramblings, some lame, some easy, some difficult. It means so much to me.

Day 45:
Apologies Never Received

My parents divorced in 2010 when I was 19 years old. I was put in a very awkward position for most of my childhood and even young adulthood. Mom would tell me her plans to leave. Dad would question what I knew and didn't know. I played dumb for peace's sake. I was put in a position I should have never been in. Most of my childhood and teenage years were spent learning how to keep secrets and fake a smile to try and keep the house as calm as possible. Mom waited until I was out of the house and in college before she left my dad.

Not long after Mom had Dad served with divorce papers, I went to his house to see him. I don't remember why. It may have just been a routine visit. My dad has always drunk alcohol; he started at a young age. He may debate on whether he is an alcoholic, but I think the time he spent in the hospital in 2018 when he needed a beer prescribed to him daily during withdrawals from the alcohol (along with pain pills he had bought) speaks for itself. He was admitted for an untreated infection in his legs, and with him not having insurance and disregarding an offer for me to pay for a doctor's visit, he thought drinking and pills were the ticket, I guess.

When I walked into the kitchen and dining room area, I saw a pile of empty beer cans laying by the trash can. There were a couple of empty bottles of Kentucky Gentleman. This was no strange scene at my house, there was just more than I remembered being there before. Dad was sitting at the bar. I can't really describe this moment for me. He was drinking and emotional. However, looking back at my childhood he was rarely what one would call sober given the amount of alcohol he consumed daily. This time was different. He was sad and mopey. He was angry at my mom, not understanding why she would have wanted to leave him. The conversation drifted in another direction, and I can't say how it got to where it did. Dad, in a roundabout way, admitted he didn't treat me well growing up. He may not even remember having this conversation with me. It was just the two of us. He admitted he had not been the best dad. Rather than say he was sorry for all of it and for all he'd put me through, he blamed it on his own grandfather and the way his grandfather had treated him. One comment was, "I guess that's why I am the way I am."

My great-grandfather, Granny's dad, is from all accounts I've ever heard one of the meanest men alive. My great-aunt Sue, Granny's sister-in-law, once told me when we were talking after a funeral that my great-grandfather was the meanest man she'd ever met. She used a different term I won't use here. In my gatherings over the years, I've figured out Granny had a terribly toxic relationship with her dad and somehow- whether out of convenience or lack of other resources- allowed him to be the primary babysitter for my dad. I was even told a story about when my great-grandmother was dying in her bed in her fifties, my great-grandfather was in the next room having an affair with her sister. Granny caught them, resulting in my great-grandfather punching Granny in the stomach. I put the pieces together a few years ago in some of mine and Granny's conversations that this event caused her to have a D&C done. Dad was about six years old when this happened.

During this talk, Dad showed me pale circles in his dark upper arms where my great-grandfather had broken off sticks and shoved them into Dad's flesh as punishment when he was very small. My dad was moving slow that day, I guess, and he was failing to put a pasture fence up correctly, or at least in the opinion of my great-grandfather. I've heard horror stories about my great-grandfather, so this alone didn't surprise me. Dad did not say sorry on this day for anything he'd done, rather he made excuses for the way he was treated as an explanation for why he acted the way he did.

I remember being stunned. I've always been a firm believer there is a difference in reasons and excuses, and at this specific moment all I could hear was excuses. I just nodded and went along with the conversation so I could make my exit as soon as possible with no conflict. I wasn't expecting this type of encounter, but I was certainly ready for it to be over with.

Years went by. I held onto a lot of bitterness about that moment. I felt like he should have apologized to me and just owned up for everything he had done. I felt a bit cheated. Once I was told by a counselor at my college that I was grieving the loss of a relationship with my dad I'd never had. The further along I've gotten through life, the more I have learned to let go of expectations for other people.

I am thankful for apologies that never come because they allow for personal and spiritual growth if you'll let them. They've allowed me to learn people's true colors. I am reminded I can't expect someone unhealed to do my healing. That is not anyone's duty, it is a job to be done between God and me. I am reminded to be in prayer for people too proud to apologize, as well as for the people who don't realize what they've done and don't know they are in the wrong.

Years down the road, during Dad's hospital stay I mentioned above, I let him know I forgave him. That certainly didn't mend the relationship necessarily, but it relieved me of some of the hurt whether it did him any real good or not. It established where we stood to some degree, I believe. During his hospital stay a family friend helped him with a prayer of salvation. I hope it was real.

I've learned to not expect a fish to dance a waltz, not to expect a storm to repair the roof it ripped off your house, and not to expect apologies you may never hear. Life's too short for it.

Day 46: Rain

Phillip and I sat in the parking lot of Bojangles' in his '93 Ford Ranger. It was only a few days after we'd started dating. It was a cloudy overcast evening. He was going to be visiting his Pawpaw a few hours away during Spring Break. It was raining. He had wanted to take things slow and we hadn't clarified what that meant yet. He held my hand, telling me he would kiss me when he got home from his Pawpaw's. He'd be embarrassed if I put the line he really said; I still tease him about it. I looked at him like he had two heads and asked him if he was serious. I was half-joking but also very shocked he wasn't ready for a kiss. I grin while writing this because he looked so anxious. Again, he'd told me he wanted to take things slow. We had different ideas of what that was, clearly. I thought a kiss wasn't that big of a deal, but obviously we were of totally different mindsets and didn't know it. He nervously agreed and leaned in. We had our first kiss while the spring rain rattled off the top of his pickup.

Any time we have stayed at a cabin, there is usually a tin roof. For my 30th birthday we went to Gatlinburg, TN to spend time in the Smoky Mountains. It is one of my favorite places on Earth. We were able to stay in a larger cabin since it was my husband and my kids, my in-laws, and my sister-in-law and her kids. Every morning I'd get up early and go enjoy coffee on the porch. There was one morning I recall where it rained just enough to get the ground wet. We were deep enough in the woods to see bears frequently. The trees were thick up top and filled the whole area with lush green. It wasn't quite Fall yet. I rocked in the rocking chair on the porch while sipping my coffee and soaked in the sounds of the rain on the roof. I closed my eyes and listened to it travel hurriedly, whispering like children trying not to giggle down a school hallway.

These are two very fond memories of rain. I'm thankful for rain because it seems to amplify special moments in a way other things cannot. However, I am thankful for rain because it can be a symbol of growth. Growing up on a farm, rain was a thing to be cussed when there was too much of it and a thing to be prayed for when there'd been none. Too much can do damage, just the right amount can bring about new life.

I believe there are a lot of things in life like rain in that way. I believe we need to take heed of what those are before we start spewing water like a wide-open fire hydrant. Take your own condition into account before moving in on someone else's weather.

Day 47:
Christmas Lights

Believe it or not, despite all the stuff I've mentioned about my parents already, there were good memories. One of those happened to be holidays. When I was small, my parents tended to go all-out on holidays. Mom loved Halloween, so Granny and Paw's yard got decorated in all sorts of Halloween get-up. Both my parents' yard and Granny and Paw's yard got decorated like a city park at Christmas time. My parents would work and make light arrangements on the wheels of my dad's excavating equipment, like the backhoe and track hoe, making it look like the wheels were moving. There'd be ice cycle lights dripping off the house. Christmas figurines such as Santa and his reindeer would be lit up in the yard. There were even a couple of times my dad pulled a trailer in the town Christmas parade. Dad had a black Peterbilt and it would be adorned in all sorts of lights to match the trailer and float. Dad enjoyed getting to drive his truck in the parade, but he decided he didn't like the lady who was over the float one year (she ended up being the mother of one of my best friends and had a huge hand in my upbringing) and never did it again. I don't know what all went down between them, but if I had to guess, my dad thought she was too bossy and probably said some ugly stuff to her. Not long after this incident, the Christmas spirit seemed to die at our house and the Christmas lights rarely ever got put out, or at least to the same degree they had before. We'd have Christmas trees and decorations inside, but not much in the yard anymore.

As I've grown up, I have not had any Christmas lights outside. Phillip and I have talked about it and have just not pulled it off. I decorate the inside a bit, and I make sure we have a nice tree each year, aside from that there isn't much of a fuss over Christmas or any holiday for that matter. We focus more on the get-togethers. We haven't deprived our children, though. We take them to see Christmas lights at least once during the season typically. We'll go to a city park or Santa Land when we are in North Alabama. Their eyes light up with joy as they run from one scene to another, taking in as much as they can. We'll hear "Come look at this!" or "Wow!" or "Look, Mom! Look, Dad!"

I'm thankful for Christmas lights and for the good memories. They give me a chance to look back on some of the good parts of my childhood and I enjoy seeing the same excitement and joy in my kids. I'm especially thankful for one specific time before Tripp was born. I want to say Anniston and Ridge may have been 4 and 3 years old at the time. Granny was still able to walk well and wasn't on oxygen then. Phillip and I took her, Anniston, and Ridge to Christmas in the Park in my hometown. She was able to walk with us and show the kids all the different Christmas lights. She finally had to sit down to rest and the kids sat down beside her. I took a photo of them smiling with the biggest smiles. Granny grinned as she stared over at them with a loving look on her face. It was the last time she was able to go to Christmas in the Park.

I am thankful I was able to give her that moment with her great-grandchildren. Perhaps she got to enjoy time travel for a moment and reminisce about her granddaughter smiling over Christmas lights, too.

Day 48: Holy Spirit

I was asked to speak at our Women's Brunch at church. It was kind of humorous how it happened. Phillip had learned from someone else that I was supposed to speak at said Women's Brunch, though no one had asked me. I, as a good little pastor's wife, went into full-on panic mode trying to figure out, when, where, and other details about this Women's Brunch while also trying to confirm that the speaker was, indeed, me. I confirmed it by worrying an unnecessary amount of people, and I began to pray about what I needed to speak about. While I did so, I flipped through my notebook and my Bible and came to the scripture Jeremiah 31:3. It was a scripture I'd previously highlighted. It says, "Yahweh appeared of old to me, saying, 'Yes, I have loved you with an everlasting love. Therefore, I have drawn you with loving kindness.'"

At the end of last year, I began to have serious doubts about being loved and if people really loved me or just loved what I could do for them. When I tell you this thought weighed me down, it hurt. It was a huge weight. I had to keep myself in a state of constant reminding that whether anyone on earth loved me, God loved me simply because I am His. While all these repetitive thoughts were going on, I laid down with Tripp one night as he fell asleep. I thought to myself how I love him and my other children and how no matter what they do in life, I could never stop loving them.

I immediately became convicted of how I love God. Do I love God because of who He is or because of what He does for me? I cried and asked God for forgiveness for those thoughts and feelings and asked Him to help me further my relationship with Him.

I ended up speaking on this topic at the Women's Brunch. It occurred quickly to me I wasn't the only woman there who had felt this way. It became clear the Holy Spirit had made known what needed to be discussed.

The following week, the tennis team and I traveled to our second tennis match of the season. On the way home that night, a few of my tennis players sitting closest to me began having what I call a "scary story" time. Now, my scary stories are the real deal. They aren't stories; they are fact. They are the stories that keep people up at night with the real fears of the spiritual world, the unanswered questions and the unexplained. I carefully navigated what I felt appropriate to say as I don't like giving evil too much attention.

The conversation organically moved in a direction about life after death. One of my players commented they were afraid there would be nothing when they died. Just nothing. They'd be gone. They said how scary it was. I took the moment to talk to God about how to proceed and I began to talk to them about what my beliefs are in a way that wasn't telling them they *should* have the same beliefs as me, but to explain how I understood things. I got to talk to them about seeing Phillip's Uncle Scottie pass away, and how that moment of his death was forever etched in my mind as proof our souls don't just stop: they keep going. I talked about my own beliefs on God, and I brought up Jeremiah 31:3, telling them what "everlasting" love meant. I could feel myself getting hyped up as we talked. The kids were pleased with the conversation, and I later messaged them telling them all I hoped I didn't make them feel uncomfortable. On the contrary, they appreciated the conversation and having someone who was willing to speak to them about it.

I messaged a friend about it because I was so excited to have the conversation. My Bible App on my phone notified me of the verse of the day. My verse of the day also fell from Jeremiah 31, only it was verse 25. It says, "…for I have satiated the weary soul, and I have replenished every sorrowful soul."

I could not have planned those events days apart if I'd tried to.

I am thankful for the Holy Spirit because the Holy Spirit is the guide we were left here when Jesus ascended back into Heaven. It lives and breathes as we inhale the Word and exhale the Truth. Its evidence is powerful and mighty in moments such as these.

Day 49: Mom

There are some prompts in these books which will be specific to me, but still relevant. I realize your mom and my mom are two very different people. Some of you may not have gotten to experience your mom. I'll also have prompts about other relatives of mine. I hope you've found someone in your life to fill those roles over the years, and if not yet I hope that person enters your life soon.

I had a hard time with how I felt about Mom over my lifetime. We were together in a far from perfect situation. We never had a lot of money. The house was not in the best condition. Her and Dad had a terrible marriage which flowed over into my life seamlessly. I have come to realize Mom *did* try to keep me safe, even though her own indecisiveness about whether to stay or leave Dad over the years ended up cultivating some distrust towards her from me. Although the situation didn't change during my time living at home, she tried to do what she thought was right for me in some way.

Mom trusted me with "grown up" jobs and it always made me feel so big. She allowed me to input data into the computer at the machine shop she worked at. I was very young at the time, as young as 4 and 5. She allowed me to have a sense of purpose and a sense of duty when I often felt I was in the way. Mom included me in just about everything she did. She even included me at the age of 9 in a speech about the Colonial Pipeline that was going to try coming through our small town. I knew very little regarding what I was speaking about, but she put me front and center and I ended up with a little blurb in the local paper about my "strong feelings" on the pipeline.

She entertained my hobbies. She encouraged my artwork and photography and often entered my work in the county fairs. I entered countless 4-H competitions in photography and won more than once. Mom tried diligently to let me be a kid while I was living in what I'd describe as an "adult problem" situation, allowing me to use my imagination, daydream, and pretend. Once I began playing tennis, she unrelentingly took me to every private lesson we could afford, some we couldn't.

Mom didn't pry about my romantic life, crushes, or relationships. She did listen, though, whenever I wanted to talk about it; the truth is I was quite boy-crazy, and she humored me. Now, she did insert herself a few times when I wished she hadn't because of my own embarrassment, and at times I'd argue now as a parent she pushed some things she may not should have, but overall, she did a good job. During my childhood, she often slept on the couch, and this continued long after I moved out. The night of my first break-up, I was destroyed. She invited me to come lay on the couch with her that night and let me cry.

Mom went all-out when it came to school. She wanted to make sure I had the BEST projects in my class. I'd argue she took it to an extreme at times, but I appreciate the commitment. She had high expectations regarding school and grades for me. At times she held her own high standards of all A's up to me, and she soon realized her daughter may have a B or two. She then realized her daughter stunk at Algebra 2/Trig and Chemistry and eased up a bit when she understood I really was trying.

Mom took me to my church youth group as often as I wanted to go. She allowed me to go on some local outings with them, which had been unheard of before. Mom also kept me in contact with my grandparents when she could, even though Dad had pushed them away from me over the years due to drama and the typical nature of a domestic violence relationship.

Mom let me pick the atrocious paint colors in my room. Mom never told me I was fat, and I can't remember many if any comments about my body coming from her unless it was meant to be constructive. Mom let me have the last bite of her McDonald's Double Cheeseburger with no pickles almost every single time I asked for it.

There are some things I wish Mom hadn't done, don't get me wrong. I don't feel it necessary to include all that right here. I had certain emotions over them as a child, but as an adult I've reflected on them all. But, again, I don't see it necessary here, and some of those instances may come up as examples in other prompts. All in all, though our relationship isn't what I'd call a typical mother-daughter relationship, it is a good one. I'm grateful for it.

Thank you, Mom, for the dedication to staying the course with me and being Mom.

Day 50:
Judas

Referencing the Gospel of John here (Chapter 18 specifically), Jesus and his twelve disciples went across a place called the Kidron Valley where there was a garden. He and the disciples had met here before on other occasions and it had become one of their spots to pray, for Jesus to teach, and more. It appears in the story that not all twelve disciples were right alongside Jesus when Jesus had called for a time of prayer. Judas lagged behind; I'll call this being distracted by things of the world. He'd already been contacted about a plot to destroy Jesus, lured by the enemy.

Judas was a money man. He was strict on budget, but also had a lust for the mighty "dollar". He had, however, faithfully followed Jesus up until this point. He had seen the miracles. He'd seen the lame walk. He'd watched how blind people regained their sight. He'd walked the miles Jesus had and believed the words Jesus had spoken. However, this time, Judas had fallen prey to the shining temptation of silver. The Pharisees and soldiers recognized Judas as one of Jesus' disciples and talked him into selling out Jesus. Those people wanted Jesus dead.

Judas took a company of soldiers and officials with him to the garden, infecting this place of peace with disruption and evil. Jesus, though, wasn't surprised. Jesus is never surprised. He knew this was going to happen. He knew just who was going to do it. Jesus had a purpose, however, and knew exactly how it was to be fulfilled. Jesus calmly played the role He was meant to play.

"Who is it that you're seeking?" he said. They replied, "Jesus of Nazareth."

I imagine Jesus stood cooly and calmly as he said, "I am he."

In Matthew 26, the account says Judas went up to Jesus and kissed him on the cheek first and identified him as "Master". Jesus would reply, calling him "friend" and asking him why he had come.

Regardless of which of the Gospel accounts you read, Judas probably felt a punch to his gut right about now. He and the soldiers and officials heard the exchange. The power it held, and the reality of the situation, caused them to fall to the ground. They confirmed one last time asking Jesus if he really was Jesus. Jesus said, "I am he." Jesus urged them to let the disciples go. Simon Peter, one of the disciples, drew his sword to protect Jesus and attacked one of the high priest's servants who'd come with the crowd, cutting off his right ear. Jesus told Simon Peter to stop, and in Luke 22 it says Jesus healed the ear of the opposer. Jesus knew it was time for the prophecy to proceed. After his arrest, according to the Gospel of Matthew, the other disciples deserted Jesus and ran away.

Not in scripture, but I imagine Judas at this point felt the lowest of low. He *knew* he'd done wrong. He understood what was about to happen. But… the money! The pay! I'm sure he thought it was going to be immense! Surely it would change his life! I imagine he asked for his pay as the soldiers took Jesus away. I'm sure one of the soldiers probably said something to the equivalent of, "Oh, yeah, 'bout forgot." The soldier handed him a small bag with thirty pieces of silver, the same worth of a servant who had already been gored to death by an ox. If I were Judas, my jaw would have dropped to the floor and my heart would have broken. I'd probably have begun to sob.

If I were Judas….? I am sometimes.

I am thankful for Judas because his character reminds me of how easily I am distracted from God. Judas is not worthy, but Jesus died for Him anyway. Judas is rotten. Judas was faithful to Jesus until his weaknesses came into play. Regardless of our weakness, Jesus is still the victor. He always was and always will be.

Judas reminds me to not allow the world to get in the way of my relationship with Jesus. I need forgiveness as I fail at this sometimes, but I'm glad I have a God who is continuously forgiving and a Jesus who bridged the gap for that to be possible.

Day 51:
Hot Showers

Reading this prompt caused me to want to go get in the shower for no real reason! Man, do I love a good, hot shower.

Hot showers are good to just wash off all the ick. Cold water doesn't get the ick off just right; for me, it takes a steaming hot shower to scrub off the day. I am a shower singer. I sing quietly, though, because I don't want commentary. Acoustics are better in the shower. Don't quote me on what scientific research paper that came from, but I'm sure it is out there somewhere in the literary world. I can be caught singing hymns, Christian music, country music, rock music, rapping something out of the early 2000's (quite poorly), or even spout off something totally off-the-wall for my normal liking.

Hot showers are the best place to cry. Hot tears mix well with hot water. Sometimes people don't even know if you're red from the water or red from tears until they look at your eyes. In my lifetime, I've made excuses to get showers just so I could go cry alone out of the way of wandering eyes. I've rested my head against the shower wall and sobbed until no sound could come out.

They're also a fantastic place for prayer time. I can talk softly to God in a place that is almost always away from everyone. When I was not married yet and lived alone or with roommates, it was a great spot. Kids can make showering alone and uninterrupted almost impossible. It seems like being in the shower is a good place to pray, too, because I don't have as many distractions there. It could also be used as a metaphor for scrubbing off the emotional and spiritual "ick" along with the mental strain of the day. Again, a fantastic place to talk to God.

Could even be a good place for you to start if you don't already. Careful, though; you may end up talking until the hot water runs out.

Speaking of running out of hot water, try living in a college dorm with three other girls. If even one of the roommates is in the shower too long, you could end up with a two-minute lukewarm shower. Talk about maddening. Spending more than 15 minutes in the hot shower was a cause for a fight, or at least a petty cold shoulder for the next 24 hours.

I mentioned kids a couple paragraphs ago. We are parents who don't mind showering with our kids when they're still small. There comes a point where Phillip and I both agree the kids are too old to grab a quick shower with us. I love that Ridge's first memory is of him and Phillip getting a shower and them singing "Old McDonald" together. Phillip threw on swim trunks and the two hopped in the shower that night. Ridge recalls them making all sorts of farm animal sounds and laughing. To know Ridge laughed meant he was probably to the point of tears. I envision his little self at that time and the goofy giggles that probably sprang out of the top of the shower.

One of my favorite things to do when we lived at the girls' ranch was to put Tripp in his baby tub in the shower with me. The shower we had was big enough we were able to do that. I'd prop him up in his baby tub while I washed my hair, shaved, or did whatever I needed to. He was happy as could be in his tub watching me. I'd wash him, too, while we were in there. But it allowed me to get much needed mom-time if Phillip wasn't home to watch him. So many people take for granted moms don't get to shower as often as they'd like sometimes when their kids are little. I am so blessed I didn't have that problem when Tripp came along.

When I was pregnant with my kids, hot showers were a blessing. Contractions would start in the small of my back every time. I could get in the shower and allow the water to hit against the small of my back for some relief. I selfishly would stay until all the hot water was gone, warning Phillip if he hadn't showered yet it would probably take a bit to warm back up. If I'd delivered my kids naturally, I'd probably have opted for water births or at least the option to rest in the hospital showers.

All those reasons are good ones, I feel, to be thankful for hot showers. In writing this, I realize how spoiled I am to be able to have this luxury. So many people only get cold showers if they get to shower at all. I get whiny when the hot water is cool after Anniston gets out of the shower now (cue a typical preteen girl comment with a following "just wait until she's a teenager" statement.) I can't imagine how miserable I'd be with no hot water heater to indulge me. Any of us who can have this, we are blessed people. I only wish we wouldn't forget how valuable things like this are.

Day 52:
Tobacco/Nicotine

I knew a prompt I am *not* thankful for would come up again eventually. Buckle up, I suppose. This one I'm a bit opinionated about. Some of you are going to get your gears wound up tight. If you'll read through the whole thing, though, you'll be ok, I believe.

I do not like vaping, dipping, chewing tobacco, anything that falls into this category. It doesn't mean I don't like people that do. I just don't like the stuff, that's all. I don't allow it in my house. We're allowed our opinions and we're allowed to make our homes into places we want to exist in. People who come visit are more than welcome to do it outside. I just don't approve of it in my house.

Mom has smoked cigarettes my entire life. The back porch would be riddled with cigarette butts surrounding the concrete block steps. Once when I was very small, Mom was pushing a buggy in the grocery store. I was small enough to still sit in the seat at the front. I blurrily remember reaching for one of her cigarettes while she pushed me down the aisle of Warehouse Groceries. I remember my little fingers getting smacked very hard, audibly might I add. I don't remember why I already reasoned this together in my head, but I didn't understand why she could have them if I couldn't.

When I was playing high school tennis, I remember one of our match days being a little colder than what I'd anticipated. I didn't have my hoodie and I was cold. Mom loaned me her grey jersey-knit jacket. She got out of her car and handed it to me. Both her car and her jacket smelled strongly of cigarettes. I began to warm up on the court again and my own teammates immediately began making snide remarks about someone smelling like cigarettes. I'm no stranger to the fact they were passive aggressively directing the comments to me. I tried to ignore it, but I was mortified. I was the kid who didn't smoke or drink and was kind of a "goody two-shoes" in some ways, and to be associated with smoking made me want to hide under a rock. I eventually took the jacket off. I was off my game from being laughed at and would rather just stay cold. The smell of the smoke lingered on my arms and in my hair long after.

I've only ever dated three guys. My first boyfriend smoked. He had enough respect for me to compromise and not smoke when I was around, or at least go take a smoke break away from me. We were 16 and 17 respectively. My second boyfriend, who I dated from the time he was 19 to 21 (I was two years younger than him,) dipped. I put in a very important rule of no dipping if he planned on giving me a kiss and he held to that. Y'all have no idea the relief I felt when I found out Phillip did neither of those things.

Dad smoked for years. When I was in first grade, we started the D.A.R.E. program and I learned smoking wasn't good for you. Talk about a rant I went on. Not only did I know cigarettes smelled bad, but they killed your lungs! Boy, I went home on a rampage. Would you believe Dad is the only one who even somewhat took me seriously? He stopped because I asked him to stop. Simply because I asked, "Dad, would you please stop smoking?" He did. He stopped that day.

The victory was short lived as he picked up chewing tobacco. He carried around a back of Red Man Chewing Tobacco, a light brown/tan bag with a Native American chief on the side of it. It smelled like burned grapes. His excuse was it wasn't as "bad" as smoking. Oh, it was equally disgusting. He often would laugh and try to get me to take a chew. The only time I ever saw any benefit to it was when I was stung by a wasp. Dad wet a wad of tobacco in his lip and applied it to the sting. There was almost instant relief. He told me it would take the sting out and make me feel better. To my surprise, it did. I guess in that one way I can be thankful for tobacco, even though hardly anyone uses it that way anymore, I'd argue. Today, Dad has picked up smoking again now that his new wife smokes.

    I think the worst part about his chewing tobacco outside of the nasty wads left on the ground outside, was the spit bottle. It made me want to gag. So many times, I almost mistook it for a drink and stopped myself. I recall one night we were driving home from Terry's Pizza in Huntsville, AL. I was around 8 years old. I was sitting in the middle of my dad's pickup. He was driving and Mom was in the passenger's seat. Someone got too close to Dad's pickup, or at least according to him. He cussed- his first language- and grabbed his spit bottle. He unscrewed the lid, opened the bottle, and poured all the nasty spit juice on the guy's windshield behind us as we sped away. He laughed and laughed. I laughed because I wasn't sure what to think and if I didn't laugh, I might have gotten yelled at for not agreeing with the humor.

    Paw smoked from the time he was a child up until he was in his late 70's. One of my favorite photos of Paw and I is him holding up a bass I'd caught when I was young, and he is grinning with his cigarette poked out the side of his mouth. He only ever smoked outside the house. He never smoked in his truck. His smoking I think, because of that, never bothered me as badly. He never even really smelled like cigarettes to me. Paw decided one day to quit cold turkey. And he did so successfully. When he passed away in his early 80's, he had a small spot of emphysema starting in one of his lungs. I say that to say, if you really want to stop smoking, you can. If someone who has smoked for six, maybe even seven, decades can quit cold turkey one day, you can, too. Paw's case alone proves it is a lot of the "want to" factor involved in the decision.

It took me reading all of this to honestly conclude how I'm thankful for these things I can't stand. I'm thankful for my experience with them because it has turned me away from it. I don't have any desire for nicotine. I have no desire to smoke. Even when my anxiety is high or I have a PTSD attack, they aren't my first go-to. I'm thankful I don't have to spend money on it, and let me tell you, just from the little I know it can get expensive. It's a habit I don't have to break. I've got plenty of habits already that need work and nicotine luckily isn't on the list. It's something my kids don't have to be subjected to at home by neither Phillip nor myself.

At the same time, I'm also thankful for people who have done much worse before and have weaned their way down to nicotine. I'm proud of how far they have come. People who have gone from heroin or methamphetamine down to just nicotine, I respect the effort. I hope one day you can come to a place where you need none of it, but I do commend you for doing what you can.

In case you can't tell, that was a tough one. Thank *you*, reader, for bearing with me.

Day 53: Grandpa

Grandpa, as you probably have figured out by now, is my mom's father. He is my last living grandparent. Paw went first, then Grandma, then Granny. Now I have Grandpa left.

Grandpa is a little over 6 feet tall. He is long-legged and strong for his age. He has blue eyes and what little hair he has left is white. A long time ago, it was practically black. He has long fingers and large hands; he came by it naturally but hard work all these years I'm sure helped their size. His wardrobe usually consists of button-up short sleeve shirts and khaki pants; blue jeans are nowhere to be found in his closet. He is a quiet presence in a room, but the silence is deceiving. The man is knowledgeable about so many things. Grandpa once told me, "I'd rather know a little about a lot than a lot about a little."

Grandpa was born in the 1930's. He was born and raised in rural Alabama. His father came from a long line of loggers and laborers, his mother from farmers and from all accounts well-educated people. Grandpa was the oldest of four children, the order going boy-girl-boy-girl. Tragedy struck when Grandpa's father died at age 37 from kidney cancer. Shortly after his death, Grandpa's mom became sick. Grandpa can recall him and my Aunt Claries overhearing conversations from my great-grandmothers' siblings discussing which children would take should she die. The two listened sadly as they learned they'd be the two no one would want; the younger two would be easier to "train" as they grew up. Grandpa and Claries were already set in their ways. They were blessed my great-grandmother survived.

Grandpa went through grade school and afterwards joined the U.S. Army. He had grown up around Grandma and had worked fields with her and her brothers. I mentioned before he asked her out on a date eventually. They broke up once. In a nutshell, Grandma believed she was dying and would not survive rheumatic fever. She didn't want Grandpa to waste his time marrying a dying woman. She came out of it, Grandpa came home from where he was stationed at the time, and the two of them got married sometime shortly after. They were married 61 happy years before her death, and it is difficult to talk about Grandpa without Grandma. They were best friends and each other's biggest fan. Together, they had all sorts of dreams. One of those dreams held a household of running feet; however, they were only able to have one child, my mom. Although I have come to understand just like any parents, they weren't perfect, they were good to her.

Grandpa is a storyteller. He can go on and on about his family history. He has talked about his experience in the Army. Grandpa used his height to his advantage during basketball back in the day in the Army. He told me about a fight he got in once, which is a shock to me because he's just not that type of person. I guess everyone has a button that can be pushed. He has told me stories about Chicago and has warned me multiple times to keep my window rolled up at a redlight or intersection.

Grandpa is a saver of money. He believes in being in debt to no one if possible. I've come to admire this the older I've gotten, especially growing up in a household where debt and repossessions had happened.

Grandpa did mechanic work and engineering work in the Army, and it carried over into his post-service careers. He has even done some logging work during his lifetime. I profess him to be a mechanical and engineering genius. The man can put anything together, fix anything, create anything, even now in his older years. He has all sorts of machines in his shop, giving him the ability to weld and fabricate whatever metal he needs to for the project at hand. The first thing Tripp does when we go to his house is ask to see the "sheens". Grandpa grins from ear to ear and takes his youngest great-grandchild to see the "sheens" every time. We've lovingly saved a piece of metal and a piece of wood cut from Grandpa's shop.

Grandpa and Grandma traveled all over the continental United States. When Mom was growing up, they took her with them. They have tons of photos from all over. One of Grandpa's greatest accomplishments is the camper he made for them to travel in. He took two vehicles and put them together to create the camper he wanted. Grandma worked on the interior and assisted with the exterior, but Grandpa did all the body work. He still has the camper today and has lovingly driven my kids around in it. They think a house on wheels is super cool!

I did not get to spend much time with neither Grandpa nor Grandma growing up. That is why I never came up with better names for them. Granny and Paw got the nicknames. Grandma and Grandpa got those names because I didn't know what else to call them. Even when they became great-grandparents, "Great" was simply added to preface the names. I was guaranteed to see them on the Fourth of July at my Uncle Frankie's house and at their church, Oak Ridge Methodist, at Christmas time for a family get-together with all the aunts, uncles, and cousins on Grandma's side. Any other time was sporadic and random, certainly not frequent. Their house was only about 45 minutes away from mine, but it seemed like an eternity away. When I started playing tennis, they came to matches whenever I was playing close by.

After I wrecked my car, I was scared I wouldn't get another vehicle of my own. The money wasn't there. I was stuck driving my dad's Chevy S10 and I was scared I'd be stuck at home, possibly not able to go to college if I didn't get another vehicle. My whole goal was to get out of my situation and get out of the house to go to college. Wrecking the car put a huge damper on that. Grandpa knew my home life wasn't great, but I'm not sure he knew exactly how bad it could be. I took the opportunity to talk to him about my concerns after they came and watched me play tennis one day. He didn't say much. He listened. That's his character. I could see the look of concern in his eyes. Later, phone calls were had between Mom and my grandparents. Within a week or so of that talk at the tennis courts, I was in a '98 Ford Contour. I drove that car for three years until Phillip bought my first new car for me.

I'm thankful for Grandpa for his calm demeanor, his perseverance, his generosity, among other traits. I am thankful I have learned by watching and listening to him and I only hope I can keep learning from his life. I am thankful he is around for my kids. My kids love Great-Grandpa. Not everyone is so lucky to have great-grandparents, but my kids get to. They get so excited to go to his house. He takes them riding in a golf court he fixed up down a trail to the cave on his property. I take pictures every time they go down to the cave with its underground spring and cool rock formations. It is a world of fascination and wonder for them. He teaches them and they listen and I'm so grateful for that. I believe they're his little dose of the fountain of youth.

Grandpa is not one to say the word "love" freely. Sometimes it isn't written in cards, sometimes it is. I believe it is just how him and Grandma were raised. I never verbally got it much from them. He may not say it, but he shows it and proves he loves with his actions. I know he loves me, my mom, and I especially know he loves these kids of mine.

I've got a good Grandpa. I'm glad he's mine.

Day 54:
Prayer

Here's the thing. I could write about all sorts of answered prayers. I could write about the most faithful prayer warriors. The important part about prayer to me for this prompt, though, is about how real the communication with God is.

I didn't listen this morning to the first part of the Sunday morning service. I wasn't purposefully trying not to pay attention, I just wasn't. I did listen to most of the sermon, I promise. Sometimes, I start the service in another way. This day, I was writing in my notebook. I write my prayers there, the ones I cannot adequately put into spoken words. I write any dreams I have I feel may foretell something, among other things. I get it all out on paper. I enjoy it because I can look back on answered prayers, but I mostly enjoy it because it causes me to focus on my prayer time rather than go off chasing hundreds of rabbits in my thoughts. As a matter of fact, I could flip through one of my journals and pull out dozens of things about answered prayers. I may do it later down the road as I continue to write.

This morning, I wrote a quick blip about being discouraged. I told God how "over it" I was. I feel so overwhelmed some days lately. I am awaiting important doctors' appointments. I am emotionally drained. The enemy has been working hard to keep me in a rough spot. I've been battling it for a while now. I wrote several times on the page about how I was discouraged. I wrote the word multiple times over. I am not just discouraged; I am *easily* discouraged right now. It doesn't take much to get me in a weird mental and emotional spot here lately. As I began to pray one more time about my discouragement in my cry out to God, Phillip spoke in his sermon about Ezra 4.

He brought up the topic of discouragement just as I prayed, just as I told God about my own discouragement. God delivered to me exactly what I needed in just the right moment. Had I not gone to Him in prayer, I do not believe He would have revealed this to me at just the precise moment He did. He reveals what you need when you to go to Him.

Simply put, I don't know where you are in your walk with God. You may even be someone who finds the whole concept laughable. If that is the case, I appreciate your commitment to reading this far. Regardless, I am thankful for prayer. I'm thankful for the real, pure, open conversation I am able to have with my Father. I am thankful He knows all my thoughts, all my faults, and all my worries. I am thankful for the ability (prayer) to directly communicate with Him whenever I desire to.

I'm thankful for His responses to my prayers even when I am not faithful to pray as often as I should. He is so much greater, so much more loyal than I. What a friend we have in Jesus.

Day 55:
Non-Believers

Non-believers for me refers to non-Christians. I've got loved ones who lackadaisically do not care for Christianity or "religion". I've got loved ones aggressively against it, either due to church-hurt, life's storms, or other reasons. I don't love them any less. That would kind of be against the "love thy neighbor as thyself" bit, wouldn't it? Even non-believers were created by God. There is a sense of respect and maturity to come with having different spiritual beliefs if people are going to maintain a friendship, a relationship, or anything falling under those umbrellas. It can be a hard spot to be in, I know. If someone asks me what I believe in and who I believe in, I'm going to tell them. If they ask me for my opinion on what they're doing or how they're living their life, I'm going to tell them in a respectful and loving manner. They don't have to agree with me. Part of that has to do with that free will we've got. Do I wish they would for salvation's sake? Oh, of course I do. However, I can't save people. It is my job to love people and share the Gospel. What they do with the Gospel isn't up to me. It is my job to be a living witness and pray, both of which I could be better at.

I am thankful for non-believers because they offer me a different perspective on life and even morals and ethics. People who have had similar backgrounds to me could turn out completely opposite of me when it comes to believing in God. People who have terrifying life experiences or vastly different ones than I also can fall anywhere on that belief "spectrum". There's no tell-tale way to determine what someone will believe one day, whether they'll accept Christ. I find it fascinating to see how people get to where they are, and I love to listen, learn, and understand what happened along the way. It's the intimacy and personal relationship-building with them I love. I long to understand the hurt, the pain, and how they came to the conclusions they have if they are willing to talk about it with me in a civil and friendly way. Contrary to popular belief, most people are wonderful to talk to if you'll just shut your trap for a few minutes instead of coming up with your next witty or "intelligent" response.

Non-believers remind me of my duty as a follower of Christ. Just as I said before, *I* cannot save someone. I can love people and I can share the Gospel. I can love the way Jesus instructed us to love. As a run-of-the-mill sinful and lazy person living earthside, I don't do what I need to as often as I should. It kills me to type that because of the conviction in my heart. Conviction, though, is needed. If it is taken correctly, it will allow for growth. Shame drowns, conviction corrects.

I am thankful for the insight non-believers can give me if they were pushed from church. Was it someone? Was it an incident? Was it something they just didn't agree with? Maybe it is something I can learn to approach differently or see my own fault in as long as it isn't contradictory to scripture. Maybe it is something I can explain in a way that wasn't explained correctly the first time. Who knows? Maybe it was an abuser in the church, which I've heard quite a bit of during my time in child welfare and working with sexual assault survivors. Maybe there's something I can help someone work through if they're ready, or there's someone I can lead them to who could help them. Again, who knows?

I'm thankful it isn't only Christians this book will be available to. I'm thankful anyone can read this. I hope anyone will read this and not dismiss it because of my beliefs. I personally find it challenging and insightful to read books by authors who aren't exactly like me. Maybe this book will bridge a gap to show people we all aren't so different at the end of the day.

I sure hope so.

Day 56:
Country Living

I wouldn't have wanted to grow up any other way. Would I change the circumstances of my childhood? Yes and no. But, as far as the setting is concerned? Absolutely not. I wish my kids could have some of the same experiences I did growing up in the country the way I remember it.

I've told you about the glory I call backroads, a huge part of country living. Refer to it for a refresher if needed. For me, country living was growing up on 52 acres of land spread between the house I grew up in and Granny and Paw's property. The total property had three ponds on it, one of which was behind my house. We had a long crusher-run and gravel driveway that circled around the backyard where the vehicles parked. Past the pond was pastureland. Barbed wire fences and metal gates sectioned the cows off from other areas.

Every afternoon when I got home from school, I was to feed the critters. Dad put metal drums by the wellhouse out back in the center of the circle driveway where we kept the feed. Dad had used a pocketknife to cut off the lid of an oil jug at an angle and washed it out, making a scoop as long as the lid was left screwed on. I'd dip the scoop into the bag of corn and spray it with my arm in a half-circle around the driveway. Fat little ducks, a few Mallards and Muscovies (also referred to as "Scobies" at my house) and Canada Gray geese would come stake their claim to the yellow kernels like they were heading for the California Gold Rush. I'd go to the next metal drum, take off the lid, fighting away over a dozen meowing and purring cats trying to get in before I could reach my arm inside. I'd scoop them out their food and go feed them at the concrete steps leading to the basement. When we had kittens, I'd make sure they had a separate pile so they wouldn't have to fight the adults. I had a soft spot for kittens. Lastly, I'd feed our outside dogs in their bowls and make sure they had water.

When the sun was setting to the west, it created an oil pastel painting over the sky of oranges and purples which cascaded over the pond creating a reflection like no other, especially in Summer and Fall. I often went down to the edge of the pond in the evenings. Just as I was tasked with feeding the other critters, I was tasked with feeding the catfish. I would take the lid I used for the other feed, dip it in the catfish feed, and haul it back down to the pond in a bucket. The closer I got to the pond I could see a large ripple heading closer to land. The fish could hear (or feel) me coming. I'd get a scoop and throw it out over the pond in the same half-circle I'd spread corn in. Mouths larger than my fist would make their rounds over the top of the water gobbling everything up. The bream would fight for their pieces closest to the bank and I got to watch their scales glisten with greens, golds, and browns from what daylight was left. Little minnows swam about as if they had no clue what was going on, they were just happy to be there. When I'd finish, I'd end the evening by listening to music on my CD player and skipping rocks, at which I am a self-proclaimed professional. Dragonflies and mosquitoes would do their dance creating circles over the water while ducks and geese swam about chasing them for a dessert after their supper. Darkness would fall and I'd hear coyotes begin to howl from the woods beyond the pasture.

I believe one of the things I'm most thankful for is the familiarity with life and death I became accustomed to. I'd find nests mama ducks made and keep an eye on them. Some mama ducks got to where I could bring them corn and they'd eat from my hand while they sat on their nests. I'd tenderly pet the tops of their soft, feathery heads while they warmed their growing babies underneath themselves. Eventually I'd stop by and find eggs cracking with little beaks poking through. They'd find a way to hatch off all their babies without us knowing and we'd catch them walking toward the pond. At our house, we tried to give the babies a chance before the snapping turtles got them, so either Mom or Dad would catch the angry mama duck while I gathered babies up into an empty bucket. They'd be caged together for a while until the babies were a bit bigger and we'd let them out.

On one occasion (I was in either fourth or fifth grade), Mom and I had been out of town came home to a calf being attacked by wild dogs. Wild dogs are dogs people drop off in the country, out in the middle of nowhere: to either be picked up by someone else or to die. The people usually don't care which comes first. The dogs eventually band together and kill livestock or other animals to survive. Mom quickly ran inside and got the 12 gauge and shot in their direction. Mom was able to hit at least one of them and the others scattered. Mom called Dad. We went over to the pasture to the calf, a very young red fuzzy bull. His right hind leg was all but mutilated. The poor boy could not stand on it and laid there in what I'd call shock. Dad squatted and hoisted the calf over his shoulders, stood up, and proceeded to walk to the barn with it.

The barn was built in the 1940's, along with the house, and was just in decent enough shape to house the little guy on the dirt floor. My parents called a local veterinarian friend who brought over some of what we called blue medicine and stitched the calf's leg up the best he could. Every day after school, I got to go down to the barn and feed the calf, who I'd named Bruno, by bottle. With every gulp, his little ears would pop back and forth. It is one of the most precious memories I have of an animal. Unfortunately, he succumbed to his injuries and only lasted a little over a week. I was devastated and cried over my short-lived companionship and the loss of my little buddy. Situations like these taught me quickly to enjoy things while they're here, because the good stuff doesn't keep. They taught me the fragility of this physical existence.

I could tell a million stories, I believe, on life and death just based on farm life. I could tell the stories of cold mornings and cranking my car to find one of the cats had crawled up in the motor to stay warm. I've peeled many a cat out from under a car hood and attempted to rescue them, often to no avail. Yes, I did try to check; I even checked tires to make sure none were hiding there. Sometimes it was just easy to miss one. There is the story of the cow whose calf got stuck and died during labor. It was a cool summer night and Dad had to pull the calf from the cow who'd found herself down in a deep holler surrounded by trees. There are certain sounds you don't forget, and that's one I won't. Dad had hooked chains to the breeched calf and had used his strength to pull the stiff body from its mother. The cow was paralyzed but Dad tried to save her. To try and get her legs working, the vet told Dad to put what we called "hip huggers" on her and have her hang that way from the tractor in a hole in the ground while her front legs were in another hole. Eventually it became evident the cow would never walk again. Paw got a pistol and went out to the cow where it continued to sit in the holes in the ground attached to the "hip huggers". I just so happened to be walking by the gate at the time and could see it. Paw's sweet soul, I knew he hated to do it. I've never liked having to make those types of calls, either. The cow looked up toward Paw and locked eyes with him. Paw lined the pistol up between her eyes and pulled the trigger quickly. Again, a sound you don't forget.

My family on both sides are long lines of farmers. I believe people in my family could look at the ground and just about anything they wanted would come up even from dry dust. I vividly remember the days of picking bushels of corn before I was allowed to go hang out with friends, being covered in dust from each footstep and battling off large green grasshoppers. The corn was ready to pick when the silks were brown. The similar method came into play when picking acres of watermelon: when the vine was brown, it was ripe and ready. Many evenings were spent shelling peas on Granny's back porch or on the swing while I smelled of Deep Woods Off and slapped mosquitos between snaps. Crickets chirped in the distance along with a low-volume radio set to a local country station playing the top hits or some old-time bluegrass.

Fishing was common at our property. The older I got, the older everyone else got, too. People found better places to fish, grew apart, or died. However, we used to have family over often. We'd have lawn chairs lined up all around different areas of the pond, fishing poles everywhere. Other times, Paw's brother, Uncle J.W. (only three years older than Paw), came over to fish. The two would go fishing and catch buckets of bream and catfish, sometimes bass. They used their old method of hammering the fish to a wood board to skin it. Two old men with cigarettes poked out the side of denture filled grins would transform from old men with slacks and button-up shirts back into two little barefoot boys with cane poles.

Although we fished, my family wasn't big on hunting; but we did have a dove hunt almost every year. Doves would be gutted by the bucket and the cats would get a delightful treat of innards and heads. People would come from all over to sit in our field, drink beer, and shoot birds while shooting the bull. One time my first grade science teacher even showed up. No clue how he knew my dad, but by the end of the day he'd learned every name of every cat on the property, I can assure you of that.

I could go off on tangents here all day, I believe. Four-wheeler riding with friends. Sun tanning on the back of a goose neck trailer in the backyard. Getting together at my neighbor's chicken house to "dump" baby chickens when they got a truckload delivered. Sitting out under the stars at night, alone or with someone else from time to time. There was just nothing like growing up the way I did.

I'm thankful for my version of country living. I don't get to revisit it often. Last year, one of my sister-in-law's chickens got out of their coop. The chickens are a 4-H project for my niece but have become a family project. I immediately sprang into action and grabbed the thing up as quickly as I could, held it up to a cheering audience, and let out a good "Woo!" For just a second, a little piece of my history came out. I felt safely present in the past just for a minute, and it was great.

Day 57: Shakettas

I don't know if she'll be surprised, maybe embarrassed, or even possibly honored by being included in here this way. I didn't know a name for the type of friendship we have, so I said "Shakettas" instead of Shaketta, in hopes maybe you've got someone like her you can identify with.

Shaketta and I met at our first day working at DHR in Alabama on January 4, 2016. We were hired the same day, began training the same day, all of it. We instantly clicked, it seemed. I don't even remember the first comments we agreed on, but we quickly did. She is physically the opposite of me. She is tall and gorgeous with an athletic built. She's got a contagious laughter. You pronounce her name like Chiquita Bananas. Only with a "shh" sound at the beginning. However, there is not mush "shh" about her. She is brightness in darkness, she is volume in silence. She is a listener when needed and bold when the time comes. She is outgoing, thoughtful, professional, and reads the room well. She gives me honesty in a constructive way. We can have hard conversations without hurting one another. We can share thoughts and opinions. We can help each other review points we may have otherwise missed when it comes to life's happenings or difficult situations. I'm sure- no, I *know*- there are times I got on her nerves. I can think of times when she may have got on mine. We never took it personally. Work was hard and there were times we'd rather avoid work and talk to each other, but the other one would be trying to work. If I were a betting woman, I'd say I pestered her more than she ever pestered me.

She left me at DHR and went on to bigger and better things before I did. She continues to work at the job she left DHR for, where she counsels and works with at-risk youth. She is a wonderful role model in the community.

Hers is a friendship I cherish deeply even though we don't get to talk or see each other very much. She came to my surprise 30th/31st birthday party (COVID-19 prevented a solely 30th birthday party so my husband combined the two) and got me gifts she hand-picked; they were gifts to remind me to focus on myself some. Hers is a friendship I've kept in a special place in my heart. Any time she's given me a card or a kind or encouraging note, I've kept it. She is a fellow Christian sister who I trust prays when she says she will. She is a spiritual sister to me. Someone I trust. She wrote *Release It!: Accept Change and Overcome*. After it was published, she asked me when it was going to be "my turn".

I started to type some of our stories in this part. Maybe they'll come up later. As soon as I wrote them, I erased them. They just didn't seem necessary right now. Right now, I just want to say how appreciative I am God placed this lady in my life. I want to take the time to remind her (if she reads this) how influential and special she is to those she meets. I hope each of you has a friend, had a friend, or will have a friend in your lifetime as delightful as her: your own Shaketta.

Day 58:
God-Given Talents

A God-given talent is defined as some sort of talent or ability that comes naturally to a person, is typically not something that has to be taught, and is usually extraordinary compared to other peoples' skills in the same subject. For instance, I feel artistic ability is something for me that is certainly God-given. Mine could be considered artistic talent. Is it incredible to me or "extraordinary"? No, not really, but I have never really had to work hard at it. I want to take some time to highlight a few of these talents which come to mind for me.

People with green thumbs baffle and astound me, the people who can lean next to a plant and ask it how things are going, and it produce juicy fruit or rich vegetables. Anything from the dirt or from a tree they touch turns to edible "gold". They can bring the plants knocking on death's door back to life with just a little tender, loving care. Granny was one of these people to me. I'm sure her talent was, well, "nurtured" from farming during the Great Depression. If I had to make a bet, though, she was probably one of those people who just knew what she was doing.

Harvey, who I mentioned before, has a God-given talent. The guy was singing beautifully even as a child who could barely brush his own teeth. His sister was the same way. They instantly became a hit to put on stage. They are still singing and still naturally gifted, seemingly having little to learn when it comes to managing their voices. Their voices leave people in awe, lost in their feelings, and overcome with emotion.

There are athletes like this. I may be wrong, but Tripp could be one of them. He has a natural ability when it comes to physical strength and finesse. There was a time this past summer when I made a game sort of like Skee-ball in the driveway using chalk and LEGO blocks (we were desperate for something to do, okay?) The middle of the bull's eye was several thousand points. Anniston and Ridge couldn't quite get the LEGO pieces where they wanted when they threw them into the chalk rings. It obviously would have worked better with something besides LEGOs, but oh well. We worked with what we had. When Tripp came up, he immediately threw his LEGO block to the center. He barely tried. Afterwards, he appeared bored due to the ease at which he was winning, and just sabotaged the game like your average little boy would do. Tripp can also hit a tennis ball to me with strangely good accuracy. I'm interested to see how this develops as he gets older.

One final example is the people who are naturally good with children. These people instantly can put babies to sleep with a soft lullaby or the perfect rocking motion. They can turn crying babies into giggling ones just by showing up in the room. They are found working in Vacation Bible School sessions with the itty-bitty kids who others get easily annoyed by. They are natural-born leaders to the tiny tyrants, and it is a beautiful thing to watch.

God-given talents bring people together with like abilities to develop relationships, bonds, and networks. They make the world a variety-filled place and a bit more enjoyable. God-given talents are unexplained but fascinating upon their discovery.

It drives the question: are you using your God-given talent? Have you figured out what yours is? Or has the world convinced you that you have none? Maybe the green-thumb folks can plant a community garden. Maybe people like Harvey can lead worship at church or even break out randomly in public to bring about praise for God. Maybe the athletes can grow to run camps for kids or be motivational speakers. Maybe the naturally-good-with-kids people can be the safe places they can come to when their little lives are just too hard.

I pray for myself and for anyone reading this that we don't listen to a world full of jealousy and hurt and pursue our God-given abilities to make the world a bit brighter while we're here. My prayer for myself and other believers is that we take opportunities received to showcase our talents not for personal gain, but for growth of the Kingdom and in some shape or form introduce people to Jesus. I pray we keep our eyes on the prize and not on our own glory.

Day 59:
Knowing No One

There are a few occasions in life when you're in a room or situation with no one you know. The first day of college or at a new school where none of the faces are familiar is an example. Another example is the funeral you went to out of politeness when your friend lost a loved one, and the only person you know there is your friend who has stepped away for a moment. Finally, there's the time you went to a training or required convention for work, and you were the only one from your workplace to go; everyone else is from another branch or county and there are no assigned seats, everyone just sits where they please. Your heart rate is a little high because you're typically an anxious person and there seems to be no feeling of safety in this room full of strangers.

Knowing no one could force you into a shell and you'll drown in your worry and loneliness. It is like a pirate forcing you down the plank of a ship. His sword is drawn; his annoying ugly parrot is copying his phlegmy laugh as you walk toward the end of the wood. Except… it's your own ship… and except in this scenario you're untied but still feel trapped, all because you're not seeing the forest for the trees, so to speak. The joke is on that stinky old pirate because you know how to swim, and I bet you could sock a shark straight in the nose with your fist if you wanted to. Go ahead and jump off.

Allow me to shed some light on why you can be thankful for situations like this. The obvious needs to be said: you know no one here, that more than likely means no one knows you! In this situation, there are no standards for you, no expectations for how you "normally" are with people. You don't have to put on a mask. You can be your authentic self.

These people, just like the prompt about "New Friends" says, don't know your history or your secrets, and this is the opportunity to live like you have none. Perhaps you could walk away from this situation with a new friend. In the situations where you know no one, you have freedom from opinions. You're not a slave to a social hierarchy of "who's who" or the "haves and have nots". This alone make being in a room full of strangers liberating.

What a grateful position to be in when you change your perspective.

Day 60: Hospice

The only experience I had with hospice care over the years was mostly negative. It was always sayings from the old folks like, "Well, they called in hospice on old so-and-so, so won't be long now." Hospice to me was death's angel: the cloak-wearing Grim Reaper of bad news coming to take the less-fortunate away to their destination. I'd heard horror stories of the caregivers purposefully killing their clients by giving too much medication or just being insensitive to the families.

When I got to UNA, I was assigned volunteer hours through the Social Work Program. I got to work with Tennessee Valley Hospice. It was easy work. I got to make crafts for the nursing home residents and pass them out with the director. I got to spend time with the director and learn a bit more about the program. I soon realized I did not want go into geriatric social work; my heart wasn't in it. It gave me a healthier respect for anyone who does the work, though.

I did not have to experience hospice for myself until Grandma passed. Grandma's body did not react well to morphine, so they opted to give her fentanyl while she laid in the hospital. Her body fought long and hard. Breath after breath it labored to keep going long after Mom, Grandpa, and I had already said our goodbyes. The decision was finally made for her to go home to hers and Grandpa's house. Grandpa wanted her to be able to be comfortable, and there was some belief she wanted to be home based on how her body was reacting in the hospital. Being sent home with hospice care was discussed. Mom immediately became very up-in-arms about it. After all, we'd all heard the negatives. We'd all heard the hard stuff. Luckily at the time, my cousin was working for a local hospice agency. She'd been able to walk us through what to expect, and later prior to Granny's passing, she helped me learn a lot about home health and what to look for with Granny's aging and beginning stages of dementia. After much discussion, everyone agreed on hospice care coming home with Grandma.

After Mom had called to let us know Grandma had passed, we left the girls' ranch as soon as we could to go be with everyone. Grandma was still laying in the hospital bed they'd put in the living room. Grandpa and Mom were there, as were some of Grandma's siblings. The nurse was fantastic. She was sitting in the corner and had contacted the funeral home. She was giving space for the family. She was polite and helpful. She remained calm. She'd done exactly what was called for: to be what the family needed her to be. She read the room well, handled emotions with care, and was an angel. She introduced herself to me, although I do not remember her name, and she kept a casual and still demeanor in a sea of chaos. I'll always appreciate her for that.

I am thankful for the people who do this kind of work on a regular basis. Being in the room with someone when they pass once or twice in life is one thing, but to live and breathe surrounded by death, emotions of loved ones, and the responsibility of administering medication, if necessary, is a difficult thing to do. I applaud the stress they relieve from families when the job is done well. Had hospice care not been an option for Grandma, I'm not sure Grandpa would have had the energy to pick up Tripp, not quite 11 months old at the time, and carry him around the house to look at pictures while his bride's body lay lifeless in the living room. I believe having someone else there helped give him peace.

Besides, he knew where Grandma really was. He knew her shell was just in the living room. He knows he's going to see her again, too.

Day 61:
Date Nights

Ah, date nights. There are too few of them. Date nights were easy when we were dating. Dating basically means date nights, right? It's the name of the game! Going out to eat, going to the movies, bowling, and more. Then, marriage happens. Children happen. Work happens. Eight moves happen. Life happens. Date nights become a distant memory and a rare happening.

As God has allowed in this book, prompts have tended to line up just in time. We were discussing tonight what our plans for Spring Break would be. I had a strong disdain for driving back to Alabama again. We went to Alabama practically once a month, if not more, for our first six months in Louisiana. We were over driving and over travel. It is an over 10-hour trip one way including stops with the kids and to fill up on gas. I was to the point I was fine with staying in Louisiana for Spring Break and just hanging out here or going somewhere local for a small vacation. Phillip called his parents and discussed with them the idea of leaving the kids with them for a couple of days while we went to Nashville, TN. They agreed. We asked the kids what they thought about staying with Granna and Pawpaw for a few days without us, and you'd have thought they'd kicked us to the curb. So, the planning began. We talked about going to see a hockey game that Tuesday night. I know I love the antique shops up in Nashville and I'm sure there'd be plenty of other stuff to do. On the way back through, I'd like to stop in Amish Country again to get some yummy deliciousness and some homemade candles. It sounds like it will be a good time and much needed.

Why is it much needed? Many folks do fine without getting away and getting a break from the routine, doing the same old thing day in and day out. We do that most of the time, and we are good. However, I recognize sometimes Phillip and I allow each other to slip through the cracks without meaning to. Being parents, him being a pastor, me coaching tennis and babysitting, along with the regular adult daily tasks we have can make priorities slide around if we aren't careful. I'm thankful we can recognize when it happens and realize our need for a time out. We know to center God first and above anything else in our priority list, then one another. Our children come next and everyone and everything else falls somewhere else down the line. Sometimes the lines just get blurry when we lose focus (as they do with a lot of people, I imagine) and we need to redraw them again.

Date nights and small vacations with just the two of us are great times to just reconnect and spend time on each other. The last date night we had was back during Fall when Phillip's parents came down to Louisiana for a few days. Phillip was able to get tickets to a late showing of a movie and his parents were okay with watching the kids. We helped get them ready for bed and we went to watch *Thor: Love and Thunder*. I felt like a youngin'. Phillip ordered the drinks and popcorn from his phone to the seat. It was a regular "what in tarnation" moment for me. That should be a giveaway for how long it's been since I've stepped foot in a movie theater. All the way to the movie theater and all the way home- after midnight, mind you; I felt like a regular teeny bopper- we talked about life, the kids, our dreams, our goals, things that concerned us for our families, things we were excited about, and more. It just gave us time for each other with no distractions. It was a great breath of fresh air in a time in our lives where things felt foggy. It was just what we needed.

I'm thankful for date nights because it reminds us, we aren't just Mom and Dad. It reminds us we aren't just Bro. Phillip and Coach C. It reminds us we are individuals, but we are also Phillip and Melinda. We are a unit that needs recharging every now and then. Date nights can be a charging station for a low battery. I'm thankful for a husband who takes an active role in planning date nights, too. I love when he plans stuff and just lets me know what he's got in the mix; sometimes he asks what I'd rather do if he's stuck. No matter what we do, I'm just grateful for the one-on-one time with my best friend whenever I can get it.

Day 62:
Lost Sheep

I grew up on a farm, but I have little experience with sheep, let alone lost sheep. I could tell you all about a lost goat, but that is for another time. This prompt is regarding Jesus' parable in Matthew 18 of a shepherd who leaves his ninety-nine sheep to go find the one sheep that went astray.

Jesus explains here if someone has a hundred sheep and one goes astray or gets lost, won't a shepherd go look for the one and leave the ninety-nine on the hillside where they are grazing or resting? If the shepherd finds the sheep, he will be so happy and overjoyed the sheep is found. He will rejoice more over the lost one than the ones left on the hillside. To summarize, it explains this is how God feels and rejoices when a sinner returns to Him.

One of my experiences that reminds me of this is about a young lady I had on my foster care caseload. I consider her the one sheep versus one of the ninety-nine. I don't want to give too much on her story here as she is another prompt all on her own if I'm not mistaken (pardon me if I can't remember all 365 prompts.) She'd fled from her foster home while I was waiting for a group home to respond back to me about her placement. She was 17 and had been using methamphetamines since she was a preteen. She and I instantly bonded when we met, and she always told me she'd never run from me. That ended up being true. She ran from foster homes, law enforcement, everyone else under the sun, but she never left my side when we were together.

At the foster home she'd been at that night, she saw an opportunity to steal a couple of tablets and take off to find fellow drug users she was friends with. She wanted to get high. Temptation had won this battle this night. I remember sitting in the car crying in my driveway after I'd heard the news, begging God to help me find her or to deliver her back to me. I prayed that He make her skin too tough for the needle to break, she'd get arrested, end up in the hospital, whatever it took for her to stay safe and allow her to get some help. I had a calling to help this young woman and I know I did; no one can tell me otherwise. I'd known it from the first night I met her. Again, I begged and pleaded with God to do only what He can do.

The next day, I was able to get a clue to her whereabouts through who I'll call "informants". I contacted one of the local police departments and one of their investigators accompanied me to an apartment building she was supposedly at. After some guaranteeing of no arrests on some old warrants, the girl's friends were cooperative in luring her back to the apartment for me. I was able to learn a bit more about the girl's history while the investigator and I waited in the apartment. I asked for her things and found her backpack with one of the stolen tablets still inside.

The girl pulled up with one of her dealers. Police took her back to the other side of the river in the neighboring county where the questioning began on where she was going to go, either juvenile detention for a three-day hold or back to the office with me to wait for further placement. As we awaited the verdict, I checked her purse. Sure enough, I found needles and baggies. I figured as much. I knew her well enough to know what she'd gotten her hands on as soon as she fled the foster home.

I walked to the room they were holding her, and I couldn't help but start crying when I saw her. One of the officers gave us some space and she and I were in the middle of the room facing one another. She sat in a chair; I squatted in front of her. She begged me not to cry as she began to tear up. Teary streaks rolled down her porcelain cheeks. Her lips quivered. She looked shamefully down at the ground and didn't want to make eye contact with me at first. I gave her a warm hug and did all I could do to hold it together, to not become a blubbering mess. She cried and hugged me back, saying she didn't want to break my heart or for me to be disappointed in her; she knew what she did was wrong, and she was sorry for hurting me. I told her yes, she'd hurt me with her actions, but I loved her… and I was just glad she was alive, safe, and with me again. I was more than happy to start fresh and get her the help she needed. I did- and still do- love her very much. We sat there and cried together before regaining our composure and taking the next steps we had to do regarding her case. She was even able to meet the foster parent again she'd stolen from. She cried when she saw the foster parent, but the foster parent hugged her and told her she was forgiven.

    I am thankful for the parable of the lost sheep. I am thankful I can see Jesus' parables played out in my own life like this story I shared with you. It allows me to have just a glimpse of the perspective of how much God loves us and wants us to come back to Him regardless of the condition we are in. Our earthly condition is sadly a condition where we battle our flesh and selfishness daily. I'm glad God loves us despite that.

    I have spent many a time in my own life where I was the sheep, too. I am sure I'll share many stories in this series where you'll hopefully recognize that and maybe even see yourself in the stories. I am thankful I have a shepherd who goes out to find me when I have wandered away or am lost. I am thankful I know who my shepherd is, and I don't wander aimlessly to just anyone or anything, the first person that shows up with a shepherd's crook to pull me closer. What a worthy God we serve, who gets excited over folks like us.

Day 63: Counseling/Therapy

I was put off by the idea of counseling or therapy at first. My thoughts were what I believe most people probably struggle with. "I'm not that bad." "I'm fine." "I can figure this out on my own." "Counseling/therapy is just somebody talking to you about your day and that isn't going to help me."

Unfortunately, I learned through social work and social welfare how long it takes to get in with a counselor or therapist. I saw so many clients struggling with appointment times set way out. There were some who were openly suicidal who couldn't get the help they needed without going into an emergency room, being spoon-fed medication after medication until they fell asleep, and then still not getting to follow up with anyone other than a psychiatrist. Sometimes mental health issues require medication, they don't. I don't believe in slamming pills at someone and seeing what works. That seems like throwing a whole bowl of spaghetti at a wall to see if any of it sticks.

In the area I lived in between 2016 and 2019, I knew some of the counselors personally. That made it awkward for me to want to get help. I knew some did their job well, others not so much. A good friend and former co-worker of mine counseled one of my ranch girls for a brief time before she left the mental health center she was working at. Sadly, she was burned out, not paid enough, and was one of the good ones who left the profession too soon. Even though we didn't have the same views on everything, she gave good-intended advice and came from a place of understanding from her own childhood and young adulthood.

The counselor most of the girls at the girls' ranch saw always frustrated me. She basically asked them how their day had been, barely took notes while they talked, to the point she would misquote things while reading the notes she took from the last session. At one point I heard one girl ask the counselor, "Are you even listening?" as the counselor scrolled and typed on her cell phone. The counselor acted startled, responded saying she was, and put her phone down on the table. This was not the only occurrence of something like that happening. The girls went to the ranch social worker about the situation, as did I. The hunt was on for someone else.

The next counselor the girls had was more helpful and I'd argue more knowledgeable. I've got my opinions about some of her methods or beliefs, especially when it comes to my maternal instinct with my ranch girls, but she did good work with them. The ranch director encouraged houseparents and staff to go see this counselor and the ranch director would see to it the sessions were paid for. I had my suspicions of the confidentiality because the counselor and the ranch director were personal friends, so I politely declined each time it was brought up. If I was going to go to a counselor, any information given would be on *my* terms and not because someone wanted to be nosey.

When I finally reached my "breaking point" I've mentioned already, I wanted a counselor who had the same beliefs as me. I wanted someone I could afford, and the lady I saw worked on a sliding scale with very generous prices. Did I mention it was very generous? It was VERY generous. I wanted a counselor who wouldn't know many people I knew. The less mutual friends we had, the better. The counselor I saw did a great job and made a believer out of me when it came to getting help for your mental health. She quickly called out my poker face in the first session after I handed her the pre-session questionnaire. I'd been told I have an "emotionless" face before, but I never really knew why. I felt the emotions, I guess I just didn't express them outwardly very well. Apparently, that is a coping mechanism. Ta-da. It is a way you protect yourself without realizing it sometimes.

After we talked and she discussed my PTSD diagnosis, we did several rounds of a very efficient therapy called EMDR. I suggest you look it up. It allows you to reprocess memories and put them in their "right place" in your brain. It can take the displeasure, pain, and level of which one can recall the memory (worst and most intrusive being a level 10) to a better score where the memory isn't necessarily involuntary anymore and manageable (best score being a level 1).

For instance, one traumatic memory I have turned into something involuntary after Grandma died. It stemmed from a question Grandpa had asked me as we sat by her hospital bed one night while she was unconscious. He'd described seeing her laying on the ground after the fall, blood pouring out of her eyes, ears, nose, everywhere. I was perfectly fine with him talking about it; he needed a shoulder. He asked me if I'd ever seen something like that. I nodded and didn't tell him the full story right then. I just kept listening to him. I'd not seen it happen to a person, or at least not out of all those orifices, but I'd seen it happen to my dog at the hands of someone else with a baseball bat. After the conversation, I'd get vivid flashbacks of the dog. I'd hear the bat meeting its skull repeatedly. I couldn't control it. It had me pulling my own hair out trying to escape the thoughts. After a very deep and thorough session of EMDR about this memory, that memory went from an 8 on that scale down to a 4. I can recall the memory and even talk about it freely. I can hear and see everything still, but it isn't as loud and doesn't get "stuck" in my mind. I recall it voluntarily now. Talking about it doesn't hurt like it did. Writing just the little detail I did only bothered me a little. I've heard of people successfully taking memories from a 10 all the way down to a 1. The therapy can work.

I am so thankful for counseling/therapy. I believe I could use more. I didn't get to continue seeing this counselor due to her schedule and mine getting a little whacky with my new job at the time. We tried; it just didn't happen. She lovingly suggested a book on how to do EMDR on myself if I needed to as she had confidence I could do it. I'm thankful for the experience because it allowed me to become an advocate for therapy if it is with the right qualified professional. I've been able to share my own testimony and how God used this counselor to heal parts of me I didn't know needed healing. When I started attending counseling, I didn't understand why exactly I needed it. I saw the symptoms and I saw the issues, but I couldn't really grasp why it was happening. I could guess childhood trauma among other things, but I did not get why I was reacting to it the way I was. I was supposed to be "tough"; the truth was I was on the verge of a bad spot most days. I'm thankful for the people who go into the profession because it is a hard one. I almost did. I'm still not convinced I won't one day. Now just isn't the time and there is no peace to continue forward in it.

    If you're questioning if you should try therapy, you probably need it. I encourage you to search out help locally or even virtually. Find the qualified professionals who mesh with you and know what they're doing, not the people who ignore you while they check their social media pages. Find the people who care and the ones who do their job. They're out there. I promise.

Day 64:
Cheap Children's Clothes

I was the kid who rarely got "new" clothes. Most of my stuff was from yard sales or thrift stores, sometimes Walmart. It was a treat as I got older to get one item from Wet Seal or American Eagle in the mall. I remember owning one pair of American Eagle jeans and they were an absolute luxury to me. My family didn't have the money to spend on more expensive clothing. Had there been consignment sales my family knew about, I bet Mom and Granny would have raided them.

When my sister-in-law had my niece, I began to realize just how much clothing for a child could cost. While I was pregnant with Anniston, I started to frequent a local thrift store for the 25-50 cent days as soon as I found out she was a girl. I'd stock up on all sorts of clothing items. While I was pregnant, I watched my niece grow up. I became accustomed to a child who didn't grow very quickly, who was very petite and stayed in clothes for a while. Boy, was I in for a shock when Anniston arrived. She changed clothing sizes every month or two for almost the entire first year of her life. I soon had to figure out some way to clothe my kid that we could afford. We had a barely minimum-wage income and were already on food stamps.

By now, we had moved to Moulton, AL. While perusing on Facebook one day, I found Lawrence County Auction Action. I'd heard rumors it was a good local yard sale group. I discovered I could sell Anniston's old clothes on there and use the money I made to buy her next size up. We'd meet up in a school parking lot on Saturday and people would make their transactions as we all parked beside one another. I was able to clothe Anniston and then Ridge the same way. I can safely say by using this method, I barely spent anything on my kids' clothes. I still went to yard sales and thrift shops, but Lawrence County Auction Action became a staple in our house.

When we moved to Muscle Shoals, AL in 2015, I became interested in consignment sales. The ones I'd heard of before were the "fancy" consignment sales, where all the stuff was boutique items, and I couldn't imagine spending $25 on a used dress or pair of pants. It made me want to clench my chest, reach for the heavens, and tell Elizabeth I was coming for her (maybe that reference isn't completely lost.) I then saw an ad for Dittos for Kiddos and another ad for Wee Swap, both seasonal consignment sales. I saw their schedule and they had half-off days. I had finally found a way to replace my Auction Action time! The half-off days left clothing items $1-$5, or at least the ones I'd buy. They were good, clean items. I could buy wardrobes for both kids for very cheap, within a reasonable budget. My motto is, "If it ain't a dollar, don't holler." I bought the used items with a lot of wear left in them. As a matter of fact, I bought the kids' winter wardrobes almost completely at Dittos for Kiddos when we were in Alabama this past Fall. The car was shoved to the windows with new used clothes to bring back to Louisiana.

For people who can buy their kids- or choose to buy their kids- more expensive items, there isn't anything wrong with it. It just isn't an avenue I choose to take. I hope you do it for good reasons and not to "keep up with the Joneses". Maybe it is from how I grew up. I can't see paying a lot of money for an item they're going to grow out in a short time. Mine are changing sizes once or twice a year right now! I don't get as bent out of shape over a thrifted/cheap item getting ruined as I would something pricier. Is it still annoying? Yes, but it isn't as though someone siphoned a whole tank of gas out of my car or anything.

I'm glad and thankful I've chosen this way to clothe my kids. They don't recognize brands as being better than another when it comes to what they wear, or at least not now. They don't see people with "nicer" clothes as more important or more valuable. I personally know little girls who bully children for not wearing Matilda Jane, Eleanor Rose, and brands like those (pardon me if I don't know the "in" brands.) These are the little girls who create clubs where girls who don't own those clothes can't play with them because of what they wear. You think I'm kidding? I wish I was. I know some who got in trouble at school for it and it required parents calling other parents and causing some serious conversations to happen. I'm a believer these kids didn't come up with this on their own, and they probably know an adult who has a similar attitude they're emulating. Again, there is nothing wrong with those brands, but when it gives someone a sense of entitlement or a sense of being above others, it becomes an issue.

I've let the kids start shopping with a budget with me when I pick out their clothes. It lets them see the value of a dollar and how far they can stretch it. It lets them have some power to make decisions, such as if they really like a more expensive shirt, they can figure out if there is room in their budget for it. I'm glad we've had cheaper options, especially during the time I mentioned before when we were very broke and getting assistance from food stamps.

I took for granted having these readily available options back home in Alabama. So far in North Louisiana, I've found one consignment store in a reasonable driving distance that meets my needs. The thrift stores as far as kids' clothes are concerned have proven to be sub-par in availability compared to the ones back home. I'm missing the Dittos for Kiddos sale in a few days, and I can't tell you how sad I am about it, especially with the growth spurts happening in my house just before Summer! I'm grateful for the few shops I have here, though, and I am glad I am still able to shop frugally for my kids.

Day 65:
Nurses

I didn't have a bad experience with a nurse until I was induced with Anniston. My doctor was a sweet older woman who had convinced me, a first-time mom, to be induced at 39 weeks because I was tired, over it, and Anniston was "measuring to be such a big girl" (spoiler alert: she was just a little over 8 pounds, not huge by any means.) I wish I knew then what I know now and maybe it would have saved me the issues I've had going forward.

I went in bright and early on that cloudy April morning to get induced. I had my plan. I was dilated to 3 cm already. I'd been walking as much as I could up and down the streets close to mine and Phillip's little apartment trying to prep my body to do what it needed to do. My nurse showed up in the hospital room. I barely remember anything about her appearance other than her dark hair with lowlights in it. She looked to be in her late thirties, maybe early forties. She started my Pitocin. She looked annoyed at my excitement for some reason. I don't know; maybe she just didn't want to be at work that day. I rocked back and forth in my rocking chair with the lights dimmed. Phillip was in the room with me. His family had come in to say hello before leaving us alone for a while. The nurse came in and asked how I was doing. I told her I felt great! I was handling the contractions well and felt fine as long as I was rocking and moving around.

Her entire demeanor became different. She looked at me like I was stupid. If I could read minds, she either was asking herself if I was indeed an idiot or if her machine was working correctly. She cut her eyes back to the Pitocin drip. I made some comment I'm sure about how I was doing well. "Oh, *really?*" she asked. It was such a dry, sarcastic tone. I'll never forget the way she said it. She upped my Pitocin drip pushing the button several times before she headed for the door.

"There. Let me know in a little bit how you're feeling." She walked out of the room with what I saw through the dark room to be a smirk. I was confused about why she'd say it like that.

Within minutes I felt terrible pain to the point I ended up getting an epidural as soon as possible. I won't go into Anniston's delivery right now, but I ended up in a non-emergency c-section that left me with new issues. These issues leave me hyperventilating in a dentist chair because I'm having to stare up at the lights and can't talk. All the things that led up to the c-section weren't ideal, but the nurse's almost sadistic attitude she had with me is something that haunted me for a long time. It took me a while to get past just that specific portion of Anniston's birth. I even considered writing something to the L&D because they posted praise notes about their staff on the wall. That means they must read everything, right? I was 21 and naïve, but also in a bad spot with postpartum depression. They probably couldn't have cared less if I'd had a bad experience. Get the mom a room, force meds down her, then cut her open if she doesn't have the baby fast enough: the business of birth. The note was never written, and that nurse very well could have gone on to treat some other poor first-time mama the same way.

Fast forward to my attempted VBAC (vaginal birth after c-section) with Ridge. I'd found a doctor who allegedly was supportive of it, then told me when I didn't want to be induced at her wishes, that if I didn't get induced at 41 weeks, she would refuse to be my doctor. Feeling what I describe as little to no support from the people on my team, I just did it. I got induced with a foley bulb and breaking of my water at 41 weeks. I have joked that all my kids would have stayed in the womb until their first prom night at the rate their gestations were going.

I dreaded seeing my doctor the whole time I labored with Ridge, but this nurse. Oh, this nurse. She was heaven-sent for me that day. My nurse was middle-aged. Her skin glowed. She had reading glasses hung on her neck. She'd let her hair go white and grey. Her smile was gentle, and gentle was what I needed. My nurse was calm. She kept a light heart and good sense of humor. She didn't comment on me not wanting an epidural. She respected the process for me because she knew what my goal was. She respected that I had a doula there to help me work through any pain I had. She was fantastic.

When I'd been in labor for about 6 hours and had not progressed past 4 cm, I was told by my doctor they thought it was time to call it. We could all hear Ridge on the monitor, his giant head hitting my pelvis every time I bounced on the birthing ball. I squalled. I felt like a broken woman. I felt the lowest of the low, like a worthless sack of crap. Typing this makes me cry, but it is the truth. I felt all the emotions of not being good enough. I just wanted to avoid the surgery that left me so empty to begin with, the surgery I believe made my postpartum depression worse than it should have been. I wanted to prove my body wasn't useless and could do what it was meant to do. I'd even been having start-and-stop labor for a couple of weeks by then. I just *knew* it was going to happen! I didn't want to have to recover from a surgery while chasing an 18-month-old girl around the house with my newborn baby boy. I very reluctantly agreed and told them to please make sure I was numb before they cut me. I couldn't bear feeling myself getting cut open again.

I got in the wheelchair and felt like I'd lost. I felt like a loser. I felt stupid. I felt no good. I couldn't even feel excited to meet my son. I cried again while my nurse pushed me down the hallway.

I gasped through sobs. "I hate myself."

The nurse stopped the wheelchair. "Do what?"

"I hate myself. I really do hate myself."

My nurse stopped in front of me and bent down to make it where we were eye-level with one another. She looked at me firmly but with love on her face. "Don't you say that."

"It's true. I hate myself. I shouldn't have got induced. I did it because I let people tell me what I ought to do. I can do this. But no one believes me. And I feel like a failure. I hate myself for this." I explained a little more. "Last time this happened I felt everything. No one believed me. I can barely remember my daughter's birth and it was horrible. I did everything right I was supposed to but now I'm here. I'm stupid and I hate myself." I closed my eyes and cried despairingly.

My nurse rested her hands on my knees and looked me in the eyes as she talked to me. I can't remember the words she said. I think I was too caught up in the fear, panic, anger, anxiety, all of it, to put her words to memory. But I remember she told me I was a good mom and that I'd done a good job. She breathed with me and told me when I went in the OR that they were going to make sure I didn't feel a thing and they were going to take good care of me. She assured me she'd stay by my side and make sure Phillip was in the room with me.

The c-section happened, and my big baby boy arrived with a scream sounding like he was already saying "mama". Phillip was with me for the whole thing. I was given a spinal block that time and she was right, I didn't feel anything. I was able to be alert for all of it. I was put back together well and didn't feel that, either. My nurse didn't lie to me once. She stayed right by my side through the whole procedure and even made sure to come check on me during recovery even after she was unassigned from my care.

Writing this has me thinking about ways I could be thankful for that first nurse. I guess I'm thankful she was there to do the job. She wasn't there obviously to do the job well, but maybe I should show some mercy. Maybe she got called into work because someone was too hungover to show up. I don't know the circumstances. Maybe she'd had to call in a babysitter short notice for her sick kid so that she could come into work. I don't hope something bad happened, but I hope something would explain her terrible bedside manner outside of what seemed to be a horrible personality.

I believe I'm thankful for that nurse so that I could appreciate my good one more. I may have taken the good nurse for granted had I not had a cruddy experience the first go-around. I'm thankful for the nurse who did everything she could do for me, from giving me some space in the delivery room to trying to ease my broken heart before going into surgery. She cared about me, and I could feel it. Any time you can feel the care from someone's soul, it sticks with you.

Thank you, nurses. Your jobs are beyond difficult. I've met enough of you to know nurses and social workers tend to have similar humor and coping mechanisms, so trust me when I say I understand laughing to keep from crying. Thank you for dealing with life, death, and the in-between every day. Thank you for your diligence and your fight against burnout.

Thank you for taking care of my kids' booboos. From the staples to the pneumonia, thank you. Thank you to the nurse who coddled my husband after he almost passed out from his tetanus shot. I was a less-than-comforting wife when you asked him if he needed a cold compress, as I mocked the situation by asking in a squeaky voice, "Yeah, do you need a cold compress??" (No, I don't feel all that bad for it; old dude got cut on the bottom of his toe by a rogue LEGO in our house and never cleaned it or put a Band-Aid on it. He did all that to himself, by himself.)

Thanks again for the servanthood. Y'all are good people.

Day 66: Cows

"**M**ooving" right along to this next prompt... okay, let me start over. Don't shut the book! I just felt the need to force a pun.

This prompt came timely with my recent mention of the little injured bull named Bruno and farm life. Cows have always been a favorite farm animal of mine, probably because I was so used to them.

One of the good memories I have with my dad is getting in the truck with him to ride over and count cows. Dad had several different pickups over my childhood, but each of Dad's trucks smelled like the blue tree air freshener he had hanging from the rear view, his cologne, and chewing tobacco. It was always incredibly messy. He had papers and bills shoved above the visor on both sides. He had spit bottles rolling around in the floor like tiny pipe bombs waiting to be deployed. He always had the radio sort of on the loud side. It was usually set to 96.9 FM where it was a blend of classic rock and current hits, sometimes a country music station.

We would cross the dam of our pond and make our way up the pasture over terrace rows. There our pasture lay with the woods in the background. Over the hillside we'd count black and red fuzzy heads, big and small, and tall and short. Ears perked up when a vehicle approached them with the anticipation of food. They'd eagerly and steadily make their way over towards us. Dad would count silently to himself. Dad would point out newborn calves to me. The little things would shakily stand to their feet and hobble around like a teenage girl wearing heels for the first time. Calves a smidgen older could be seen running circles around them as if they were showing off.

Another good time I remember was being a teenager and getting to put tubs of molasses out for the cows during early Winter. I rode in the back of a pickup while Mom was driving. We got out in the middle of the pasture behind Granny and Paw's house. I donned a cotton canvas jacket, white t-shirt, and jeans. My hair was pulled back in a ponytail. The day was cloudy and dark; the ground was still green, but cold. Mom stopped the pickup and let the creaky tailgate down for me. Dad had put out hay already for the cows and this was an extra treat for them. It was my job to slide out the heavy tubs onto the ground. As always, dozens of ears stood peeking over the hay bales and the cattle began making their way to us. A few "moo" sounds bellowed from the herd. I slid the molasses tubs onto the ground and you'd have thought someone had dropped a bar of gold in a grocery aisle at Walmart. It was funny watching them all come and enjoy the sugary goodness. We had to pull off quickly to another area of the pasture to get the rest of the tubs unloaded otherwise they'd have surrounded us and blocked us in while they ate.

Years later, when we lived at the girls' ranch, we came to realize the ground beef we ate at the ranch was bred and grown on the ranch property. The house we lived in was surrounded by pastureland with Black Angus cattle roaming the green hills. I'm fond of a view with livestock, so this made the landscape even better for me. The girls did not believe Phillip about the cows being "ranch food". Once they realized it was true, I joked about naming the cows things like New York Strip, Filet Mignon, and Hamburger Steak. It became an inside joke.

I'm thankful for cows obviously because I am a beef eater. I love just about any type of beef to eat. I'm grateful for having the opportunity to take care of cattle and even herd cattle from time to time. Nowadays, if I see cows on the side of or in the road and I have the time, I'll stop and see if I can figure out who's they are and maybe offer to help put them back up. I've seen Phillip shake his head over this, but I believe is the right thing to do and I know firsthand how scary, aggravating, and potentially life-threatening to other people it is for cows to be out. I'd want someone to do the same for me.

Living a childhood where I got to partake in responsibilities like this helped grow a nurturing and motherly spirit in me. I think opportunities like this are great for kids to not only learn responsibility, but to learn the truth about life and death and to understand and appreciate the fragility of it all. In short, yes, I'm thankful for a good hamburger, but I'm more thankful for the lessons learned and for that part of my upbringing.

Day 67: Sobriety

My hope when I drew this prompt was that I would receive multiple stories of sobriety. I see them all over my social media. I see ones that are successful for years and years, sometimes for the remainder of their life. Sometimes I see successful sobriety stories celebrated only to see them disappear from social media for a time. I later learn they fell back into old habits and into their old struggles.

When I asked for stories of sobriety, I had a few people come to mind. I directly asked my friend, who I used to work with at the girls' ranch. She is now not only a houseparent there, but assistant director. The following is her story she shared at a ranch event and gave me permission to use. I summarized it for this book.

The lady's name is Miranda. Miranda's childhood was not a lot different than the childhood of most of the girls who come to stay at the girls' ranch. Her childhood was wrought with abuse and things no child should be subjected to. She married young to her husband. God brought them three children. God called the whole family into ministry. Life was hard, but life was good. Life was worth it. Perfect living wasn't in the picture, but they were living what some folks would call the dream.

Somehow, somewhere, the road got rocky. Satan eyeballed the situation and threw curve balls left and right at the family like they were a Skee-ball game, looking for any bullseye he could hit. He found it. Discouragement sank into the holes of the young mother's heart left over from those who'd hurt her. The liars, the abusers, the evildoers. Doing her best to save face and persevere on, for a time she placed more importance on keeping on' keeping on than her prayer life and her relationship with God. Whispers of temptation convinced her dealing with all the trauma was too difficult, that there were substances that could do what God wasn't doing on *her* time the way *she* wanted.

The spiral started, and soon it landed her in the back of a big white van with seventeen other women. The van belonged to a place called The Dream Center. The van was affectionately named the "druggy buggy". The Dream Center, a drug rehabilitation program, worked closely with a church and the ladies enrolled at The Dream Center would clean the church facilities. They were cleaning while getting clean, so to speak. She sat on the hump of the large van one day, uncomfortable, just like her life had been up until now. The women on this bus were all remnants of what heartache, abuse, battering, and addiction had done. Some of these women had even lost their children and been estranged from their families and loved ones.

As some looked out the window, lost in thought, a song came on. Songs are one of the coolest ways God commands attention, and in this moment He not only commanded it, He demanded it. "Beautiful Day" by Jamie Grace played through the speakers of the old van. Dry bones awoke. Souls sat at attention. Miranda and her "druggy buggy" sisters sang and worshiped right then and there. Frowns turned to smiles. For a moment, it didn't seem like the end of the world. There was joy and hope. Miranda's quote to describe this was: "I began to break in that moment. Walls started to fall! My heart started to melt as wax!" Those holes discouragement had once filled were emptied and refilled with God's mending love.

Guess what? Miranda completed the rehab. She has now been sober for 10 years. Two of her children are grown; one is almost there. Miranda and her husband have been married for over 20 years now. They continue to work in ministry. As for her story, well, she still drives a big white van. Only now it is not full of broken women, but broken girls. God brought her full circle into a life of sobriety and has continued to heal her heart while she assists in healing others.

I don't know if you're dealing with those pills calling your name from your medicine cabinet, the ones you just can't find the nerve to flush. I've heard the familiar whisper of whiskey call me from a cabinet after only buying it to mix with honey for a bad cough. I had to pour it down the drain and throw the bottle away as fast as I could. I don't know if you are trying to escape the hauntings in your mind and just want to sleep it away, only for them to return the next day. I don't know if you're fighting the urge to stop at the liquor store on the way home like you always do. Maybe being high and hallucinating is the only way you believe you find joy anymore because you feel like life just sucks that badly? If that's the case, I believe her story can tell you there's something better. You're useful. You're valued. You're loved. There's more to life.

I am thankful for sobriety because without it, we wouldn't have stories like these. We wouldn't have rebirth. I find the term "recovery" subjective because to recover means to go back to what you once were. The truth is, you'll never be your old self. That is gone. But you could be someone even better. How amazing that could be, not to be your old self but be greater and used for good!

I'm thankful for sobriety in my life because I've never not been sober. Though I come from a long line of addictive personalities, I've been determined to send that curse back to hell. I'm thankful my children will never have to see me drunk. They'll never have to see me high. What they see is what they get. I'm thankful for all the children who, because of parents like Miranda, will never have to endure seeing those they love most go through it again.

Change today. Take the step. If not now, when? A crowd of witnesses you don't know and can't even see is cheering you in the right direction now if only you'll close off the world and hear their shouts. Don't wait.

Day 68: Losing

Today, my tennis team traveled to a beautiful tennis facility about an hour away. There are several courts to play on. The bus was full of excited guys and girls decked out in their tennis uniforms. There are great places to sit and watch every match at this place, including shaded seating up on the hill where the restrooms and shopping area are. Today's match included only a handful of singles matches and a lot of doubles matches. It was a sunny, humid day and we even beat the rain just an hour before it began an icky evening shower. What a fantastic day for a tennis match!

And... we lost. We lost a lot. We won two of the matches we played. We lost the rest of the other fifteen... Losing is one of the lesser fun times in life. In life, though, we'll lose more often than we'll win, it seems.

We'll lose competitions. We'll lose county spelling bees over a heavily accented word. We'll lose our keys when it is time to pick the kids up from school. We will lose our cool when after we've found our keys and are now right on time, the train will block our way to school per usual. We'll lose patience when the small child flushes a mountain of toilet paper for the 4,329th time after we've instructed them not to and even shown them how much to use. We'll lose control of our tongue a bit when the guy facetiming his girlfriend cuts over in our lane and almost causes us to wreck into someone else. We'll lose the matching socks in the dryer.

We'll lose our security of our day-to-day when a loved one gets the diagnosis of dementia. We'll lose our own minds trying to navigate the ins and outs of moods and gradual loss of abilities. We'll lose the idea of the future we had in mind and must accept the reality dealt in the best way we can. We'll feel like we are losing valuable time with who we knew our loved one to be as we watch them shrink away behind dementia's ugly veil.

In competition, losing means you showed up and did the thing. I tell my players every time they get on a court, it is experience and a chance to get better. In losing the keys, it maybe means you were distracted by kiddos when you sat the keys in a different spot before you gave a piggyback ride or helped with homework. In losing your cool, you were frustrated over something you find important, meaning you have some sense of priorities. Losing patience with your kid shoving toilet paper down the commode means you've been working with them on changing the behavior instead of just letting it happen. Losing it with a bad driver probably means you were paying attention to your surroundings and the road, as you should be. When you lose some socks in the dryer, it shows you were doing the laundry!

Losing our daily security over something like a diagnosis means we've had a routine of some sort. Losing our minds learning how to provide for and treat our loved one means we want to take care of them exactly right; we want them to get the best care. Losing our idea of the future means at least we had plans and dreams.

Feeling like we're losing time? Well, that can be a good place to be. It means we understand someone's value and know what they mean to us. It is often a motivator to change things up. It can be just what we need to rearrange schedules we've been putting off. Sometimes it forces us to let loose of things and realize what is worth keeping… and what is worth losing.

Day 69:
Delayed Flights

I've only flown once. Well, I should say for one occasion. In 2010 when my tennis team went to Tucson, AZ, we had to fly. We drove from Boaz, AL to Birmingham, AL where we boarded the plane to go to Atlanta, GA. From Atlanta, we flew across the lower half of the continental United States to Phoenix, AZ. From there, we drove in a rented 15-passenger van to Tucson, AZ. The plan was to be in Arizona for about a week regardless of how far we got in the tournament. Coach had plans for us to go on the guided trail ride, to see the mountains in Arizona, and even go to Tombstone in our spare time. The plan was for us to get the airport on the last day bright and early and fly straight back to Birmingham from Phoenix.

We make plans and God laughs. I don't think it was us getting up late. I don't think it was anything specific that caused the issue. I think it was just the little things. The hotel checkout taking a bit too long, traffic being just a little inconvenient, and time was simply misjudged. I remember booking it, really knees-to-chesting across the airport while lugging our bags. We were trying our best to make our flight. The lady at the counter very sweetly told our already-agitated coach we had missed our flight. The only other flight to Birmingham that day would mean we'd fly to Detroit, MI first and immediately get back on the plane to Birmingham. The lady, in her most perky way, informed us the flight would leave that night. This meant we had an entire day to kill.

Coach was able to get us the van back for the remainder of the day. We ended up going to a local outdoor mall. I remember reading the temperature on a digital sign at the mall and being amazed that it was 102 degrees outside when it felt so good. Alabamians are used to the humidity. That temperature in Alabama would mean your skin is starting to cook like the chicken boiling on the stove. I remember the waiting period at the mall very vaguely outside of the scenery. The whole day was just big, tense, stressful blur.

We made our way back to the airport. We found a spot, parked our luggage, and made camp on the airport floor. There were eight of us girls and our coach. Coach and a couple of the girls had brought decks of cards. We played a game we'd all grown to love. Oh, I wish I could remember the name. It was intense with a lot of screaming at your partner, perfect for competitive young women, most of whom had been living in close quarters with each other for the past year. We laughed until we cried, rolling in the floor of the airport over a silly card game. We'd had our differences that trip, but we were enjoying the moment.

Supper time came. We all got our food and sat cross-legged on the airport floor. Coach always said the blessing before we ate. He always said the longest blessing, putting the Gettysburg Address and the book of Psalms both to shame. After what seemed to take a couple of decades, the blessing was finished, and we ate.

A man who appeared to be in his late sixties walked over to our group. He told our coach how much he appreciated us blessing our food and how he didn't see it done often anymore. Pleasantries were exchanged and Coach talked to him about us and why we'd traveled to Arizona, where we were from, etcetera. The man was impressed with our good attitude about the whole situation and made sure to compliment us. If memory serves me right, he prayed over our upcoming flight.

The late hours of the night came, and it finally came time for us to board our flight. I was incredibly excited. This trip had been my first time flying and I'd gotten to see America's landscape change underneath me, fly through rough turbulence, and have a window seat. Everything I'd gotten to experience had filled me with so much wonder. Now, I was going to get to witness the sunrise from the view of a plane. I didn't sleep. I just couldn't. I felt my eyes get heavy a couple of times, but I just couldn't let myself do it. A couple of other girls stayed awake for the same reason. I don't remember which of my teammates I sat next to, but they asked me to wake them up when the sunrise was happening. I remember a head laying on my shoulder as I sat quietly on the flight.

The airplane was dark except for a few lowlights to see by. Suddenly, through the window, the dark clouds got a little whiter. The stars said goodbye and spun out of the way like ballerinas. A gold glow peaked its way out of the horizon. I calmly woke my teammate so she could join in on the view. I don't think I have good words to describe the scene. The sun was directly to my left; it was awe-inspiring. The only thing I could think about was, "Wow. God did all this. He created the sunrise, and it is so beyond beautiful." I had a huge smile on my face. My mouth widened from one side of my face to the other. My eyelids were peeled back to absorb it all.

We landed in the desolate land that was Detroit. I was in shock at how abandoned it looked back then. The airport was surrounded by boarded-up buildings, which looked like someone had dumped a bowl of graffiti and vulgarity from the sky. We were maybe at the airport for an hour. We then made our way to Birmingham, AL. As we flew over Alabama, I immediately recognized our state. I saw the Tennessee River. I saw the hills and tree lines. I knew home when I saw it.

I'm sure there was some reason we weren't meant for the other flight, whether it be just for me, for safety's sake, for some mighty purpose I won't understand until later. I'm thankful for the safety and God's watchful eye on us. I'm grateful for the blessing we gave in the airport that blessed a stranger's day. I was able to see part of the country I may never get to experience again. The free time in Arizona was wonderful. I got to spend just a little more time with my teammates. I'd only see them each a few times more. My wedding was one occasion where one of my teammates was a bridesmaid; another got sick at the rehearsal dinner and couldn't join the wedding party the next day. Another time I'd see them at another teammate's wedding; I believe all of us were there. One of my teammates had a daughter one week younger than Anniston. We were able to meet up once for a playdate when they were very small. I've seen none of my teammates since these moments and keep up with them on social media now.

I'm thankful for delayed flights for these reasons. I'm sure for frequent flyers they are an annoyance, but I hope those that fly often can stop to just live in that moment. Sure, schedules may be thrown off, but at the same time you're right on God's schedule. Your time isn't your time. It is borrowed. Hopefully this is a reminder to soak in all the time you're allotted.

Day 70: Eve

A few readers may not have immediately guessed who or what Eve is. Some may have pondered about Christmas Eve, New Year's Eve, or even Thursday afternoon which my high school English teacher lovingly referred to as "Friday Eve". Some may have guessed I know someone named Eve, but I do not. I know an Eva or two, but no Eve. I'm referring to Eve in the Bible, Adam's partner, the one folks tend to blame for periods and pain in childbirth, and the one we blame for being kicked out of the Garden of Eden.

I'm going to do a little background on Eve for those who don't know much about her. She was the last being God created specifically in the Story of Creation. The seas were filled with swarming fish and creatures already. The skies were filled with squawking birds. Flowers grew. Trees provided shade. Sun and clouds, moon and stars both were "dressed to impressed" already. Then, God made man and gave him the name Adam. He made Adam in His own image and likeness (Genesis 1:26) and charged him to rule over the other living creatures and the whole earth. I imagine God's plan at the time was for Adam to rule over it with love, care, and an authority mirroring God since, as it said, Adam was created in the image of God.

One day when we get to Heaven, we'll have all the answers. I don't know if we'll just know the answers or if we'll get to ask God everything we want to know. My belief is we will be made perfect when we are in the presence of God. Any questions we had would then immediately be answered. For whatever reason, God decided man shouldn't be alone.

God decided to make a helper corresponding to Adam (Genesis 2:18). It doesn't say He'd make a helper lesser than Adam, a doormat for Adam, or a servant for Adam. He'd make a helper corresponding to Adam. What I interpret, rather inquisitively, is that when God gave Adam the task to name every animal and creature He had created, the task must have been tiring. Most folks I know can barely pick out a name for their own children. My thoughts are this is how God made Adam fall into a deep sleep (Genesis 2:21).

If all the creation story isn't cool enough for you, check this out. While Adam was asleep after a long day of naming critters, God went into Adam's side and removed one of Adam's ribs. He closed everything up as if it had never happened, good as new (all things considered, Adam was still in mint condition.) With this rib, God crafted Eve.

How do I imagine Eve? Why, she must have been stunning! In Eden, there'd been no way she had any sort of acne, blackheads, or blemishes. She'd have had no cellulite. She would have been perfectly healthy. Every part of her body worked exactly the way it should for her. I don't think hers (or Adam's) flesh was probably quite like ours. I like to think she had a beautifully eclectic skin tone encompassing every fair to dark complexion her descendants would have. I can close my eyes and picture a glowing woman with no flaws and skin glistening in the sun. I believe she probably had speckled eyes of every color we know, maybe even some we can't even imagine. Her hair maybe was dark with glistens of blonde, red, brunettes, and silvers when the sun hit it just right, full of every texture from straight and fine to dense 4C hair. I bet every living thing loved being around her. I bet she radiated growth, passion, and peace in every breath and step she took. Eve became Adam's corresponding helper, and I bet Adam was just as mind-blowing as she was. Eve was bone of his bone, flesh of his flesh. They were married together as one. They walked with God daily together in the Garden of Eden.

God had commanded Adam before Eve's creation that he could eat of any tree in the garden, except for the tree of knowledge of good and evil. Adam was told, "For in the day you eat of it, you will surely die." I can only assume either God told Eve this after she was created, or Adam told Eve. After all, they'd became one flesh at this point so obviously there was a little more than some small talk going on.

We see in Genesis 3 there was something suspicious going on in the garden. The serpent, who scripture calls the most cunning of all the wild animals, approached Eve. Eve had everything going for her at this point. She had absolute perfection and right fellowship with God. The serpent looked to her and asked Eve if she *really* couldn't eat from any tree in the garden. Eve told the serpent she and Adam could eat from any tree in the garden, except for one. Eve said for the tree in the middle of the garden, God had told them they could neither eat it nor touch it (uh-oh, the first mistake; refer to what God said...) or they would die. The serpent probably scoffed for dramatic effect. "No!" he said. "You will not die." The serpent told Eve that God knew it wasn't true, and the only reason God didn't want them eating from it was because they'd be like God. What a rotten old thing, that serpent.

I imagine Eve's glow was a little dimmer at this point, kind of like when a lightbulb starts to shine less brightly before it goes out. Her mind was lost in wonder as she looked toward the tree. The further her mind wandered from God and His direction, perhaps part of her spark went out. Little did she know she'd moved closer to it already as she and the serpent wandered along. That's what evil does. It will have you moving ever so slowly, drifting further from where you need to be before you can even recognize what is happening. The fruit looked delicious, lush if you will. It probably looked scrumptious, just itching to be plucked.

With a twist and a tug (I imagine in Eden this probably didn't take as much effort as it does today; it probably barely took a touch,) Eve got some of the fruit and handed some to Adam, who'd apparently fallen for the trap as well and was right beside of her. I can see them now, looking into each other's eyes, putting more faith and trust in one another than God thinking, "This is it!" A crunch sound is heard by every ear, the vibration is felt by every plant. The first bite was swallowed. The deed was done.

Genesis 3:7 says, "Their eyes were opened, and they both knew that they were naked. They sewed fig leaves together and made coverings for themselves." It is hard to imagine exactly what went through their minds. I don't think it was just embarrassment over realizing they were nude. I think they quickly realized the gravity of what they'd done. Their minds flooded with thoughts they'd never had to think, emotions they'd never had to deal with. Everything they'd been spared from now burdened their hearts. The looks in their eyes were even different. They knew immediately they'd betrayed God. Imagine feeling every emotion all at one time: excitement, anxiety, depression, anger, sadness, panic, all in a place and time where just seconds before had been nothing but complete perfection and peace.

I don't want to go into the entire story for longevity's sake, but God knew what they'd done. When confronted, Eve owned it. Did she try to hide first? Yes, but when called out, she owned what she'd done. She admitted the serpent deceived her and she ate the forbidden fruit. For Eve's part of the punishment, God would intensify her labor pains and she'd bear children with painful effort. God told Eve her desire would be for her husband, yet he would rule over her. Don't worry, Adam got his fair share of the deal, too. Adam and Eve were sent away from the Garden of Eden physically with nothing. However, God stayed with them anyway, though their relationship was not as close as it had been in Eden.

I'm thankful for Eve. In a joking way, I'm thankful I'm not the only woman tempted by some good-looking food. My spare tire and upgraded pants size speak volumes about some of my less-than-perfect food choices. On a more serious note, she reminds me I am God's creation as she was. I am capable of a great relationship with God, but it is my choice on how good that relationship is. Typing that is convicting and caused me to stop and reread what I wrote... Eve reminds me when my gaze drifts from God to anything else, I begin to shift into someone I am not supposed to be.

She reminds me to own my mistakes and not try to put it off on anyone else, to own my mess and allow God to work on me without trying to grab the tools out of His hand. I am reminded she was the first wife and the first mother. Adam probably got on her last nerve some days. She had to watch Cain and Abel say "look what we can do" until her ears rang. I bet if we sat beside one another today, we'd have a lot to talk about; we'd probably have a list of similar accomplishments and similar things we wish we could do over.

In doing all this, though, in enduring this consequence for hers and Adam's lack of contentment and lack of gratitude in Eden, she learned what love was. Being a wife and mother in the imperfect world they were banished to allowed her to finally understand how much God loved her. I think she grew to understand what God's love looked like.

I am thankful for Eve because she is a reminder that we do deserve consequences, but God uses the same consequences He deals us to grow us and make us more like Him. We've got to stop and just be the rib in that way. We've got to let the Master do what the Master does. The masterpiece we'll be created into will be beyond anything we could have ever imagined on our own.

Day 71: Tantrums

It was Sunday. It was a nice Sunday! The weather was a bit cool, but the day was pretty. We'd walked home after church (understand our church is beside our parsonage, so we rarely ever drive to church unless it is raining.) Phillip and I rested on our bed watching TV after we ate lunch. His phone began to ring. The screen read "Spam Risk", but he answered it anyway. Sometimes, especially when we don't know everyone's phone number in our area, it's better to just answer.

Phillip politely answered the phone and said, "Hello?"

"Hello! Your table at De Soto's Seafood Kitchen is ready." The automatic prompt was happy to inform us our party was ready to be sat! How exciting and what a relief! The only problem was it wasn't us who had the reservation.

Another call came in. Phillip answered.

"...Hello?"

"Hello! Your table at De Soto's Seafood Kitchen is ready."

Phillip hung up. Out of curiosity, he looked it up. The restaurant was in Gulf Shores, AL. We sort of assumed it would be local seeing as we have a Desoto Parish close to us. Finally, one more call came in. Phillip laughed this time. He answered just in case someone- a real person and not an automated message- happened to be on the other end of the line and we could correct the mistake. No such luck.

If I had to take a guess, I'd bet some poor soul at De Soto's Seafood Kitchen had either misspoken their friend's phone number or their own. That, or the host or hostess had misunderstood them. I've frequented

Lower Alabama several times, but I've never stopped at that specific restaurant. I had to Google it. It's not on the strip right beside the beach, but it is just a couple of blocks away. It looks like they serve some good food and have been around a while. This time of the year falls right around the time of Spring Break, but it also falls at a time of day locals may want to go out for Sunday lunch after church.

Once I pulled up the restaurant's photos, it was easy to tell there wasn't much waiting room outside. You either have to go inside to wait or sit out in your car when it comes to finding somewhere comfortable to sit. This is where I imagine the frustration came in. The poor soul whose number was miscommunicated probably became frustrated after waiting so long to be seated. Then, the people who came in after them got seated. Maybe people with a bigger party. Now, that really must have burnt their biscuits! Phew. How *dare* those workers sit the people who came in afterwards! What nerve!

There's a chance this person was chill, relax, and a go-with-the-flow kind of guy or gal. After all, they're at the beach, right? Unfortunately, folks in this situation more often tend to be more like an angry Donald Duck, taking their hat off and stomping it on the ground making hard-to-understand screaming noises. They do it so that people know just how upset they are. They want to make sure everyone knows life isn't fair, *especially* for them.

I've seen my fair share of tantrums. I've seen toddler meltdowns over the wrong color spoon or fork. I've seen teenage girls throw a complete fit when they get caught doing something they weren't supposed to be doing and now must deal with the consequences. I've had my own share of tantrums throughout my lifetime. Now that I am older, most of mine are in front of God and God alone because I know God can take my questions and take my anger.

Being thankful for tantrums comes as a difficult prompt to write on. I am thankful for seeing tantrums, I suppose, and I guess I'm thankful for having had them. Seeing tantrums reminds me of how *not* to react and causes me to check myself. I don't want to be that person and want to present myself well. Seeing other people's kids have tantrums gives me some ease that maybe- just maybe- I'm not the only parent who has had to deal with them! I'm thankful for tantrums I've had though, too. In some way, it shows I care about something. I believe that raises another question for me: is the tantrum over something worth caring about? I'm thankful for my own tantrums because they can reveal weaknesses or struggles in my own life that perhaps I've been trying to hide or deal with on my own without God.

A sweet lady I used to work with used to sarcastically tell her teenage granddaughters to "pitch a fit" whenever they were throwing a tantrum. Sometimes "pitching a fit" is warranted, other times not so much. I encourage you (and I remind myself) to recognize what is worth "pitching a fit" over.

Day 72:
Courage

To withstand danger, to withstand difficulty, to persevere regardless of the circumstances... to be scared and to "do the thing" anyway... that is courage. Courage is knowing the outcome may not go well or may not be easy, but doing what needs to happen regardless.

A man was in a youth pastor's position at a medium-sized church. There was tension in the church from the word get-go, it seemed. The youth pastor was hired on in a God-led vote, there was no doubt, but with a new pastor in tow and some hurt feelings by a long-time church member over who "should" have been youth pastor, the youth pastor's time was coming to an end. It was obvious. After a private meeting with the new pastor, it was put to the man as this: either you get fired or you need to resign. There was no explanation as to why. There weren't many comments made other than "some people" were not "happy". There were only vague answers to questions, and it was a very short meeting between the two. The man prayed over what to do. His wife prayed. Their loved ones prayed. After some time, the man chose to resign. The heartbreak was real and so was the struggle in his heart. The whole situation stunk. Just stunk.

The following week, the man had a fun night with the youth. It was close to Halloween. There were fun games in the youth room/church basement of tasting gross foods, food-eating contests, and just a good time of fellowship. After the games were finished, the youth pastor informed the kids of his resignation. He was unable to give much of a reason as to why, because even he didn't know what was happening, but he explained the best way he could. The youth pastor explained he had to walk into the sanctuary and openly deliver his resignation letter in front of the church. There were tears. There were questions. There was a young man who stood up and said he, for one, was going with the youth pastor to support him. He asked the youth who was going with him. The whole group agreed to go with the youth pastor to the sanctuary.

The kids followed behind the man down the hallway toward the sanctuary. It looked very official. Heads of all height bobbed up and down slowly as they followed the man. It was silent. It was heartwarming and moving to see the unexpected support from the kids in this very collective way. This group of young people had been a very rowdy one, so to see this togetherness out of them was extraordinary. The youth pastor went into the sanctuary and sat down with the kids behind him on the next pew. The adults of the church were shocked to see them all there, and the boy who stirred the crowd said the youth pastor was not going to do this alone.

The youth pastor delivered the resignation speech to the congregation. He fought through tears. There was sorrow and pain because it was a decision which he'd felt trapped in. He'd felt caught between a rock and a hard place. There was peace in the resignation to some degree, but it was not in the man's plans. The resignation letter was read, but not without a broken spirit. The sanctuary was full of shock and mixed emotions. The job was over. The time at the church was finished for the man and his family.

The man could have bowed out and not given a resignation. He could have just not shown back up, not said goodbye to the kids or the friends he and his family had made at church over the last two years. He could have even taken being "fired". Despite his feelings, his embarrassment by the situation, the worry, he did what he had to do. He showed courage in one of his weakest moments. It was a moment where a position he held dear was taken away. He was hurt. His income for his family was taken from him. Rather than run and hide, he stood tall. He "did the thing" because he knew he had to.

There's a bunch of examples of courage I could give. I planned to put them all here, but after I jotted them all down and started writing, it just didn't feel right. Therefore, this was the story given.

I am grateful for courage. Without it, we couldn't move on to the next step in life. We couldn't be who we need to be for others. We wouldn't step forward in our callings without it. Without my husband facing this situation head on, we wouldn't have moved on to the girls' ranch. We wouldn't have met the people at the wonderful churches he has served at. We wouldn't be where we are now. The adventure we've had together would have never happened without courage.

I tried to find the right sentence to end this. I am stuck on the word "applied" and it brought me to a hymn lyric about the blood applied. I was reminded of the courage Jesus displayed on the cross. He already knew what was going to happen. He was reminded daily of what His fate was. As a carpenter, surely, he had scars on his humanly flesh. Every scar accumulated was just another reminder of the scars Jesus would one day receive at the crucifixion. Jesus could have called down leagues of angels. Jesus could have walked right off that cross. But he stayed. He was courageous and I don't express my appreciation half as well as I could.

I believe a thought to ponder on is whether you can have courage without love, or love without courage. As you ponder, I pray you have both. You know, just in case they do, in fact, go together.

Day 73: Chad

As I have mentioned once now, I've only ever dated three guys. In order, they are Zeke, Chad, and Phillip. My joke for Phillip is "the third time is the charm." Bless Phillip's heart, his prompt will happen sooner or later. In his defense, he gets mentioned a lot.

The funny part of this prompt for me is my counselor had wanted to work through this relationship with me in therapy sessions before our sessions came to an end. I didn't see the need and I don't recall how it got brought up to begin with in therapy. I think it happened when she asked how Phillip and I met. If I'm being completely honest, I've forgotten a lot of my relationship with Chad. If I want to remember it all, I really have to work at it. It was an important part of my life, but all seems like a blur. She saw something in this long-term relationship resonating in me that maybe I hadn't noticed. I guess this will be a form of processing the memories for me, too.

I began my senior year of high school in 2008. I was single at the time and had been for a while. I'd went on a date or two and talked to some guys, but either none of them resulted into a relationship or I'd shut it down quickly. Homecoming was coming up in October 2008 and I wanted to go with a date. A friend of mine had been talking to my best friend and was now going with her to homecoming. This friend suggested I talk to his friend Chad, who he'd gone to high school with. I quickly navigated Myspace to find Chad. If I'm being truthful, I was bored, and high school friends were pushy and a bit judgmental when it came to if you were in a relationship or not. Not only that, but I was also jealous of friends who found relationships so easily. I hadn't put two and two together that multiple relationships weren't exactly a brag. I was tired of catching flack for being single from friends. Chad and I exchanged numbers and began talking. If memory serves me correctly, the first time I met him in person was at the tennis courts at the city park.

Chad was a little taller than me and two years older than me (one year difference in school; I was one of the youngest in my grade and he was one of the oldest in his.) Chad claimed to be 5'9", but I doubt it (I'm sorry if you're reading this, man; no hate, I just don't buy it.) He had curly black hair, fair freckled skin, and blue eyes with gold specks. He was a stocky and strong former football player. He was attending a local community college and his plan was to become a teacher and football coach. It was so cool to be a senior in high school and talking to a college guy, as dorky as that sounds. Chad was- and if I had to guess, still is- a natural-born comedian; he immediately made me laugh, especially watching him attempt to play tennis with me. He had a fun sense of humor, and it won me over in a lot of ways. Chad was very outgoing and friendly, a class clown if I'd ever seen one. He was a flirt and gave me a huge confidence boost. It didn't take long for me to dive right into a relationship with him after the homecoming dance. Looking back, it was convenient, he was fun, and I just wanted to date somebody. Plus, his friends quickly became close friends with me. It all fell together well.

I had some strong opinions back then. Still do, in a lot of ways. I've already said I didn't drink, smoke, or do drugs as a teen, and I still don't. I was very adamant about that. I also liked going to my youth group at church. Prior to us dating- and I suspect some during our dating I didn't know about- Chad partied some. He also dipped and he occasionally smoked, but I didn't find out about the smoking until a few weeks into the relationship. Chad had gone to church on and off and went to my church with me once or twice. However, it didn't last long. My priorities went from growing my relationship with God to growing my relationship with Chad and trying to create a happily-ever-after for myself. Chad had told me he was saved, and we didn't have much of a conversation beyond that. Months went by, class rings were exchanged, and futures were discussed. We were in it for the long haul.

Our first year of dating came and went. There were disagreements, some things I'm sure were pushed under the rug and other things neither of us should have been doing were going on. We were young and dumb, period. I don't want to go into all of it because I don't want to say anything negative about him here. It was just obvious back then we were starting to grow apart and were in denial about it because we were comfortable. Our relationship was each other's security blanket. There was a time when a concert he'd bought tickets for got rained out and the concert was rescheduled for the next day. However, it was my first day of college. I wasn't missing my first day of college and he ended up wasting the money on the tickets he'd bought and was not happy with me. His point was all I'd miss was orientation and doing nothing the first day. While that's a real point, I just couldn't miss the first day. I'd worked too hard to get the opportunity to go to college and I had made up my mind it was more important. Again, we just had different opinions and priorities.

When the time came for me to transfer to a university from community college, UNA was the obvious choice. Chad was there, and after all, I was convinced I was going to marry him one day. That's what you do when you've been together a long time, right? I'd visited UNA several times by then and liked it, even toured it with a friend of mine before. I don't like to say I moved to Florence just for Chad, but let's be real. I went to UNA for Chad and because it was the easy thing to do. I didn't even consider other schools. I ended up living with Chad starting in Summer 2010 and our two friends, who were also a couple. It was the four of us in a two-bedroom, two-bathroom apartment.

By the time year two rolled around, living with him had given me a whole new perspective of him. Living together will do that and you will learn a lot about a person. I made some mistakes and so did he. Red flags abounded when both of our minds began to wander about other people and what other relationships would be like. That is as far as I'll go on that note. It became very clear very quickly we were not on the same page anymore. I remember lying in bed with him one morning and God specifically speaking to my heart, telling me I didn't need to be living like this and I needed to stop sleeping with Chad. It was so direct and straight-forward. I became immediately convicted about living together. After a discussion with someone I'll call a Christian mentor I met at UNA, I told him I wanted to have separate bedrooms. Our roommates agreed and the guys ended up with one bedroom and the girl and I ended up with our own bedroom. God was working on me and even though I made mistakes over the course of the next few months, He revealed to me Chad and I were moving in totally different directions. I just didn't want to see it because it was hard, and keeping the relationship going was simpler. Again, the relationship was as security blanket. I even almost broke up with Chad in Fall 2010, but just couldn't do it. Around that time, I'd wanted to start going back to church and he seemed less than interested. I was becoming more financially mature, too, and it seemed to me he was not. There were just textbook issues going on I didn't want to deal with because we'd been together for so long, and things were "okay".

By the time Valentine's Day rolled around in 2011, I realized I didn't want to be with him anymore when he wrote me a letter talking about possibly getting engaged the following June or July. The moment I read that, my mind panicked, and I thought to myself, "I've *got* to get out of this relationship." It was an involuntary thought. I began thinking about how I'd afford living on my own or with a roommate. It wasn't feasible. I was working full-time making minimum wage while being a full-time student. I felt very stuck and trapped, and it wasn't fair to either of us.

In early March 2011, my best friend called me as I was walking into my Human Sexuality Midterm. She told me her boyfriend was gone. She said he'd left a suicide note and no one could find him. I got out of class and Chad let me drive his truck down to where they lived, since my car would never have made it. It was about 2 ½ hours south of Florence. Just months before that, the four of us had taken a day trip together. This news came as such a shock when I heard it. I stayed down there for two days, just being a support for my friend in the best way I knew how. I was interrogated by police; they were trying to figure out if my best friend could have killed him or had something to do with it. Her boyfriend wasn't found while we were there. The police couldn't locate him. The trail went cold. His remains wouldn't be found until years later. He'd hung himself in the woods in the only area not searched. The whole experience shook me. I got to know some of what was in his letter. I decided life was too short to be unhappy and be with the wrong person. I knew I had to break up with Chad, but like I said, that was hard. What was I supposed to do? Live with someone I broke up with or potentially be homeless? What a mess I'd got myself into.

While all this was going on, I got to know Phillip at work at Bojangles'. I'd had no intention of dating Phillip, and as a matter of fact he got on my nerves because everyone just loved him so much. He was someone who made me roll my eyes as I scrubbed dishes and took orders. He got away with a lot because he was Phillip and a lot of people liked him, and for whatever reason that drove me crazy. I found Phillip to be a genuinely good guy, though, and we believed the same things. I never thought of it more than that, just someone at work I thought was a good guy. Did I think he was cute? Well, yeah. Outside of that, though, I had no intentions of dating him. The only strange memory I have that suggests otherwise was sometime in February when he'd talked about quitting Bojangles'. I was at the redlight on my way to work thinking about him and others who'd talked about quitting, and a voice came to my head and clearly asked, "Are you going to be okay never seeing Phillip again?" Shocked, I replied audibly, "No." I have no explanation other than God trying to guide me in the right direction and I didn't know it.

For the sake of not overlapping prompt topics because Phillip will have his own prompt, I'll say this: my relationship with Phillip was not planned by any means. It was God's timing, hands down. The moment I knew I was supposed to be with Phillip was something God himself told me. But, in my cowardice, it took me two whole days to break up with Chad after that. I barely ate. I was sick from my nerves. I could hardly sleep. I chose to break up with Chad the day he was going to his family's house for a gathering so he wouldn't have to be at home alone or be around me for the rest of the day. I stood in the parking lot of our apartment complex and did what I had to do, leaving him broken and in tears. That hurt. I had never broken up with someone before, let alone someone I'd been with for over two years. Our friends had known for a couple of days I planned to do it, and one of them was upstairs while it happened. As soon as it was done and I was back upstairs, my friend hugged me while I cried with guilt-ridden relief over the ordeal. I started dating Phillip the following weekend.

I lived with Chad for two months until my lease was up, and boy was it awkward. We'd never really fought or been ugly with each other until we had to live together after the break-up. There were some awkward moments during our last weeks of living together, that's for sure. Years went by and he reached out to me in a message to make peace over the whole situation. He apologized for his actions, and I apologized for how the whole thing went down. I know it wasn't pretty, it just had to be done. There were no hard feelings between either of us. He is now in what seems to be a happy relationship with a family of his own.

I'm grateful for our relationship, first off, because he exposed me to things I had never done before. I didn't go out to eat much because of my financial situation at home. I got to go to Applebee's! Man, that was a treat. It was so cool. I didn't know how to order from the menu, really. I was a bit overwhelmed. I'd never had steak before that date. We traveled all over the place, whether my parents knew or not. We traveled across the Tennessee state line once just to say we'd done it. I was still in high school then. I got to go to different events because he could take me, such as a rodeo, a professional tennis match, and much more. When I went to college to play tennis and he transferred to UNA, if I wasn't driving to Florence to spend the weekend with him there, we'd go on weekend trips or trips over our school breaks. We got to go to Gulf Shores a few times, Myrtle Beach, even Rock City and Chattanooga. He took me to my first college football game. I had never gotten to experience a freedom like that before dating him and I genuinely appreciate those experiences. I grew a bit more independent because of it.

On the other hand, there are things I don't want to bring up in detail but for the sake of finding ways to be thankful, I need to address. There are experiences with him I wish I could take back, the kinds of experiences that leave you cringing and humiliated. Additionally, in a nutshell, I felt a bit pushed in directions I didn't want to go in, all for the sake of me wanting to make him happy. I have a tattoo on my back now (which he paid for) I got mostly because I thought he would like it and because he told me I was too scared to get it. The tattoo isn't anything embarrassing, just not something I bring up all the time. I think at the time I lost myself all for the sake of keeping a relationship and trying to make him happy. My personality changed in a few ways I'm not proud of because of his influence, and I lost some beloved people over it I've never gotten back. People's opinions changed of me because of who I was while I was with him. I guess if I look back on these parts, I'm thankful for all those things because they allow me to relate to other people when they are going through similar relationships. The bad parts of the story allow me to minister in good ways now. I'm thankful for this part of our relationship experience because it reminds me to never let it happen again, to be myself and not be ashamed of what I believe in to make people comfortable or to keep them around. The right people will stick around. It took me this relationship to learn that.

I'm thankful for the relationship because without it, I'd never have moved to Florence. I never would have met Phillip had I not lived in Florence, and I wouldn't have the life I have now. My marriage wouldn't exist. My kids wouldn't exist. It all happened for a reason, and I'm more than okay with that.

Day 74: Control Freaks

The title probably seems a little harsh, but here we go. Put your boots on because some toes are about to get stomped.

I believe people fall into being control freaks for a few reasons. Sometimes, people are born into this world bossy. At some point, one can only hope they realize it is both a strength and a weakness. Another reason people turn into control freaks is because they need just some sort of semblance of control in their life. Everything else- or even just something very important- in life may be going down a spiraling black hole, and for these people to feel some kind of peace, they over-exert control on everyone and everything in their lives.

I've had supervisors and bosses micromanage everything I did at work, causing me to want to leave the job sooner. Some of these people would call me every thirty minutes to do a random "check-in" on where I was, sometimes catching me in the middle of an interview with an alleged perpetrator or in the middle of knocking on the door of a home visit. On several occasions, a supervisor would hand me back a court report saying it was too long, and I'd bring it back with corrections only to be told I should not have changed it to begin with. I've had co-workers/equals I partnered with in classrooms and on projects who would go behind and redo well-done jobs I had completed only because *they* had not done it and it was not to *their* liking.

There will probably be some books slamming shut in a moment over this example: people who must load the dishwasher a specific way. Picture a moment when you are teaching a teenage foster child how to wash dishes for the first time in their life with a dishwasher. They're in a home they've only been in for about three weeks; they're still the new person in the house. You show them how to load the dishwasher a couple of times and they do okay. The next time, they do it solo. Proudly, they have you come look at their chore before they push the start button. The smile on their face searching for approval is broad and excited. They messed up how you wanted it done, but the dishwasher is ultimately loaded sufficiently. Rather than tell them they did great for their first time and offer them some tips for next time so they can improve, you glare at them and correct their loading job, complaining they didn't load the dishwasher right. Now all the teenager sees is they can't do anything right, so they may as well not even try. Danged if they do; danged if they don't. In their mind, they weren't good enough for their own family (which is probably far from true, but kids' minds think this way a lot) and now they're not good enough for you, either. How stupid they must feel. However, you feel like a champion for getting the bowls exactly how you want them. What an accomplishment. You press the start button like the winner you are. The wind flows through your hair and lifts your cape as you prepare to soar off like the hero you were born to be. You'll live to fight crumbs and drips another day, thank goodness.

 Tripp is 4 years old now and has been learning to put his own clothes away correctly. I taught all my kids the same way. I drew pictures of t-shirts, pants, underwear, etc. and taped them to the appropriate drawer. It has been an effective method, but Tripp is just an entirely different kiddo. He is rebellious and finding motivation for him is hard. I really fight the urge to not just put his clothes away because it is easier on me. It is a skill he must learn himself. Sometimes I lose my cool and just start putting things away, complaining he isn't doing it right or fast enough. At times, he doesn't' care; other times, his little lip pokes out and his face saddens. So, believe me when I am talking about control freaks, I am talking about me, too. I hurt my own heart when I say these things.

 I'm thankful for control freaks and even for the times I can be one. Sometimes they can be annoying and get on everyone's nerves, but when you can look past it at the underlying reasons these people could be the way they are, it offers some equality. It reminds us to be patient with one another even when we can be unbearable. Although, I'm thankful because there are times when having a control freak in my life has encouraged me to do better in my duties. I'm thankful because when I am a control freak, I'm reminded just how little I do have control over. I only have control over my thoughts and actions and how I treat others. Everything else is out of my hands, and your hands, too.

Lastly, I want to share with you a story about a woman named Martha. She can be found in Luke 10 and John 11. While Jesus and his disciples traveled, they came to a village where a woman named Martha and her sister Mary lived. Martha became overcome with being the perfect host. Scripture says she was distracted by many tasks. I bet she was making sure the food was placed just right and that all the dishes were in their proper place. Everything had to be perfect. Mary was nowhere to be found. How dare Mary! She was sitting there at Jesus' feet, and He was the guest Martha was trying to ensure had the perfect visit! I bet Martha was infuriated over her sister's behavior. Martha brought up to Jesus Mary's behavior and asked Jesus- no, *told* Jesus- to have Mary assist her. Martha was slowly losing control of her home and the situation. Jesus' answer to Martha was not to be worried or upset about everything, and He urged Martha to understand Mary was doing what mattered.

Martha was a control freak. Sometimes we want to have total control of the situation, when, in reality, Jesus is in the room and has control the whole time. Martha was too concerned about other things and wanting things to meet her standard to see the standard was staring right at her. Ouch.

Take this toe-stomper as a time to reflect on your own behavior and how it can be perceived by others. Reflect on how your need for control reveals areas in your life that may be lacking faith and trust. I sure will.

Day 75: Comedians

Phillip and I went to see a comedy group in Birmingham, AL last November. We've never gone to see a comedian or a stand-up comedy group, so it sounded like something fun for us to try. This group was one Phillip was familiar with from social media and I'd heard of them before. Their sketches are about SEC Football. Now, I was born and raised in Alabama. Most babies born in the state are born with an emblem on their chest representing which school- Alabama or Auburn- they will root for during their lifetime. The vast majority of Alabamians, even stretching that out to Southerners, are brought up in the culture of football. They either play it, go to football games from pee wee to high school throughout their lifetime, or watch it with their grandfathers while they scream absurdities at the television. I enjoyed it as a kid and even on up into young adulthood, but the older I got the less I cared. Phillip is a huge Alabama football fan and for his sake, I enjoy it.

I was so impressed by the comedians. Their sketches appealed to not only the football fans in the audience, but to me as well. I appreciated their humor and their talent. Boy, they were something! They found a way to bring humor to the whole building and not just to a specific group of people. We had a wonderful time and I'd be more than happy to go to an event like that again.

I'm thankful for the laughter comedians bring, the smiles, and how relatable they are. They make people feel like someone else understands, that you aren't alone, and in a fun way. I'm thankful for the natural-born comedians, the people who are just naturally funny who can turn the worst situations into light ones.

Let us not forget there are times when these people are fighting their own battles and choose to bring joy during dark times. What an important role they play in often mundane days.

Day 76: Waffle House

You can go almost anywhere in the Southeast and find a Waffle House. A fine eating establishment, it is. Large, yellow squares with black letters stand proudly on a skinny post in front of a diner-style building where you can watch everyone dining on breakfast food or chili. I didn't frequent Waffle House much until I started dating Chad. Our friend's mom was a waitress at Waffle House and sometimes we went there at night with our friend group to go eat and see her. Later, the same friend would serve at a different Waffle House.

I met a variety of good people in Waffle Houses and met at least one I almost got in a fight with. Lots of laughs have been shared among friends and people I loved at Waffle House. I heard my first Louisiana accent at a Waffle House (it was later I learned there are different Louisiana accents just as there are different Alabama ones.) The cook's accent was as thick as the batter mix. It was as if it poured out his mouth and sizzled, like the mix hitting the waffle iron. He was a peculiar character with a gold tooth.

In 2018, a man fell through the ceiling of one of our local Waffle Houses. He was either drunk or high and had gone into the bathroom, taken his pants off, and crawled up into the ceiling. Some creaking and a crash were heard before he fell amongst the patrons. He staggered his way out the front door and was later faced with felony warrants.

In late September 2014, Phillip and I were on our way to the hospital to deliver Ridge. I'd done my homework on this pregnancy. I'm telling you, if there was a mile, I'd walked it. If there was a book or a theory, I'd read it. I had talked over just about every decision in detail with my labor doula. Before the induction, I wanted to be ready and energized. The only place worth eating at that was open was Waffle House.

We were welcomed by the smell of coffee and the sight of several sets of eyeballs staring at my gargantuan belly. I'd actually *lost* weight throughout this pregnancy, but Ridge was a big fellow and demanded attention even in the womb. To explain, I lost 15 pounds at the beginning, gained it back, and he weighed almost ten pounds when he was born. Talk about a strutting-out-of-the-hospital moment when we went home. I weighed less than before I'd gotten pregnant!

We sat and the waitress took our order. I don't even remember what I had, but I'm sure waffles, eggs, and bacon were involved. The waitress was as sweet as the syrup and asked me when Ridge was due. Her response, like most other people's, was always fun to watch when I'd reply with, "A week ago." We were wished good luck and given prayers as we finished our meal, all by staff and other customers who had heard the story of how we were about to have our second child in a few hours.

I'm thankful for Waffle House because it is usually open 24/7. It is a solid place to eat. I'm thankful for the sweet memory of it being the last meal before Ridge was born. We've been able to take our kids to Waffle House and it is always fun watching their faces light up over some chocolate chip waffles and as Ridge calls it, "bankin".

I recommend you give it a go if you haven't. I hope you have a great experience and maybe, just maybe, you won't have a random man land on your head.

Day 77:
Old Friends

I referenced old friends in the "New Friends" prompt to explain the difference. I touched on sharing a baby crib with a friend growing up. His name was Luke. I've known him since I came home from the hospital. He is 10 months older than me, and Granny babysat him when we were kids. His mom took us to school together a lot before he began homeschooling and I'd listen to her childhood stories from the back seat. Luke was hands-down my first friend. Luke's mom gave me my first job at the tack and saddle shop. I've got pictures with Luke and his parents just like I would any of my own blood relatives. Luke is also one of the first people to rally the troops when Granny and Paw's house burned down, including gathering friends to help us get Paw a new lift chair and unload it at Dad's house. After all, they were Granny and Paw to him, too. His dad was even a pallbearer when Paw died.

Another friend, Arwen, is the one I met in the bathroom in second grade. Why we hadn't spoken to each other before then, I don't know. We were in the same class. We chased the same two boys on the playground every day without fail. She sat in one stall, and I sat in another. One of us asked the other if they wanted to be friends; the other responded, "Sure." We became best friends after that. She assisted me to the nurse's station after a skinned knee on the playground (like I really needed assistance, but we got out of class for a while.) She listened to all my boy-crazy obsessions. I dealt with her anime and *Lord of the Rings* fantasies. We used to email each other stories back and forth and had a whole chapter book going, only to finally dwindle off. I'm fairly certain that email address I was using was later hacked by some guy with a funny name in another country. She introduced me to *The Office* and that alone makes me grateful for her (comedy genius!) Arwen is the friend who called me years later during college about her boyfriend leaving a suicide note. I did the only thing I knew to do and that was to go and be present with her. I made breakfast for her and her roommates.

Not to burst Phillip's bubble, but I got married in first grade to a kid named Clark. Technically we still aren't divorced. Call that a scandal if you will. We had a whole ceremony under a tree on the playground while another girl in our class played a fake organ under the tree. Years went by and the marriage was full of infidelity on both sides. I mean, at one point he ended up with the organist as a crush for a couple of years! Of all things... Through it all, we remained friends. We received tutoring together in high school, did homework together almost every night, and even had a spurt where we almost dated. Prior to that brief time, his parents had become parents to me and had given me an example of a married couple to look up to. Time went on, some feelings got hurt over an apartment in Florence I'd wanted that he and someone else took out from under me, or so I perceived. Regardless, he called me as soon as his relationship went south. Law enforcement was called due to a very violent physical altercation between the two of them. I went to his side as quickly as I could. More years passed and sadly, his dad's death came. I made sure to go to the funeral and was able to speak a bit on what his dad meant to me.

I have other friends I could go on about, but we'd be here forever, and this book is already longer than I anticipated it to be. Why am I thankful for old friends? They shared the earliest experiences of life with me. They were there for school plays, crushes, navigating through teenage romance and the humiliation of puberty. They're the ones I've got funny and embarrassing photos with and of from all those years ago. They were there for the nitty gritty, the first aches and pains of childhood and adolescence. They were people I got to watch fail and succeed, fall, and get back up again. They were there for a chapter in life's story and are fun pages to look back on. Sometimes they grow with you, sometimes they grow apart, but either way there are threads always linking you together.

Day 78: God's Voice

God's voice has already been addressed some. Most recently, I brought it up in the prompt about Chad. The moment I was sitting at the redlight on my way to work and a voice- not mine -posed the question to me about if I'd be okay if I never saw Phillip again. God told me very plainly later I was going to marry Phillip and to break up with Chad. It's an indescribable moment in time when you know it is not your voice, it is not your thought, none of it is something you concocted. It is the voice of God that shuts out every other distraction. It demands your attention.

However, there are times where God's voice isn't necessarily audible, but His message is clear. In Fall 2010 when I was at UNA, my two roommates and I had been having a discussion on whether it was okay for all of us to be living together like we were. At the time, we were all coupled up in our apartment. We were in the GUC, a place where the college students could all eat lunch and look out the giant wall of windows to see the amphitheater at UNA. It was perfect Fall weather for Alabama, a comfortable temperature in the 70's accompanied by soft wind knocking off the orange and red leaves from the surrounding trees. They effortlessly found their place on the ground. After our discussion, I walked outside to hang out before my next class. The amphitheater was a nice spot to take a break and sit a while. This day, a church group had set up outside the amphitheater with a question written on a chalkboard.

I couldn't remember the question if my life depended on it, but I was greeted by a woman about my mom's age. She was so kind and seemed so happy. I can't remember how the conversation started, but I remember asking her what she thought about people living with each other before they were married and telling her I wanted to find a church home in Florence. She and I ended up on the lower steps of the amphitheater away from everyone and I told her the situation I'd found myself in. I sat one step lower than her on the marble-looking concrete steps. She witnessed to me and loved on me in a way I desperately needed.

As I talked to her about my concerns with my living situation, financial situation, and my relationship, she encouraged me in my convictions and helped me find ways to address wanting to change bedrooms so the guys would have one bedroom and the girls would have the other. We ended up praying together over the situation. I opened my eyes as she said "amen". We exchanged phone numbers. During our goodbye, an orange leaf caught my eye. It floated down through the air directly into my hands, which just so happened to be sitting open on my lap. An instant peace came over me and an assurance I was moving in the right direction. Leaves were scattering everywhere at the time, but for one to fall right there, just at the right time on that day during that conversation, I have no answer for… other than God.

This morning was our first day of revival at church. The Sunday School lesson just so happened to flow well with the message our guest preacher delivered that morning. There's no doubt in my mind this is a way we can "hear" God's voice, too, letting us know it is certainly Him reaching out to us.

I am, from the bottom of my heart, grateful for God's voice. It gives me confidence in His will and plan for me. It reminds me I am His whenever I have doubts. Finally, I am glad I do my best to listen to it, not ignore it. Some of what He tells us may not be easy to do and the enemy will certainly use our fear to deter us. God's desire for us is so much grander, though, and if we will turn off our own desires, see past our own noses, and listen to more than only what we want to hear, His voice will make our paths clear.

Day 79:
Cringey Moments

Cringey may not be a word some of you use, so for those of you who aren't sure what I'm referring to, I'm talking about embarrassing moments. These are the moments you'd love to forget or wish everyone else could forget. These moments are the ones that can wake you from a deep sleep at night only to have you lay awake with regret. Ridge watched me draw this prompt out of my jar this morning now that he knows I'm writing a book. I told him what it said. His face bunched up and he looked confused. "Why would you be thankful for being embarrassed?" I answered him explaining that was my job: to figure out why. I've got a lot- when I say a lot, I mean probably hundreds, maybe thousands- of these moments and I could spend all day trying to remember them. Each one makes my gut hurt.

    I'll give an example of the kind of embarrassment I'm talking about. I believe it was early 2011 (apparently those years were the hot mess time of my life) or possibly late 2010. I wanted extra money. I was working full-time in fast food and going to school full-time, but I was strapped for cash and trying to find ways to up my income. I'd tried selling AVON, but learned I was not much of a saleswoman. It was not my strong suit by any means. I started identifying what areas I was good at, and I thought to myself, "I like kids and I'm good with kids... I could babysit?" I joined a website and created an account to put myself out there for babysitting work.

    It wasn't long before a young couple in the area contacted me about babysitting their three-year-old daughter and infant daughter while they went out on a date. I was supposed to get there around 6 p.m. that evening and they'd be back around 10 p.m. or so. I don't remember what I was supposed to be getting paid, but what I do remember is that it was a bit of a trainwreck. I didn't know these people... at all. They were total strangers. When I arrived at their house, it immediately felt awkward. This should have been my first red flag. They were quiet but friendly people and their three-year-old was a ball of energy. Their infant daughter appeared to hate every living thing and looked like she could cast spells with her eyes and wish evil on her enemies. They were two completely opposite kids.

The parents left and gave me specific instructions as well as their phone numbers. They left for their date, and I was left to entertain the children and make sure they didn't destroy the house or hurt one another. The three-year-old wanted to watch *The Little Mermaid*. I put in that DVD and then she wanted popcorn. I popped popcorn and she sat on the couch while watching the movie. About this time, the baby decided she hated me and began to cry. Incessantly.

Here's the point I figured out I had screwed up. I had hardly dealt with babies in my life up until now. I'd tutored small kids, gave tennis lessons to little kids, done VBS several times... needless to say, I could handle small kids. Babies... I think in my dim mind I thought this would be simple. Ha. Oh poor, naïve Melinda.

I remember for a fact I changed the baby. I played with the baby. I believe I fed the baby. Surely, I'd have done that. The 9 p.m. mark was approaching, and I had been dealing with a crying baby for the first time in my life while the three-year-old had created a pillow fort for herself in the living room. I caved and put the baby in her crib in the girls' bedroom upstairs. I was at a point I didn't know what else to do for the baby and there was only one hour until the parents got home. Surely nothing else would happen, right?

The three-year-old followed me upstairs and began to show me her snow globe collection on an easily accessible shelf in the bedroom. First of all, even *I* knew better than to have something breakable where a three-year-old could reach it. The first one she picked up she dropped on the thick, shaggy carpet. Water, flakes, and glass shards went everywhere. "Whoopsy! I get it!" the little girl said as she went to grab the glass. I jerked her hand away and yelled, "No! Don't! You'll get hurt!" The baby, who had continued to cry non-stop, glared at me from her crib throne as I squatted on the ground trying to keep the little girl away from the glass. On cue, the baby paused her crying while continuing her glare to take a deep breath before crying more. The little girl began crying because I told her, "No." I brought the three-year-old back downstairs with me while I searched for cleaning supplies only to find the family dog had knocked the bowl of popcorn into the floor and tore up one of the kids' stuffed dolls.

    The parents came home to me bringing the baby downstairs. Their happy faces greeted me and asked me how things went. I was polite but honest, informing them of the broken snow globe upstairs and told them the baby hadn't stopped crying for a while no matter what I'd done. I handed the baby over to her mother. The baby instantly stopped and looked at me like I'd murdered her best friend. The three-year-old was sitting in the pillow fort she'd made as if nothing had happened. Her crying fit was over. I never got a call back to babysit again. I've often woken up from a deep sleep wondering if I'd done something wrong at that house and cringed at the thought of what a terrible and inexperienced babysitter I'd been.

    There's plenty of other times that life rent-free in my mind, squatting on prime real estate and I can't seem to kick them out. There's the time in fourth grade when I didn't know what sex was. My only knowledge was a kid named Guy saying his mom went on dates and had sex. Bless his heart. In my mind, sex equaled dating because of this one conversation, and I knew you hugged on a date from what I'd watched in movies. So, I deduced sex was hugging. Cool, got it; a core memory was created.

    Soon after on a field trip, a fellow classmate was hugging a tree and pretending to kiss it, claiming he was a "tree hugger". The crowd of kids laughed, I laughed, and I used my new-found knowledge to tell the crowd, "He is having sex with a tree!" Granny came to my side faster than The Flash comes to save the day and I got a whooping worthy of champions right then and there. Being unaware as to why I got a whooping, I screamed out, "What? All I said was he was having sex with a tree!" The whooping continued and so did the tears. Granny was not one for explanations. Mom was forced to have "the talk" with me after that.

I've got a long list of embarrassing moments I may get into later. Now comes the part Ridge mentioned: figuring out why on earth I would be thankful for all those memories that make my stomach churn. I guess they help me to remember how dumb I was; they help me to recognize how much I've grown… thank goodness. They give me ways to relate to other people who've made their fair share of mistakes. The fact they hurt my heart and bother me makes me aware of my conscience. Embarrassment falls into a category of conviction, which isn't a wrong place to be if shame doesn't anchor you down. This leads me to realize I've got to let go of my anchor on some of these ridiculous memories and not let them become the monsters they aren't.

To finish, a big thank you to everyone who was patient with me when I didn't deserve it. I pray I remember it as I watch my own kids grow and learn. Lastly, a big apology to the people I babysat for all those years ago and I hope your girls survived the one night of the terrible babysitter. I'm sure they're fine young ladies now with a healthy respect for snow globes.

Day 80: Bible Stories

From the time I was old enough to go to Granny's Sunday School class, I was learning the ins and outs of all the "fun" Bible stories. I was also learning how to pout just right if Granny wasn't teaching that day so I could go be with her instead of being stuck in class (Granny was slick and didn't fall for this trick for very long.) I can remember some of the ways I interpreted those stories. Somehow or another, Noah got all those critters on the ark. Must've stunk on there. Poor baby Moses floated around in some water like a bobber with crocodile bait. One of my favorite depictions of David and Goliath was a show called *Wishbone* which aired in the late 1990s. Watching a Jack Russell Terrier playing the role of David while he took down a large man with only a slingshot and a rock really put the story in perspective for five-year-old me.

I remember trying to pay attention in big church. I really did try. However, hearing that old man hee-haw about Kiah's, Hiah's, and Miah's lost me quicker than a football fan loses their temper. I appreciate the effort adults made then, though, I really do. Some of it stuck. Enough of it stuck to keep me coming back and to give me a desire to learn more.

I remembered Joseph thrown in the pit by his brothers. It gave me enough interest to reread it later and see what else he went through. How he ended up in Egypt. How he was wrongly accused. How he was able to reconcile with his brothers eventually and see his father again. I recalled Daniel in the lion's den. I can recall the cartoon images of a happy-go-lucky guy in a rocky pit full of smiling, sleepy lions. As I've gotten older and seen God's wonders for myself, I've listened to and read the story again and God really did shut the mouths of those starved lions, and what a miracle it was.

I'd vaguely been taught about Job. Adult Bible studies have allowed me to delve deeper into his sorrow and the older I've gotten, the more I empathize with some of his pain. The loss of his home, his children, his health, everything. Even through it, though, God spoke directly with him. God dealt with Job. It's a good one. You should check it out.

I'm thankful for Bible stories I am familiar with. I'm thankful for those I'm not. Being married to a preacher as knowledgeable as my husband made me realize quickly how few Bible stories I had in my old filing cabinet. When we first got together, he was shocked I didn't know some of the stories he mentioned, and I was shocked he knew as much as he did. He's a joker and I questioned the validity of the stories a few times in the early years before I looked them up for myself! I'm thankful for the lessons these stories teach me, the lessons I am reminded of that I so easily forget when I allow myself to be overwhelmed by life's junk. Bible stories give me examples of faith when mine is tested. They give me strength when I am weak. They encourage me by showing me "it" can be done.

Lastly, I'm thankful for Bible stories. They remind me that God, per the King James Version, can even use an "ass" to do His works (Don't believe me? Go to Numbers 22:21-39.) If God can do that, I am sure He can use average people like us for something extraordinary.

Day 81: LEGOs

All my kids love LEGO building blocks. They love them so much that before we moved into our new house in 2020, Ridge and I made a project out of an old cabinet, spray paint, and LEGO boards to create a LEGO bench just for him. Tripp wasn't old enough to do anything but cause havoc with LEGOs yet, so the bench was to go in Ridge's room under his window. He was over the moon.

Not long after we moved into the new house and everything was- for the most part- in its place, Grandpa came over to see his great-grandkids. The kids showed him around the house, and he spotted the LEGO bench. Grandpa, still nimble in his late 80's, bent his tall frame down onto one knee and knelt beside the LEGO bench. Ridge joined right in beside him and began to build ships, cars, and structures with Grandpa. They talked about the different colors, how all the pieces fit together, and much more. Two mechanical geniuses made fellowship that day and had a meeting of the minds. I took a picture on my phone to document it. Moments like these are few and far between and one day will be just memories.

Ridge, unlike Anniston, did not inherit the "artsy" gene from me. He has his own type of creativity, but not the "traditionally artsy" stuff people instantly think of. Ridge's creativity can be found in his engineering abilities which seem to come natural to him. The kid gets an idea and immediately wants to put it into existence via blocks, cardboard, or in this case LEGOs. Tripp is yet to be determined. Ridge didn't inherit much from me except a witty (some would call it "smart") mouth and, in some strange way, the talent of being a math whiz. Once I get past Algebra 1 and Geometry, I'm practically useless in the math world, so he must get the greater ability from his Great-Grandpa or someone else.

I'm glad for LEGOs because it is a way my kids get an outlet to create. Things like this are the spark my kids- and many other kids- need in order to figure out their passions and desires. Maybe they'll turn my kid into a construction worker? Maybe a mechanical engineer? Perhaps he'll design skyscrapers one day.

I'm thankful for the chance to watch him and his siblings build and to watch through their eyes the little gears turning in their minds while they put their masterpieces together piece by piece. I'm glad for likeminded great-grandparents who can still turn into little kids when brought together by colorful little pieces of plastic.

Day 82: Bonus Kids

I have a soft spot in my heart for bonus kids: the kids who aren't mine but may as well be. I believe it is because I was a bonus kid. I can name a handful of families and individuals in my life who took me under their wing; there was even one who had me at their house almost every single day and fed me supper most nights. I found these people and bonded with them not only because I could feel the love, but they gave me a reason to not have to be home all the time.

When I was growing up, I dreamed of having a ton of kids. I wanted a minimum of five kids. Seven, eight, nine, or ten would have been nice, too. I would daydream of which winner from my school I'd end up with and come up with creative names our kids would have. Full disclosure? I had a whole document on Paw's computer that held my top girls' and boys' names. Typing that didn't feel good at all. I guess admitting that will go down as another "cringey" moment.

Phillip and I went on to have three earthside biological children of our own. After our first two children were born and I began working in child welfare, I began developing close relationships with some of the kids on my caseload. I mentioned one already before when I talked about the lost sheep. I have fed that child, parented that child, and much more. If I had thought it would have been safe for my small children, I'd have found a way to take her home. This experience along with a calling on mine and Phillip's heart to possibly adopt one day led us to become licensed foster parents. We went through the Alabama Baptist Children's Home for our classes, and our plan was to take one kid at a time younger than our two small children. Through a series of events which I'll go into another time, we ended up being live-in houseparents at a girls' group home (the girls' ranch) with up to eight teenage girls at one time in our care.

Through this process, we've ended up with girls being close to us, some closer than others, but nonetheless close. Without taking away from other stories at the girls' ranch, we were there for two years treating these young ladies like our own children. We got pregnant with Tripp while we lived there, and they were a part of that pregnancy journey and first year of Tripp's life just like any other member of our family. MK eventually came to live with us after we left the girls' ranch. One young lady became pregnant and was not in a good place in her life and asked us if we'd take her baby when it was born. We immediately agreed, but tragically the baby passed. We've given money when girls needed some extra help. There's been conversations had at the wee hours of the morning when we were at the ranch and even after we left concerning life's problems, why things are so difficult, general advice, just to chat, and even what to pray about. We were able to be a safe place for these kids, these bonus kids. We were- and still are- bonus parents.

One of my prayers since childhood was to be a mom. Not just to be a mom, but a good mom. The best mom. I wanted to have a great husband and have lots and lots of kids just like I mentioned earlier. God did not see fit for me to have a lot of biological children. He saw fit for me to have three c-sections, a 6-week miscarriage in 2017, and an ectopic pregnancy in 2020 after my tubes grew back together following my tubal ligation in 2019. However, God answered the desires of my heart in ways I never considered. I have been able to have my own biological children, bonus kids who call me "Mom" through the girls' ranch, bonus kids from my caseloads I've had special relationships with, and even some of our youth groups over the years.

If I'd had the large number of biological children all those years ago, there's a chance I would have had neither the time nor energy to give to all those bonus kids. I may never have had the opportunity to be a positive influence on their lives. They may never have had the chance to have a positive influence on mine. I look forward to more bonus kids over the coming years as long as they keep coming.

I'm thankful for the opportunity this bonus kid had to have bonus kids. If I can show them in some way what love is supposed to look like, I've done my job.

Day 83: Barbers/Hairdressers

There have been people who have done a good job on my hair, and there have been people who have done a not-so-good job. There are people who charged me part of the rights of my firstborn child to cut and style my hair and there's people who have done it for free. I became most grateful for barbers/hairdressers when the COVID-19 Pandemic happened. My sons needed haircuts. A time ago, Phillip's grandmother's husband Rick cut the boys' hair, but we simply weren't getting out much during 2020. My daughter, on one hand, was somewhat easy to trim. I've done it before just to cut split ends and manage her hair. The boys' hair, however, was a challenge. Poor Ridge's hair had gotten down in his eyes and with his hair as straight as it is, there's not much else to do other than cut it off.

I've talked about being artistic, and having this trait, I assumed I could put this talent to good use with some clippers and a YouTube video. I'll say this: it wasn't the *worst* job someone could have done. However, it made me realize just how much practice and patience it took to get the fade just right and to get the hair even on an impatient kindergartener. I haven't cut Ridge's hair since then. Phillip's hair became scraggly and messy around this time, and he needed a haircut, too. He tried to cut his own hair after seeing the massacre I'd made of Ridge's, and it looked rough. He ended up buzzing it all off.

When we first came to visit here in Converse, LA, we were introduced to a woman named Beverly. She, her husband, and others in her family attend our church. She is petite with brown eyes, glasses, and short hair she keeps just right. Her beauty shop is just down the driveway of our church beside a busy highway. It is a small building with a sign that says, "Bev's Beauty Shop". She's cut most of the hair of our church members and many citizens of this small town for years. She's been my go-to for a haircut for all three of my kids whenever she's been available. I can trust she's seen it all when it comes to the sporadic behavior of my four-year-old. And, believe me, if it's happening or is happening in this little town, I can make a bet the news enters her doors before almost anyone else's.

During my recent surgery, I found it difficult to lift my hands over my head for an extended period. This was due to the abdominal incisions which were very tender and tugged a lot when I moved too much to begin with. I've already mentioned my "soupy" belly button in a previous prompt, so now you can put together the kind of shape I was in. Sadly, there came a point where I needed my hair washed. I couldn't let it go like it was any longer. Phillip was more than happy to give it a go, but as much as I love him, I'm not sure he could manage to get this entire head of hair clean. I've got a lot of hair. My first thought was to ask Beverly if she had time to wash my hair for me. When I texted her, she was in the middle of cutting someone else's hair but said when she got done, she'd be happy to do it.

I drove down from my house to her beauty shop. Like I said, her beauty shop is very close to us, and I could walk there if I wanted to, and have several times. It's beside our mailbox. It did not take Beverly long to finish up and she had me sit by her sink. She scrubbed and massaged my head. Under her hands and the warm water felt like such a relief to finally feel clean again. She took no payment from me. I even offered to pay her back for the emotional damages Tripp had caused during his last visit with her, but she would not take it. She asked if I was sure I could dry it on my own. I assured her I had a new hairdryer that would do the trick. I could sit and dry my hair or just let it air dry for now. I told her I could recruit Phillip if necessary.

I'm glad to have people who can take care of us when we can't take care of ourselves. I'm thankful for hairdressers and barbers for the uplift they give with a fresh new 'do. I'm so glad there are people out there with better skills than me, otherwise my sons would have buzz cuts and my husband would probably be the one to do that because I would find a way to mess that up, too. I think there are some people we take for granted during our lifetime and I feel like these people fall into that category. I appreciate the attention they give and the time they spend.

Day 84:
Love

I wasn't sure how to approach this one. I typed, erased, typed, then erased again. I had multiple examples, but then I nixed them all and stuck with just one.

When I was a child, I was told a story. I even remember seeing the remnants of the scene. It was a true story, but one I don't know specific details on as far as the people's names and backstories are concerned. I don't believe it matters here.

A man working for the Department of Transportation years ago was working a jobsite on the side of a mountain. He was on the downhill side for traffic. It'd been a nice day so far, and if he just got another hour done, he could go home to his wife and kids. Everyone on the crew was ready to go home after a hot Alabama day. Before he had a chance to realize what was happening, an 18-wheeler came flying towards him. The brakes had gone out. The truck's driver lost control and was barreling down the mountain. Most folks did not obey the speed limit down this mountain. I can only imagine this fellow may not have been, either. All the crewmembers but this man somehow had time to see it coming and get out of the way.

Blackness, a blur, a small lapse in time, and the man awoke. The only thing he could think about at first was the overwhelming immense pain he was in, but somehow at the same time parts of him were numb. He quickly realized his horrible situation. He was pinned between a large tree and the truck. Somehow the driver had survived, wiggled his way out, and was searching for help. There was blood, lots of it. Black circles tried to swallow up the man's vision as death stood nearby whispering to him. There was ringing in his ears. His soul wrestled with his flesh. Adrenaline flipped on like a light switch.

He began to see flashes of red and blue lights and hear sirens. A man in a uniform approached the scene. Assessing the situation and seeing the horror before him, the uniformed man sighed and asked the man who he could call. The man responded immediately, "My wife." He was able to softly speak his wife's phone number, because this was a day and age when you remembered stuff like that. The wife was called, the situation was explained, and she came to the scene as fast as she could drive. She had no idea what awaited her at the bottom of that mountain.

While they awaited the wife's arrival, other uniformed men and crewmembers jumped in to try and get the truck off the man. Maybe they could get him out and have him med flighted, something! The worst happened. It was realized if the truck was moved, the man was going to die immediately. The humbling reality and gravity of the situation, along with the blood loss, chilled the injured man and the others to their bones. The silence was loud. The man, calm, said he wanted to wait for his wife to get there before any decisions were made.

About thirty minutes later, the wife pulled up to the scene. In tears she rushed to her husband's side, demanding to know why they had not got him out yet! What were they doing! The man quietly told his wife it was going to be okay, and he and the uniformed men explained what was going on. Through sobs, the wife reluctantly accepted what was to come. The two were allowed to sit together for a length of time I'm not sure of. That part of the story wasn't told to me. I just know it was a while. The police officers, firefighters, and EMTs all waited patiently while the two lovers talked together about life, their babies, what Heaven would be like, laughing like they had all the time in the world. It sounds like they both really believed they did. I wasn't there, but I bet there wasn't a dry eye on that hillside.

The sun had gone down, but who could tell with the number of headlights and spotlights out there. The time came eventually for the wife to tell her husband "See you later" and "I love you." He answered, "I love you, too."

A few nods of agreement were exchanged amongst the response crew. The right equipment to move the truck was at the scene now. The wife let go of her husband's hand and backed away. With a careful but calculated movement, the deed was done. Her heart broke into; his heart stopped. He left; she stayed. Love is patient, and if she hasn't left this earth yet, I'm sure he is patiently waiting for her to come worship God face-to-face with him.

Love is not only patient, but kind. It is not self-seeking. It isn't irritable. It doesn't keep a record of wrongdoings. It doesn't find joy in unrighteousness. It rejoices in truth. Love bears all things. Love believes all things. Love hopes all things. Love endures all things.

I am overwhelmingly thankful for love. I don't know what we would do without it. The good stuff, the real thing, the real deal. Some people will cook up a cheap imitation and label it as the original work, and it's important to know the difference. I'm glad to know what love is and to experience it. My prayer is you understand this love and come to know the One who created this love and who *is* this love, the One who is the reason this love exists.

Day 85:
Clean Water

I've never lacked clean water. I already know based on the little knowledge I do of the world I am a blessed woman for never having to search for or desire clean water. The closest I have come to having unclean water was the well water at Granny's house. It stained my teeth yellow from the minerals and had a strange taste. My poor kidneys learned quickly to filter sweet tea, Pepsi, Coca Cola, and Mountain Dew rather than attempt to drink the faint yellow liquid that came out of the sink faucet.

On the other hand, Grandma and Grandpa's property has some of the best water I've ever tasted. There is an underground spring on their property that a long time ago, had the perfect, cold, crystal-clear water. Mom would get the large plastic water jugs locally and we would take them down on the property to fill them. The water was crisp and refreshing. I don't know how it is anywhere else in the world, but North Alabama had plenty of refreshing hidden secrets like this. I remember going to a small bridge at the bottom of a mountain once with Mom and filling the jugs from the underground spring there someone had told her about. It is a beautiful thing to see nature take care of itself and us.

I'm thankful for clean water simply because I know how blessed I am to live in a place with it. There's been places even in the continental United States who have sadly had to deal with the unsettling reality of unclean water. I've been fortunate enough throughout my life to not have this happen to me.

However, there is another type of clean water I am thankful for. This water is nourishing. This water is delightful. This water is the safest and most satisfying water you have ever had.

Jesus, a Jew, asked the Samaritan woman at the well for a drink of water in John 4, which was a big no-no for the readers who are not familiar. The Samaritan woman in verse 9 asks Jesus why a Jew would ask a Samaritan woman for a drink. Jesus answered her in verse 10, "If you knew the gift of God, and who says to you, 'Give me a drink,' you would have asked him, and he would have given you living water." To paraphrase, the Samaritan woman, confused, asked how he was to get this water if he didn't have a bucket. Jesus said to her, "Everyone who drinks of this water will thirst again, but whoever drinks of the water that I will give him will never thirst again; but the water that I will give him will become in him a well of water springing up to eternal life."

Any water besides this water will not do. It will not quench your thirst. It will not sustain. I encourage you to read the rest of this story on your own to learn more about the living water we all need.

Day 86: Ruiners

Sociopaths, when put in a search engine, come up under antisocial personality disorder. The definition explains people with this disorder are often characterized by a blatant disregard for others. They don't care about others' feelings, pain, and have little-to-no empathy. Or, if they do have empathy, they disregard that as well. Sometimes these people become "leeches", or people who suck the life, energy, and resources right out of you if you allow them to. A lot of these people are not formally diagnosed, but I bet at least one has already crossed your mind. For those that ride the fine line of knowing what they are doing and not understanding the seriousness of the evil they are inflicting, I'm going to call them the "ruiners".

I've known people to suck dry the financial resources of their significant other after they've run their own accounts into the ground. I've seen people make it impossible for those they allegedly love to succeed at anything. These people are the ones who use others as steppingstones to their own success, not caring if those they step on sink in the mud in the process. Ruiners find joy in others' downfalls, not out of some form of vengeance, but for some sick form of entertainment. Others' downfalls are what these keep these people feeling alive.

I remember one occasion when I worked in child welfare that I was accused of stealing. There was a program in the area who raised money and obtained Christmas presents during the holiday season for the state foster kids. All the items would be unloaded off the large truck and lined up down the hallways of the child welfare office. Workers sorted through bags, including myself, and began to schedule times the bags could be delivered. A sad reality for some of these kids is there were runaways. One seventeen-year-old boy had specifically told his worker not to come look for him and he ran away. The worker had commented once before the boy's location was known, but the worker wasn't going to be "bothered" to look for him.

I looked down at the seventeen-year-old boy's bag and the few items he had left there. One woman, who had worked there for years, was walking out of her office down the hallway. This woman was kind, not malicious at all, and someone I had a good work relationship with. I asked her what happens to the leftover items. She said, "They're up for grabs!" I had just reached my mid-twenties and was still under the impression I could trust people I worked with to have the correct information. That is hardly ever the case in child welfare, unfortunately, and there was a lot of training and information not properly distributed at that office. When I heard "up for grabs", I understood that to mean I could have something if I wanted it. I saw a small bottle of knock-off brand cologne. I thought to myself, "Phillip would like that!" I thought it would make a nice stocking stuffer. I only told two people that day at the office what I'd found and what I had been told, not because I was ashamed or thought I'd done something wrong, but because I kept my circle small in that catty work environment.

My foster care supervisor requested I come to her office the next day. I went in not knowing what the sudden meeting was about. My supervisor informed me she was told I'd stolen from the foster care closet. Unsure of what she meant, I asked her to clarify. She asked if I had a bottle of cologne. I said I did, and I'd put it in a drawer at home. Words were thrown around about how she wasn't sure what the director would say, if I'd have a job, etc. I became upset and told her I'd go home right then and there and get the cologne. She said, "That isn't necessary." I interrupted her and told her no, that it was indeed necessary otherwise it wouldn't have been brought up, and that I'd be right back.

I made the 30-minute round trip home in about 20 minutes, crying the whole way because I had no idea that I'd done something wrong. I felt bad about the whole thing. I put the cologne on her desk and demanded to meet with the director right then. My supervisor said it wouldn't be necessary. I angrily replied, "It was necessary earlier, why is it not necessary now?" My supervisor talked around it, beat around the bush, and said the director was busy and it was probably fine now. It was never brought up by my superiors again.

I was livid. I found out who had caused the issue and who had reported me as a thief. It took everything in my power to make myself turn the other cheek that day. I sat in my car and just screamed for a while. I cut off everyone I needed to cut off to survive there just a little longer. I was mocked openly in front of others after this occurred, called a thief and a liar, and much more. I took it because I needed to feed my kids. There was a small group of people at the center of all of it. Two of these people had such a disdain for the supervisor that when they found out I had put in my two-weeks' notice in 2018, they planned their exits at the same time to purposefully leave her short-staffed when she was arguably one of the best supervisors there.

What these people failed to care about was when they blew the cologne situation out of proportion, they almost cost my kids food. They almost cost me income. We'd gone down to one income at that point and outside of that, the stress of this workplace and its inconsistencies was already slowly breaking me down. I'd let my mouth slip back to the way I'd grown up talking. I'd turned into a person I didn't like in some sort of attempt to survive that place. These people didn't care that their supervisor, who'd taught them everything they knew and had done right by them, was short-staffed and drowning in her own problems. As a matter of fact, these people laughed. They laughed at me. They laughed at her. They'd also become cold to the children they were there to serve.

There'd been times before when I had worked in investigations, I taught these people how to do my job because I thought I was being helpful by cross-training. Apparently, that had backfired and had been used to try to prove I did not do my job well, when in fact I did it well enough that state reviewers took notice. I guess it took my job being threatened to understand the great lengths of horror they'd put anyone through for a quick laugh.

Even typing this rattles some anger still left in my cage. I felt so humiliated dealing with these people, and the thought of having my family's livelihood stripped from me for someone's excitement over a misunderstanding made me sick. Figuring out a way to be thankful for these people is difficult for me. I guess I can be thankful because ruiners teach me to cover my actions in writing, recording, whatever I need to do. They taught me to have witnesses. I am thankful because these people re-instilled in me the need to keep my circle small and close. I'm glad I've typed this because it revealed to me there's still some tiny piece of bitterness left from the incident in the deep corners of my heart. However, it also shows me that the further on in life I get, the less it bothers me because I can recognize the path I'm blessed to be on and all the ways God has worked in my life. I'm reminded even if those people had been successful in getting me fired, dampened my reputation, or worse, God would have taken care of me. I have no doubt about that. I'm thankful for ruiners because when I'm up on a hill in life, they remind me they lurk in the low spots and that I need to be on my game when it comes to my prayer life and relationship with God.

I pray for these people. Maybe they've found happiness and have learned what love is. I hope whatever roots of bitterness they have in their own hearts they are dealing with appropriately. I hope they are successful; I hope they find themselves convicted and their hearts changed for the better.

Day 87: Moochers

Moochers may not just refer to people who overstay their welcome when it comes to money, but people who overstay their welcome in general. Moochers are constantly without money or in less-than-ideal situations who ask for advice and help, but when both are given, neither are taken seriously. These people see you again with new jewelry after you gave them grocery money to make sure they were fed. These people are the ones who go on weekend-long trips after complaining they had no gas money and you loaned them some so they could get to and from work. People who are smarter than me would suggest the giver stop giving and be done with it. I never claimed to be all that smart, anyway.

Over time, I've had to really work on how I address these types of people. The first time I felt led to give money was when I was working at Bojangles'. I don't remember when it was; I had two stints of employment there. A man came in seeming a bit nervous to ask for help, but he did anyway. He said he had to get to Tennessee (roughly 30 minutes away) and needed gas money. I had a $20 bill in my pocket and felt led to give it to him. I handed him the folded money and he thanked me repeatedly before leaving. My manager looked at me like I had lost my mind. He commented something like, "You know he's probably gonna go buy alcohol or something with that, right?" In that moment it hit me the man may go do that, but I still had felt led to give the money. "That's okay. I did what I was supposed to do." My manager shrugged and we both got back to work.

The past few years have brought me to deal time after time with a lot of people who fall into this category. While it gets on my nerves and can leave me feeling unappreciated and foolish to help these people, I've found myself drawing nearer to God each time. I'm thankful for these people because they've forced my relationship with God to be stronger by asking Him whether I should give or not, how much I should give, etc. What I just realized, though, is how little I take the opportunity to pour out the Gospel to them while I am doing this giving. In hindsight, I guess I am thankful for this prompt about these people because it has convicted me to use these moments rather than just mull over whether I should give or not. My job isn't to decide if people can or should ask me for stuff, my responsibility is what I do with the moment when they ask.

Day 88: Sunrises

I really wish I could have put into words the beauty of seeing the sunrise from an airplane when I mentioned it earlier. Maybe a prompt only about sunrises will give me some creative freedom.

Where I grew up, sunrises came quietly. They rose gently yet powerfully over the field across the road from our long driveway. The sun worked its way up through scattered clouds. Its yellows and oranges took over everything in its path, like God tipped over His glass of orange juice at breakfast time. The black, muscled backs of neighbors' cattle would glisten red and gold in its presence. Ripples across their hide were highlighted as they moved across the pasture. Dew on hay and grass would sparkle and spray up as the beasts stomped about. Sometimes in the distance a neighbor's rooster could be heard.

Sunrises at the girls' ranch were different. The house sat on a hill, and we could see through the kitchen windows of the large 1960's style home. The sun would ease up over the tree-covered hills and shed light on everything previously unseen. Each morning was the one quiet part of the day to count on. For a houseparent, it was just you and the sunshine as you sipped your morning coffee before girls came barging down the stairs to grab breakfast before school.

Our house now has a different view of the sunrise. We live right beside our church, which means we always have a view of the church and parking lot. When we moved here, one of my favorite views was the sunrise hitting the three white crosses on the front lawn of the church. Cardinals come and go. Hummingbirds visit their water cooler and move on. The sunrise remains one of the most beautiful things about our new home as it hits those crosses. Beams of light shoot over the beams of white. Shadows are cast on the ground bowing down to their master.

Sunrises reveal what darkness cannot. They cast truth. They symbolize second chances as our eyes open and start a new day, not the same day all over again. They mean we survived. They mean we still have purpose, that though life may feel as if it is over, it is far from it. They are new beginnings. They are a gift.

Each day I see a sunrise, I now try to find gratitude I get just one more. It doesn't guarantee the day will be flawless, perfect, remarkable; we weren't promised these days would be. We weren't promised a certain number of days, either. I pray we don't forsake the sunrise, for it is one way the Son tells us to rise again because our journey is not yet through.

Day 89:
Daydreamers

I'm a person who can make an argument about letting your mind wander being a not-so-great thing. It probably is dangerous a lot of times depending on where you let it wander, what about, and how long you stay there. Though I have this opinion, I've also got another side to consider.

Daydreaming morphed as I got older. When I was very small, I daydreamed Barney was my best friend and that we did everything together. I daydreamed about being a princess. Later, I daydreamed when riding in the car by imagining a dancer or some sort of hero leaping across the trees as we drove past them. When I got older and had a CD player, I'd imagine them doing it to the music. I drifted off in class- a lot- and would dream about leaving my hometown and becoming someone not necessarily famous, but just someone successful. I'd daydream about everyone who picked on me or treated me like a loser would feel when I showed back up, fresh and fabulous. I daydreamed about boys, so many boys, and how they surely were the key to my happiness. Everything from my childhood movies to the teen dramas on VH1 and MTV said so. All the books and magazines I was recommended agreed.

There are people who daydream about having a spouse and children. People who daydream about becoming a surgeon one day to save lives. There are people who daydream about being heroes when they grow up. I can see my kids right now, throwing on their Velcro capes and felt masks while clambering on our furniture through the house. In this moment, my kids are living their wildest dreams. They believe they can do anything.

Daydreamers make me thankful because where would our world be without them? Ideas are the very first step to change. I'm pausing to consider when people stop their daydreaming. When they were children because they were forced out of it? When they got into their teen years or early adulthood because their dreams collided with harsh reality and came to a screeching halt?

I hope if you are daydreaming for productive things, for what is good, you don't quit. I hope you pray for guidance to know if your daydreaming needs to become something real and if so, when. Maybe your daydreaming will lead to a discovery, a work, a blessing that makes this physical life just a little better while we are in it.

I hope you never stop believing you can do anything, but I also hope you believe you can do the right things for the right reasons.

Day 90: Smiles

I'd argue my children have some of the best smiles. Am I biased? Absolutely not! Maybe? Possibly? Anyway, my children have some of the best smiles. They are dimpled and cute. They have great, straight, beautiful white teeth. Their smiles light up a room individually and together. It's one of my favorite parts of motherhood out of all the good things motherhood has to offer.

Last year, Anniston came to me on her birthday as she got ready for school.

"Mom, my smile is broken."

I was sitting in the living room when she approached me. I looked up to see her and sure enough, her smile was broken. The left side of her face was completely limp. She could not blink her eye; her mouth was drooping. I have been trained to remain calm. It didn't take much training because I still had a poker face I'd perfected from childhood. For some unknown reason, I immediately knew it was Bell's Palsy. I don't know why. I've seen it once or twice before, but not enough to diagnose it. I could call this time mother's intuition. I calmly told her to let me see her face and she got closer to me. I asked her to blink. One eye blinked. I asked her to smile. The right side of her face made a cheesy grin while they other one sagged.

I got her into the doctor's office as quickly as I could. A couple of nights prior, she'd had an episode I can only describe as "seizure-like". My child has never been diagnosed with seizures, but she's had some bedwetting incidents she doesn't realize are happening during the moment, and she's also struggled on and off with sleepwalking. In retrospect, we probably should have taken her to the ER the night it happened, but she snapped out of it after a few minutes, and we thought she was fine. Her pediatrician saw her and confirmed she had Bell's Palsy. We were instructed to give it some time as there wasn't much to be done. She'd had COVID-19 in January, and it was now April. There was talk this was a side effect they were now seeing from it. However, they did put us in a referral to a neurologist at my request that turned out to be months away.

I brought my beautiful baby girl to the car, and we started to drive home. She asked me the difficult question, "Mom, will I smile normal again?" I didn't know the answer. It was a real possibility at the time she may not. I told her we were going to do everything we could to make it happen.

I began my research as soon as I got home. I learned about the causes, treatment methods I could do at home, all of it. We bought her an eye patch. We bought her eye drops because she couldn't blink. She was miserable. She wore sunglasses when she went outside. I spoke with a friend who is a long-time physical therapist and discussed some gentle exercises I could do with her. I did those for the first few days until she told me they made her face uncomfortable. I then began heat therapy and had her lay on a heating pad every single night before bed to try to relax those facial muscles when I realized they were tensed up. We weren't going down without a fight to save our little girl's smile. If God chose to never let have her smile back, well, she was going to be the most confident half-smiling child you've ever met if I had anything to say about it. There'd never be a shortage of compliments given to this girl.

She had so much support from family and friends. Her Great-Aunt Janet sent her a children's book about Bell's Palsy that she still enjoys reading. Her friends at school loved her and were extra sweet with her. Her teachers were fantastic. When we needed the support, we got it from all sides.

Her Bell's Palsy "lasted" for about a month until it was what we'd call "healed". Her smile never quite went back to what it was, but unless you just know what had happened, you wouldn't see the difference. A few months down the road after we'd already moved to Louisiana, we had our neurology appointment at Vanderbilt Hospital in Tennessee. I drove her back up in July and prayed the whole time something would tip the doctor off and prove to him something wasn't right. Sure enough, the day before her appointment, she had what the doctor later determined was a "flare up" of her Bell's Palsy. Her left side went partially limp again. The doctor could tell and although we didn't- and still don't- have any definitive answers, my prayers were answered, and the doctor had no reason to doubt the realness of her facial paralysis. I was given direct orders to take her to the ER if it got worse that night or if she had another seizure-like episode, because that would mean it wasn't a flare up but something they could pick up on an MRI. By the grace of God, it was just a flare up and her face went back to normal in a few days.

We take smiles for granted. I never in a million years thought that would happen to my child. There's another mother where we are from who recently lost one of her four small children (as well as her own mother) in a tragic car accident. I'm sure never in a million years did she think she'd be living life without one of the four gorgeous smiles she'd been blessed with.

I'm glad for smiles because I can say from a personal position that I almost lost part of my daughter's. I'm heartbroken for that mama back home because I can't imagine how I'd be if I ever lost any of my children's smiles permanently. Smiles remind us of life, of youth, and of happiness. They remind us of tenderness. They remind us jokes are funny, food is good, and people love us.

They remind us of life's uncertainty. No matter how uncertain it may be, you just never know when "lasts" will happen. Soak them all up while you still can.

Day 91:
Broken Dishes

I drew this prompt out this morning knowing it would be the last one for my first book. I was hoping for something snazzy. I was hoping for some deep thought-provoking piece to finish off this first chunk of the series. I drew out "Broken Dishes" and I thought to myself, "Really?" I brushed it off and for a moment thought about the prompt. I thought about how many times my kids had broken dishes. I thought about how many times I had. Then, my thoughts trailed off. I started wondering if I needed to put my book into more parts rather than four because of how long it is looking to be. At this point, I could go ahead and publish one with seventy-three days in it rather than ninety-one (plus or minus) at a time. I sat in bed to finish my Saturday morning coffee while I pondered how much work this has been. Then, I heard it.

Crash!

It was the unmistakable sound out a broken plate. I looked up toward Heaven as I have before during this book. God knew exactly what I was thinking when I did.

I got up to see what had happened. Anniston had taken the plates from the kids' table and put them in the already-full kitchen sink. One of my antique saucer plates I use for their sandwiches, pizzas, and small foods had fallen to the floor. She looked at me and immediately apologized. I told her it was okay and told her to move out of the way while I swept up the mess. I didn't want her to get hurt.

Used to, I would not have been so nice. Unfortunately for my older two kids, they got the first-time mom version of me. They were stuck with that for a while. They had the mom who had dealt with postpartum depression after Anniston was born; they had the mom who struggled with guilt and failure after Ridge was born. They had the barely grown woman who, although she'd set out and dreamed of being the best mom she could be, was not all that great. This woman was once a child who'd been screamed at over almost every wrong she'd committed. She was hurt, angry, grieving, and unsure where to begin on processing everything she'd been through. I mean, goodness, she didn't even really know what "processing" meant. This mom was short-fused. This mom was easily irritated by every little thing. This mom was once a small daughter who was made to pick up her father's trash- papers, Dr. Pepper bottles, whiskey bottles- in the living room floor beside his recliner. She was cussed at and even on at least one occasion kicked across the room for not moving fast enough. She was reminded how bleeping stupid she was. Though this mom had sworn to never be that angry with her own kids, sometimes a sliver of that same angry reaction crept in, rearing its ugly head. The humiliation and the anger at herself would drive her out of her own mind into her own mental downward spiral. That first-time mom had for sure flown off the handle before over broken dishes, inconsistencies, and inconveniences.

Broken dishes have happened a lot in our house over the years. With each crash, with each sharp shard I've pulled out of a small foot, God has offered me redemption and chances to be a better mom. He's offered me chance after chance to improve my patience, my tone, my reaction with my children. This time with my almost ten-year-old daughter, I was aggravated it had happened, but I recognized why it had happened. I'd lapsed on my own responsibilities from the day before on loading the dishwasher, so the sink was totally full. On the other hand, they'd lapsed on keeping their kid table clean from the day before. I pulled her and Ridge into the kitchen with me to explain to both I wasn't upset it had happened, but that we all needed to do better on our chores. I told them I was sorry for sounding irritable. They said it was okay.

I apologized; they forgave.

I confess my sins; my Lord forgives me. 1 John 1:9.

I am thankful for this correlation and the way this book can end because I hope you know your sins can be forgiven as well if you call out to God. You are going to fall short. You're going to fall short every single day you're breathing on this big old spinning rock. However, I'm glad we have a wonderful God from whom we can receive the forgiveness we so desperately need.

The question remains: have you asked for forgiveness from Him? If not, why? Do you recognize your need for it? I hope you think on those as you close this book and go about your day. I hope it stirs you. I hope it grabs your heart and doesn't let go.

Made in the USA
Coppell, TX
08 March 2025